Policing the peace in Northern Ireland

MANCHESTER
1824

Manchester University Press

To my mother and father

Policing the peace in Northern Ireland

Politics, crime and security after the Belfast Agreement

Jon Moran

WITHDRAWN

Manchester University Press
Manchester and New York
distributed exclusively in the USA by Palgrave

The right of Jon Moran to be identified as the author of this work has been asserted by him in accordance with the Copyright, Designs and Patents Act 1988.

Published by Manchester University Press
Oxford Road, Manchester M13 9NR, UK
and Room 400, 175 Fifth Avenue, New York, NY 10010, USA
www.manchesteruniversitypress.co.uk

Distributed exclusively in the USA by
Palgrave, 175 Fifth Avenue, New York,
NY 10010, USA

Distributed exclusively in Canada by
UBC Press, University of British Columbia, 2029 West Mall,
Vancouver, BC, Canada V6T 1Z2

British Library Cataloguing-in-Publication Data
A catalogue record for this book is available from the British Library

Library of Congress Cataloging-in-Publication Data applied for

HV
8197.5
.A2
M67
2008

ISBN   978 0 7190 7471 4 *hardback*
ISBN   978 0 7190 7472 1 *paperback*

First published 2008

17 16 15 14 13 12 11 10 09 08   10 9 8 7 6 5 4 3 2 1

Edited and typeset
by Frances Hackeson Freelance Publishing Services, Brinscall, Lancs
Printed and bound in Great Britain
by CPI, Antony Rowe Ltd, Chippenham, Wiltshire

Contents

List of tables

Abbreviations

ASB	Anti Social Behaviour
ARA	Assets Recovery Agency
CAB	Criminal Assets Bureau
CHIS	Covert Human Intelligence Source
CIRA	Continuity IRA
DAAD	Direct Action Against Drugs
DCU	District Command Unit
DPP	District Policing Partnership
DUP	Democratic Unionist Party
EU	European Union
FARC	Revolutionary Armed Forces of Colombia
FATF	Financial Action Task Force
FSA	Financial Services Authority
HET	Historical Enquiries Team
HMIC	Her Majesty's Inspector of Constabulary
HOLMES	Home Office Large Major Enquiry System
IMC	Independent Monitoring Commission
INLA	Irish National Liberation Army
IPSIG	Independent Private Sector Inspector General
LVF	Loyalist Volunteer Force
MIT	Major Incident Team
MLRO	Money Laundering Reporting Officer
NCIS	National Criminal Intelligence Service
NICS	Northern Ireland Crime Survey
NIM	National Intelligence Model
NIO	Northern Ireland Office
NPM	New Public Management

OCTF	Organised Crime Task Force
ODC	Ordinary Decent Criminal
PIRA	Provisional IRA
PIU	Performance and Innovation Unit
POCA	Proceeds of Crime Act
PSNI	Police Service of Northern Ireland
PUP	Progressive Unionist Party
RHC	Red Hand Commandos
RIPA	Regulation of Investigatory Powers Act
RIRA	Real IRA
RSF	Republican Sinn Féin
RUC	Royal Ulster Constabulary
SARS	Suspicious Activity Reports
SDLP	Social Democratic and Labour Party
SF	Sinn Féin
SOCA	Serious and Organised Crime Agency
TFU	Terrorist Finance Unit
UDA	Ulster Defence Association
UDP	Ulster Democratic Party
UFF	Ulster Freedom Fighters
UUP	Ulster Unionist Party
UVF	Ulster Volunteer Force

Preface

What are we to make of crime in Northern Ireland, particularly what is termed organised crime, and within this ominous term, paramilitary related crime? Former Secretary of State Peter Hain assured the province that the Provisional Irish Republican Army no longer organises crime 'from the centre'. It seems now just reckless individuals or groups of them who must be 'off message' commit crimes only for personal gain. The Independent Monitoring Commission, the body established to monitor and report on paramilitary violence and criminal activity, argues that the PIRA continues as an organisation but this is a good thing: all the better to make sure its members desist from crime. David Ervine, before his untimely death was leader of the Progressive Unionist Party, the political counterpart to the loyalist paramilitary group the Ulster Volunteer Force. Ervine often argued that the UVF was being smeared with the accusation of criminality, and that neither the PUP nor the UVF has control over everything Volunteer Force members do. In any case, the argument goes, focusing on crime detracts from the main issue of 'conflict transformation' via which the UVF moves to 'non-violent responses'. The Irish National Liberation Army also engages with the question of crime, arguing that it is not involved, but,

> we are however aware that a small number of pseudo gangs and former members of not only the INLA but other republican armies are engaged in extortion, racketeering and drug dealing using the name of the INLA. Some of these gangs are operating with the full approval of the so-called security forces.[1]

The Ulster Defence Association issues statements condemning criminality while its members are charged with drug trafficking, extortion and attempted murder. Like the UVF it is 'struggling' with criminality, although the leadership seems to accept some concrete responsibility for the practice, since it has repeatedly requested public funds to aid in its move from violence and criminality. The day after it had been awarded public money in early 2007, the police argued that it was still heavily involved in extortion. Possibly the police do not understand the Byzantine complexities of paramilitary 'conflict transformation'.

As implied by Peter Hain's comment in the opening paragraph, the British government does not provide any more clarity. According to a former Security Minister, the Irish National Liberation Army is not a security threat, and its main role is to engage in 'civil administration'. This abstract formulation in empirical terms means the punishment of anti-social behaviour, with INLA members putting a teenager down a manhole, informing him they are going to find a gun to complete their work.[2] We are told by the government's Organised Crime Task Force that no crime is victimless, in its attempt to win the psychology war and stop some of the citizens of Northern Ireland driving around in cars fuelled by tax-free petrol, guzzling counterfeit vodka, smoking smuggled cigarettes or buying fake CDs. Yet at the same time, other government agencies when confronted by crime adopted the position that it indeed may not be victimless, but nevertheless needed to be viewed 'in the round'. Thus the Ulster Defence Association leader Johnny Adair continued to encourage pipe bombings and other forms of sectarianism and manipulate others in the UDA to murder in an internal loyalist feud before being returned to prison, because his presence/absence had ramifications for the peace process. The UVF was responsible for the deaths of a number of people before being declared off ceasefire by the government. Similarly, under the guise of Direct Action Against Drugs republicans murdered alleged drug dealers. Others faced death if revealed as agents of the police or military. Thus in 1999, Martin McGartland, a Provisional IRA member who had also been a police informant was shot six times at his new home on the Northumberland coast (but survived) and in 2006, after admitting to being a long-term British informer, Sinn Féin worker Denis Donaldson was shotgunned to death. Others faced discipline for speaking out against their former comrades. Thomas 'Slab' Murphy had sued the *Sunday Times* for stating he was a senior member of the Provisional IRA. Eamon Collins, a former member of the Provisional IRA had appeared in the libel trial and stated that 'Slab' Murphy was indeed a senior PIRA man. Murphy lost. Collins also had publicly criticised the PIRA in his book *Killing Rage*. Collins was horribly murdered in 1999, certainly by PIRA members. Responsibility for these actions was either impossible to pin down or did not get in the way of the British and Irish governments in their search to bring the republican movement and Sinn Féin into the peace. However, in another action the republican movement's

£26 million raid on the Northern Bank ended what prospects there were for political agreement, made international headlines and led to sanctions on Sinn Féin. This crime, as well as the murder of Robert McCartney could not be 'read' within the peace process.

Here we are in an almost post-modern world, where the actions of organisations, or actions by those within organisations are 'read' in order to construct a meaning about an intact ceasefire or organisational culpability. These types of discourse may be developed for concrete political purposes but the result is still a disengagement from a genuine analysis of change. Truly, when considering the responsibility of republican and loyalist paramilitary organisations for crime it seems that 'all that is solid melts into air'.[3]

Discussing crime implies a discussion of how it might be controlled. The police are of course central to this. They were also central to consolidating the peace, since any genuine peace process would have to involve substantial reform of the police. Thus the RUC became the PSNI. Many unionists and police officers believed the police were being downgraded. In fact by the end of the reforms the police had been modernised along the lines of a major urban British police service. One of the reasons for this was a number of external reports which had criticised police practice and also the rising levels of crime in Northern Ireland, which the police could not halt. Although much attention was focused on the Patten Report as a blueprint of police change, the report had said little or nothing about criminal investigation, and it was reform here that modelled the PSNI on the London Metropolitan Police Service.

In terms of the practicalities of crime control, politics was no less present. The role of the British government in 'seeing no evil' in terms of paramilitary crime has already been mentioned.[4] Paramilitary organisations on both the republican and loyalist side were given some room for manoeuvre before the authorities moved to tackle them, often in response to criminal activity which could not be 'spun' away. Meanwhile dissident networks of individuals within certain paramilitary groups or separate groups (such as the Real IRA and the Loyalist Volunteer Force) were consistently heavily targeted. Political policing was evident with regard to the Assets Recovery Agency, supposedly the magic bullet for organised crime.

In 2005 the PIRA announced its war was over and began to move away from crime, the latter an intrinsic part of its demobilisation. Later, its political counterpart, Sinn Féin, accepted the role of MI5 in Northern Ireland and voted to accept policing structures after devolution was restored. These developments must be truly hard to swallow for many republicans, but the circle seems complete and the problems of crime and policing acceptance (if not legitimacy) are finally being wrapped up.

If loyalist and republican paramilitaries are in a process of desistance from crime, this demonstrates how central crime has been to the peace process and the demobilisation of paramilitaries. If in 2005 the Provisional IRA finally issued a statement that its war was over this was partly because it had boxed itself into a corner after the Northern Bank robbery and the murder of Robert McCartney. If loyalist paramilitary organisations are ordering their members to desist from crime it is because they realise the negative effects it has had on their legitimacy, and because the police have effectively targeted sections of loyalist paramilitarism such as the anti-agreement LVF and the North Belfast leadership of the UDA. Their political and academic sympathisers might not accept this as a variable in loyalist change but that signifies their (often naive) over-concentration on formal political strategy and internal debates.

Certainly fundamental change is evident: beatings and shootings are down, as are murders and there is a move away from crime officially sanctioned by the paramilitary leadership. However, issues of paramilitary criminality are still on the agenda, despite the fact that official actors (governments) have framed crime as an issue which has been resolved and thus no longer exists. Loyalist paramilitaries are a long way from ending crime. The Provisional IRA is still engaged in criminal activities although this is at a lower level and tolerated by the leadership as a smoothing mechanism towards demobilisation. Dissidents still engage in criminal activities. Finally, there is the question of the role of organised crime in Northern Ireland, not in a melodramatic 'mafia' sense but simply that if paramilitaries are demobilising we should expect to see a drop in the crimes for which Northern Ireland is disproportionately recognised: serious armed robbery, extortion, counterfeiting, smuggling and so forth. If not, questions remain about who is doing what crime.

This book then, stresses that crime has been central, not peripheral to the peace process and discusses some basic issues relating to crime in Northern Ireland following the Belfast Agreement. A couple of notes concerning methodology are in order. Firstly, interviews were semi-structured, notes made contemporaneously and written up in full afterwards. Copies of the interviews were then sent to the interviewees for correction/clarification. If requested, anonymity was provided. If no response was received, anonymity was provided. At least three of those police officers spoken to were, or had been very recently, under threat from paramilitaries, a rejoinder to those who believe paramilitary activity is a fading ghost about to be dissolved in the unending sunshine of the peace.[5] Secondly, Northern Ireland is interesting in that accusations of partiality are often aimed with force by those whose own position on the chair of Solomonic wisdom seems shaky at best. Those who write works seen as sympathetic to republicans and loyalists are clearly in the metaphorical firing line but this is particularly the case for those who write on the police. Much of what has been written on policing in Northern Ireland is overwhelmingly negative. There is nothing wrong with this if it is deserved, but this methodology of endless discontent lacked context before the peace and began to look archaic after 2001 or so. Maybe some of the individuals who adopted the position that nothing has changed and that the Patten Report was the shibboleth which must be worshipped and implemented without deviation might accept something had altered by 2007 if Sinn Féin leader Gerry Adams and its policing spokesman Gerry Kelly accepted the level of police change. Perhaps not. Further scorn is reserved for those who concentrate on crime rather than 'the real politics' of paramilitary organisations. Of course, crime is part of the real politics of Northern Ireland and particularly paramilitary politics.[6]

A note on terms: small letters are used to refer to republican and loyalist organisations, except where capitals are appropriate to denote a reference to overall political ideologies. The term 'republican movement' is used interchangeably with the Provisional IRA. This term does not include Sinn Féin. When discussing Northern Ireland, it is often compared to the 'the rest of the UK'. This denotes the current constitutional position, as recognised in UK domestic and international law, that Northern Ireland is part of the United Kingdom.

Notes

1   Quoted in *Starry Plough* (May/June 2004), 2.
2   A. Chrisafis, 'Teenage suicides bring new fear to Ardoyne', *Guardian* (17 February 2004).
3   Marshall Berman, *All That is Solid Melts into Air* (London: Verso, 1983). The quote comes from the Communist Manifesto.
4   C. Knox, 'See no evil. Hear no evil: Insidious paramilitary violence in Northern Ireland', *British Journal of Criminology*, 42:1 (2002), 164–185.
5   For an overview of research into the police see R. Reiner, 'Police research', in R. King and E. Wincup (eds), *Doing Research on Crime and Justice* (Oxford, Oxford University Press, 2000), pp. 205–235.
6   It should not need to be pointed out that while this book is about crime and paramilitaries it does not argue that all current paramilitaries commit crime. It does not suggest all paramilitaries live high on the hog from the proceeds of that crime which brings financial rewards. It does not suggest that those who have left their organisations, particularly recently, live on the proceeds of crime. As McEvoy and others point out, the social problems of, and official restrictions on, most ex-paramilitary prisoners at the lower level stand in contrast with those former prisoners who have assumed high positions in the

Northern Ireland Assembly and other public bodies. K. McEvoy, P. Shirlow and K. McElrath, 'Resistance, transition and exclusion: Politically motivated ex-prisoners and conflict transformation in Northern Ireland', *Terrorism and Political Violence*, 16:3 (2004), 646–670. Most former paramilitaries have not turned to crime. Many current paramilitaries resist and condemn crime, at risk to themselves. But there is a need to recognise that there are many who engage in crime, and that crime is of core importance to these organisations.

Acknowledgements

A number of people have made this book possible although as always, and particularly in this case, all interpretations and errors of fact are the author's. Foremost among these people are the police officers who agreed to be interviewed. Thanks to Colin Goddard for his vital help, unfailing hospitality, good humour and generosity. His assistance made this book possible. Thanks must also go to Victoria, Felicity, Harriet and Julia. Many thanks to all the members of the PSNI who gave generously of their time, including former ACC Sam Kinkaid. Thanks are due to Essie Adair and Sam Sittlington, and for help in the latter stages of this book thanks also to Johnston Brown and Liam Clarke of the *Sunday Times*. I am also grateful to help provided by officials at the Northern Ireland Office, Lorraine Calvert of the Northern Ireland Policing Board, Alex Attwood MLA, Danny Kennedy MLA and Ian Paisley Jr. MLA. This book has also benefited from the brains of Professor Clive Walker of the University of Leeds, Dr Peter Sproat of the University of Teesside, Dr David Weatherston, Cleveland Police, and the reviewer of the manuscript. Thanks also to Colin Knox, University of Ulster and Mark Phythian, University of Leicester. Praise is due for the excellent website, TheyWorkForYou.com. Inspiration has been taken from Steve Bruce and Ian S. Wood. Thanks to the History and Governance Research Institute, University of Wolverhampton for funding support and for a sabbatical which made the writing possible. Cheers to Steve Griffin for professional help with the above and chats about Irish politics, and to Phil Whittingham. To Jimmy Hilton thanks for the beers, Pete thanks for the absence of dead bees, thanks to Ian 'Mash' McKim and Michael 'Even Keel' Tonge. Thanks and love to Edward and Moyra Moran, Lisa, Paul and Sam and Charlotte Booth. Finally but certainly not least, to Harriet with all my love. Thanks for so many things.

1

Politics, policing and crime as an issue in Northern Ireland after the peace process

Paramilitary organizations are rarely the monoliths presented by their opponents; rather they are complex organisms performing a variety of functions and providing an umbrella for different interests. The diversity allows paramilitary leaders to assume the high moral ground by emphasizing their political and civil roles while turning a blind eye to punishment beatings and murders.[a]

Experience elsewhere has shown that a decrease in paramilitary related crime is frequently offset in a peaceful situation by growth in other types of organised crime, often involving violence.[b]

Politics are central to policing.[c]

Ten of our comrades endured the agony of hunger strike and died defeating the criminalization strategy. We will not betray their courage by tolerating criminality within our own ranks.[d]

---

[a] J. Darby, 'A truce rather than reality? The effect of violence on the Irish peace process', in M. Cox , A. Guelke and F. Stephen (eds), *A Farewell to Arms? Beyond the Good Friday Agreement* (Manchester: Manchester University Press, 2006), p. 218.

[b] *A New Beginning: Policing in Northern Ireland. The Independent Commission on Policing in Northern Ireland* (Belfast: The Stationery Office, 1999), para 12.12.

[c] Author interview with Ian Paisley Jr. DUP, MLA, Belfast, 5 October 2006.

[d] PIRA statement, 23 March 2005.

Introduction

The period of conflict in Northern Ireland from 1968–1998[1] claimed over 3,600 lives. The republican paramilitary organisations (dominated by the Provisional IRA (PIRA)), in their attempt to remove Northern Ireland from the United Kingdom and unify the island of Ireland, murdered over 2,000 people. The opposing loyalist paramilitary organisations in their aim of preserving Northern Ireland's Britishness and maintaining it as part of the United Kingdom, murdered over 1,000 people.[2] Amongst the dead were approximately 1,600 civilians, 500 soldiers, 300 policemen, 200 members of the local British army regiment the Ulster Defence Regiment, 290 PIRA volunteers and 150 loyalists. The Belfast Agreement of 1998 promised a peaceful settlement of this basic political dispute over the status of Northern Ireland.[3] It promised a devolved government composed of representatives from across the Catholic and Protestant, Republican and Nationalist and Unionist and Loyalist communities. It promised a reformed police force, the decommissioning of paramilitary weapons and the end of the organisations themselves. Shot through the document was the idea of a peaceful and democratic means of dispute resolution.

Policing and justice were absolutely central to consolidating the peace by appealing to the republican and nationalist community groups with whom the police had little support and less legitimacy. The fact that crime might change was not really vocalised as a core issue, although it was accepted by observers from a number of quarters that the crime which was linked to paramilitaries was important since it funded their existence and capacity to return to 'war'. However, crime and particularly paramilitary crime assumed a central role in the developing peace process following the signing of the Belfast Agreement, as did issues of police reform, police effectiveness and the notion of political policing in controlling it. This book examines how crime became central to the peace.

The issue of crime has been central to politics in Northern Ireland in a number of areas. Crime was and is important as an issue in its own right. Prior to the peace process Northern Ireland had a relatively low (but rising historically) crime rate. Some of this was due to situational factors – simply the spread of physical security controls made some forms of crime difficult if not risky, particularly for ordinary criminals. Social controls also played a role in keeping down crime, including the role of paramilitaries as controllers of anti-social behaviour and drug taking, and the role of tight-knit communities in minimising scope for such forms of behaviour. Following the peace both types of controls loosened and serious and volume crime became an issue akin to that in the rest of the UK or the USA; a topic for politicians, media reporting and phone-ins.[4] This is the most straightforward manner in which crime became an issue, but other crime issues raised fundamental concerns about the prospects for a stable peace and about change within paramilitary groups themselves. The role of paramilitary organisations in crime also raised difficult issues for policymakers, and raised issues about the role of the British state in the transition process.

Paramilitary organisations, by most estimates, increased their involvement in criminal activity following the peace process. This was often rejected by their spokesmen and sympathisers. They used the same mechanisms of denial, arguing that reports of crime were biased due to their official nature, or sensational because they came from the popular media. Of course when other official analyses suited these organisations (such as public funds which were directed at loyalist community work based on their efforts at political change, or government statements accepting the change within the PIRA), they were welcomed as proper accounts of paramilitary activity. This form of partiality is the stuff of politics but often affected academics who have paid little attention to paramilitary crime.

The role of paramilitary organisations in crime reflected processes of consolidation and transition within the groups themselves. In terms of violence (paramilitary beatings and assaults) these performed a number of functions. For example, they were a response to community demands to take action against anti-social behaviour. But they also worked as mechanisms of social control. In terms of organised crime activity this performed a number of functions: to gain revenue to maintain capacity in case the struggle should resume again (financing recruitment, the payment of members, the purchase of arms etc.); to keep the military men occupied in time of peace; alternatively to provide for retirement funds in the case of a long-term winding down of paramilitary groups; crime was also a reflection of the disorganisation of some groups in that units and individuals decided to 'go it alone' and employ their management of violence and illicit entrepreneurial activities to raise funds for personal use. For dissident groups opposed to the peace agreement, crime was a mechanism to rapidly raise funds for capacity building in order to continue the struggle. Thus it should come as no surprise that there was a logic to crime by both loyalist and republican paramilitaries that saw it expand in the more propitious conditions created by peace and British government policy. Further, this should not be seen as controversial. There is ample evidence of a tight link between crime and organisations engaged in political violence.

Crime became an important barometer of change within paramilitary organisations. As the peace process wore on, a focus on the high level leadership and political policy of paramilitary organisations and their political counterparts widened to encompass the idea that crime was a central issue in the demobilisation of republican and loyalist paramilitaries. Not only was the British government forced to acknowledge this after the Northern Bank robbery in 2004, but the groups themselves realised that crime was affecting their legitimacy amongst their own supporters. The murder of Robert McCartney in 2005 cast a shadow over the PIRA's claim to be defender of the community and the involvement of loyalists in drug dealing was a similar problem. Indeed in 2007 the revelations of the Police Ombudsman who inquired into the crimes committed by elements of the UVF while they were police informants highlighted not only the burning issue of the need for police reform but also the crimes perpetrated by loyalists on their 'own people' in Belfast's Mount Vernon estate. By 2005 the PIRA had officially declared its war was over and began a process of demobilisation and turning the organisation away from criminal activities. The loyalist paramilitaries commenced a slower process of desisting from crime. These were not irrelevant processes. Accounts of paramilitary involvement in crime from British and Irish governments and other official bodies such as the International Monitoring Commission, as well as the statements of paramilitaries themselves on crime became central to judgements of whether they had demobilised or not.

This criminal activity raises the issue of the response of the authorities. The position of law enforcement is often controversial in processes of political transition.[5] In a number of countries the issue of law enforcement is managed away or resolved after a certain period. In Northern Ireland it was still central in 2007–2008. A process of police reform was seen as central to consolidating the peace, and following an external inquiry (The Patten Report) a substantial change programme was instituted. The Royal Ulster Constabulary was superseded by the Police Service of Northern Ireland in 2001. The question was whether this reform would foster police legitimacy, or at the most, acceptance of the police. Police reform raised a number of questions. The reform aimed to take the politics out of policing by emphasising responsive and community based policing. Police reform did achieve results. However, the state in Northern Ireland was itself still contested with the nationalist Social Democratic and Labour Party (SDLP) and Sinn Féin still seeking a unified Ireland. The SDLP agreed to enter policing structures in 2001, Sinn Féin tentatively in 2007, a major break with republicanism's rejection of anything smacking of a British police force. Furthermore, the process of reform had unpredicted results. The Patten Report had said little about criminal investigation but a number of controversies and external reports led to a modernisation of policing which ironically remoulded the Police Service of Northern Ireland (PSNI) along the lines of a major British urban force.

However, while this reform process took place a rise in crime took place, a rise that a demoralised police could not prevent in the 2000–

2001 period. This raised the issue of how to confront the crime problem. In institutional terms, reform of the police was only one part of law enforcement. The British state increased its capacity to combat crime in Northern Ireland with the setting up of the Organised Crime Task Force (OCTF) in 2001 and the Assets Recovery Agency (ARA) in 2003. However, the response to paramilitary crime was deeply affected by politics and here the role of the British state was particularly controversial.

The British state was concerned to solidify the developing peace process. The Belfast Agreement set the overall framework but a period of institutional development, political competition through elections and the negotiation of issues such as decommissioning, police reform, the release of paramilitary prisoners and so forth needed to be resolved. On the one hand, for a long period the British state had displayed a studied ignorance of crime committed by republican and loyalist paramilitary groups. Finally, the Northern Bank robbery and the murder of Robert McCartney pushed the government into action and the republican movement was targeted by the PSNI and the ARA, although even here targeting was measured. Similar treatment was aimed at loyalist groups, however, when Ulster Volunteer Force (UVF) violence and Ulster Defence Association (UDA) activity looked to be too destabilising action was taken, although here also some targets were more equal than others.

Questions were raised as to whether the British state was following a coherent policy of conflict resolution and peace building or stumbling through via a mechanism of carrots and sticks, hoping to institutionalise paramilitaries in the new political universe of Northern Ireland. The British state acted in an inconsistent manner in which the need for political policing affected the PSNI. Although police resources are always stretched and the police retained independence, it is also clear that the police were involved – and still are – in the politics of policing the peace. Whether dealing with paramilitary related crime or normal crime, the police operate in a highly charged political context. This raises questions of whether the state undermined the rule of law in order to secure peace.

Indeed these processes: the persistence of paramilitary structures, the reform of the police, the development of organised crime and black markets, the tolerance of crime by the state, the targeting of some groups over others, could make us conclude that Northern Ireland and even Western Europe is not a quantum leap or category difference from other polities around the globe that are accused of lacking rigorous governance and strict adherence to the rule of law. Political violence is difficult to neutralise, particularly when crime has been an important not marginal part of its operation.

Finally, as implied above, there is the practical question in terms of effectiveness. Obviously this is affected by the political context since some targets and activities might be effectively off limits. But the policing of the peace raises questions of the effectiveness of the magic bullets currently on offer for controlling organised crime and terrorism. The use of asset recovery, special agencies and increased powers may all be less effective than supposed or trumpeted by their advocates. Traditional focused tactics of criminal investigation remain key, boring as this might be to policymakers. This may even have lessons for the war on terror.

Crime in Northern Ireland

Three points need to be made about crime in Northern Ireland. Firstly, crime in the province must be seen in context. In the post-peace universe, volume crime (the numerous offences concerned with property and violence, e.g. theft, criminal damage, assault) and organised crime became symbolic of the bitter fruits of peace, but overall crime remains lower than the rest of the UK, and low by international standards. However, secondly it is important to note that crime has risen. Official sources argue that the rise in crime is largely a result of statistical changes. However, crime was rising on the previous trajectories, and the changes in crime recording affected volume crime more than others.[6] Thirdly, and in connection with this, Northern Ireland is out of proportion to the other parts of the UK and many jurisdictions in Europe in terms of serious crime, and in the social power of organised crime. Fuel smuggling, cigarette smuggling, counterfeiting, cash-in-transit armed robbery, and extortion all rose markedly after 1998 and the murder rate remained well out of proportion to country size. Out of 128 cases of fuel smuggling detected in 1999–2000, 17 were in England and 111 in Northern Ireland. The revenue value of these cases stood at £2,500 in England and £901,000 in Northern Ireland. Revenue loss for petrol and diesel (from fraud and legitimate cross-border shopping combined) stood at £1,880 million overall in the UK, with a disproportionate £380 million (approximately 20 per cent) in Northern Ireland.[7] In 1998–1999 counterfeit goods worth £376,159 were seized by the RUC.[8] In 2003–2004 counterfeit goods worth £7,625,000 were seized.[9] An estimated £10 million is taken via extortion each year, a practice which worsened following 1998. High-level armed robbery remained out of proportion to the rest of the UK. Further, all the greatest years in terms of 'take' have come following the peace process, including £7,405,000 in 2001–2002; £3,034,000 in 2003–2004 and over £28,000,000 in 2004–2005.[10] Northern Ireland has the highest rate of crime against businesses in the UK.[11] Thus we cannot examine crime in Northern Ireland without examining organised crime, and paramilitary crime. And it is this form of crime which had such important effects on the developing peace process.

Paramilitaries and crime

Crime is a complex issue but this is particularly the case in Northern Ireland, where it is linked to the political strategies of paramilitary groups. Yet in many studies of paramilitarism crime is relegated as an issue. In many books on republican and loyalist paramilitary groups it does not appear in any index. Why might this be? Many political scientists, sociologists and historians marginalise it as an issue, concerned as they are to place ideology, strategy, organisational development and internal politics at the heart of their analysis of paramilitary groups. As Horgan and Taylor point out:

> All too often, we are beguiled by the rhetoric of political violence into focusing on the political agenda of terrorism, but in doing so we frequently fail to appreciate the sometimes substantial organisational and financial context to terrorism … this has especially been the case in Ireland, where images often substitute for reality at all levels of the political process. Terrorist groups from both Nationalist and Loyalist sides of the Northern Irish community may well have their roots in ideological and historical processes but they exist very much in the here and now, and have required considerable financial resources to sustain their existence.[12]

These financial resources come largely through crime. There are international donations and local donations (although these of course are illegal if done via intimidation or to finance a legally proscribed organisation) but the dynamic of paramilitary funding has been through local illegal activity.

Yet there has been, and remains, a tendency to politicise crime down, often almost out of existence. What many academics often imply might be caricatured as 'organisation such and such commits murders, sells drugs/ licenses dealers (delete as appropriate), and commits sectarian attacks but at the same time has a political vision, displays ideological development, aims for formal representation and engages in community work. This is vital activity, and therefore it should be judged dispassionately and in context.' And this is surely correct: academic analysis is about context and disaggregation. But this approach, evident in recent analyses of loyalist groups in transition, also smacks of presenting paramilitary organisations as though they were politically committed Citizens Advice Bureaux with a sideline in punishment beatings and counterfeiting training shoes. Their *raison d'être* was not community advice, and when they do perform such functions what might be the variable behind them which gives authority? These groups are engaged in serious criminality which is an important, not a marginal dynamic in their operation, and whether in the form of murders, assaults or economic crime beaches the principles of the Belfast Agreement to which they gave support. The neglect of crime as a variable in paramilitary political development in Northern Ireland is one manifestation of the long-term neglect in political science of variables such as criminality or violence in political development and change, or their over-determination by formal political models of explanation.[13]

Criminologists and some journalists tend to adopt a reverse analytical framework, viewing paramilitary organisations as basically criminal groups with more muscle.[14] Official sources sometimes fuel this perception, with apocalyptic talk of 'godfathers' and the looming 'mafia' society, sometimes as part of the desire of law enforcement for resources, or the creation of a policy consensus.[15]

If many political scientists tend to over-politicise paramilitary groups while criminologists under-politicise them, the point then is to *integrate*. In context, there is nothing unusual about political organisations being involved in crime, or vice versa, and there is nothing unusual about criminality being a generator of conflict or (in)stability at some points and not others.

Crime versus harm in paramilitary activity

This over-politicisation has led to a suspicion of the use of traditional terminology and law with regard to paramilitary organisations. English, in his analysis of the PIRA, argues that terrorism is not a proper term to employ when analysing the republican movement because it is pejorative. However, his replacement, 'guerrilla force', might not be pejorative but lacks clarity.[16] The mistrust of the term terrorist is also linked to a suspicion of the legal framework for defining acts of political violence because this was of course central to the security policy of the British state in Northern Ireland. The British state tried to normalise the conflict via the policy of police primacy. This stated that the local police, the RUC, were in charge of counter-terrorist policy, even to the extent of directing the military who were provided with limited powers of arrest. For republicans this was irrelevant. They were struggling against an illegitimate state and the laws of that state were null and void. This tactic was also adopted by loyalists who employed war terminology in arguing their actions were in support of the state. Offences such as murder, explosives and public disorder were 'military operations'. When they were sentenced, the paramilitary groups rejected the idea that they were 'normal' criminals. The removal of special category status from republican prisoners was resisted by them, eventually resulting in the hunger strikes. (Loyalists also successfully resisted). In terms of those offences which contravened the 'normal' criminal law: theft, extortion, robbery and so forth, on one level the argument continued to shine: the state was illegitimate, or a war was in operation and acts committed in the course of maintaining 'the struggle' were not crimes in the normal sense.

These arguments became more difficult following the Belfast Agreement with its implication of the acceptance of democratic and peaceful means of political activity and dispute resolution. Further, even if the idea of analysing crime through a formal framework is rejected, if we employ the arguments of the critical criminologists paramilitary actions can still be subject to critique. Their argument is that the normal legal framework is insufficient to characterise the effects of distributions of social power and the way in which powerful actors in society can have their actions not seen as crimes or even misdemeanours. Thus actions by states and large corporations are not classed as crimes, or are negotiated away via compliance; the authorities focus on petty theft and volume crime but not large-scale corporate and state pollution or deaths at work; large-scale fraud and corruption is under-policed and breaches of health and safety treated as regulatory offences. Thus these critics substitute the notion of harm, a non-legally bound definition of the negative effects of the actions of these powerful actors.[17] We can apply this to paramilitary crime, particularly since in the urban and rural zones of Northern Ireland these groups constituted powerful actors, and in many micro areas were the dominant actors.

It is clear that crimes committed by these groups cause harm in terms of the effects of their actions on victims (the emotional and financial loss from extortion, those injured in robberies, the physical and psychological effects of the intimidation of witnesses or punishment attacks) and they also cause harm in terms of the social cost of fraud and smuggling, while the involvement of the republican movement in fuel smuggling and illegal waste disposal has the same environmental cost as that done by any small business of the same size. In fact, the argument might be taken further: to those on the left, the actions of these organisations might be seen as a form of predatory capitalism, rather than as capacity building in support of 'the cause'. The notion of harm has rarely been applied to paramilitaries, but interestingly it is beginning to be used in a general sense by official (government, parliament, police) accounts of paramilitary related crime.

However it should also be noted that 'harm' has no clear infrastructure and risks dissolving into a list of what certain observers most dislike in a particular society.[18] Thus the criminal law will still be employed as a framework within which the notion of harm can be pursued. If the criminal law is insufficient to characterise the actions of republican and loyalist paramilitaries (as their academic sympathisers often assert), a more contextual approach still demonstrates the harm caused by such organisations. No more clear example of this might be in the clinical legal term of assault, to label a punishment attack, a term which disguises the long-term effects on the individual, and the role of such attacks (even if welcomed by many in the community) on the space for community development.

Paramilitaries, crime and communities

The issue of crime raises the issue of the relationship between paramilitary groups and communities. This is treacherous territory, and even the term community immediately raises conceptual and practical issues.[19] What is 'the community', a phrase which falls so easily from the lips of politicians and paramilitaries and the plethora of community action groups in the province? In relation to paramilitaries the concept has a double, even triple meaning. We hear that paramilitaries 'prey' on their communities, particularly in relation to crime, and control 'their' communities in relation to punishment attacks. Indeed, with regard to punishment attacks, they facilitate control but as has been pointed out repeatedly, there is also a demand for them. As Democratic Unionist Party MP Sammy Wilson recounted:

> On one occasion in my council ward in East Belfast someone came to me about people who were behaving antisocially next door to them. I went through all the normal channels – the environmental health department, the noise monitoring service, the police and social services – but still the behaviour went on. The lady met me in the road one day and said 'It's okay Sammy, I got it sorted out.' She named one of the people who sat with me on Belfast city council and said, 'I went to him. The boys came round and they sorted it out on Friday night.'[24]

But it is also clear that paramilitaries could not expand or operate (as for example the republican movement did), without community support. This leads us on to a final point: paramilitaries are, of course, part of these communities. Republican and loyalist groups also defend community boundaries and provide social support. Thus, the relationships between paramilitaries and crime are unstable: certain paramilitary criminal actions may see them losing legitimacy with their communities, either with their concrete supporters, fellow travellers or those whose support (via elections, nominal support, acquiescence or tolerance) varies with their distaste of certain actions or individuals. As Cavanaugh argues: 'communal support is conditional'.[25] In other words, paramilitary activities, particularly crime, may, in Peter Shirlow's framework, see a territory oscillate between 'sanctuary' and 'prison'. Indeed, as Shirlow tentatively points out in a recent study of geographies of in/security:

> The truth, by its nature was impossible to ascertain in particular cases, but we got the distinct impression that the very substantial scaling down of offensive operations since the 'ceasefires' has meant that 'internal operations' and the 'prison side of the territoriality coin' have become relatively more pronounced.[22]

Having discussed crime and the role of paramilitaries in it, we cannot examine these things without examining the state response, particularly the police, since they underwent a compressed and radical process of reform during this period. The actions of the state highlight important debates about the coherence of state policy, its effects on the rule of law and the simple effectiveness of state policy towards paramilitary (and other) crime.

The State and crime control

The state's response to crime has raised a number of controversial issues, not least the fact that a process of police reform was central to solidifying the peace. As this was proceeding there were debates over police effectiveness. However, policing takes place in a wider context, and the wider political variables affecting policing and other types of law enforcement require examination.

Policing and political transition

Policing was and is central to change following the Belfast Agreement. Republican supporters had always felt the police were by nature illegitimate because they secured the peace in a part of Ireland which should not be under British rule. This was exacerbated by their complaints about police heavy-handedness, police recruitment of informants, and police collusion with loyalist paramilitaries. Nationalists who sought negotiated change rather than the violent removal of the British nevertheless had similar complaints. The Patten Report set the framework for a large-scale reform programme which involved substantial cultural and organisational change. The latter involved the establishment of a new Crime Department and the application of New Public Management reforms to policing. Bureaucratic reforms to policing were accompanied by a process of modernisation, which was evident in homicide investigation, the use of intelligence (involving the National Intelligence Model) and financial investigation (although this had been evident under the RUC from the 1980s). The result of these reforms is that the police were not effectively phased out of existence as a major police organisation; in fact the PSNI has become more like a major British force than at any previous epoch, a process discussed in Chapter 6. This new structure was central to the investigation of sensitive crimes such as homicide but also long-term problem areas such as extortion and a rejuvenated spate of armed robberies, particularly cash-in-transit robberies (see Chapter 5).

The politics of policing and accountability

The Patten Report also called for a new framework of police central and local accountability. The reforms engendered marked change. The Police Authority of Northern Ireland was replaced by the Policing Board, with greater powers to call the Chief Constable to account, in both private and public briefings. The Policing Board is evidence of accountability and 'local ownership' and is currently distinct from any policing accountability structure in the UK. Locally, police decentralisation matched local authority districts and was coupled with the establishment of District Policing Partnerships. 'One thing policing is not, however, is political', the Policing Board argued on the basis of these reforms.[23] It might be the case that one type of politics has been taken out of policing (the close association of the RUC with Protestant hegemony) but more have blossomed in its place. This is to be expected. Policing is increasingly political in the UK, driven by successive Home Secretaries and crime panics.[24] The political component of the Board naturally reinforces the political profile of policing. Some of the political drive is short-term, for example, the politics which were clearly evident if actors including the Oversight Commissioner (who reports on police reform), the Policing Board, and the PSNI Chief Constable repeatedly made public remarks about getting Sinn Féin on the Policing Board.[25]

The Police Ombudsman has been a vigorous and independent buttress to the system of accountability and has also been intensely political. The Ombudsman's Report into the Real IRA bomb in Omagh created evident controversy as it also fuelled the process of organisational change within the PSNI, particularly in the area of homicide investigation. Further reports have continued to raise the role of police and military informants inside paramilitary organisations.

However, the long-term political component is the balance between the police as upholders of Northern Ireland and the consumerist debates about police service and efficiency which are evident in most polities. If debate about the police becomes focused on 'normal' crime and police effectiveness in the long term de facto acceptance of the police, or even police legitimacy may develop across the community divide.

As implied, these issues centred on the PSNI also raise issues of the wider context of policing and law enforcement.

Government policy, policing and the rule of law

By the 1970s the British state had effectively 'quasi-nationalised' the conflict in Northern Ireland. This process was not planned, but it did stem from the 'British way' of policymaking and counter insurgency.[26] Obviously the main plank was direct rule from London. Then a massive security budget funded the expansion of the RUC, the presence of British and Northern Irish Army regiments and the development of a physical security infrastructure of checkpoints and watchtowers. Furthermore, police and military intelligence, it is now increasingly clear, developed a network of informants in both republican and loyalist paramilitary organisations, which was buttressed by a web of technical surveillance.[27] In fact if revelations concerning the number of informants inside paramilitary organisations continue, it will be shown that the British state was often effectively fighting a 'war' with itself.

Clearly, the British state remains central to security and crime control. The Organised Crime Task Force is run from the Northern Ireland Office (NIO). This has been the case partly in the absence of devolution, although devolution would not mean an end to the state's role rather its localisation. Further, important functions remain UK controlled: the Assets Recovery Agency has an active Belfast office but is answerable to the Home Secretary. By 2006 MI5 was in the process of taking over national security intelligence from PSNI Special Branch, in preparation for the official handover in 2007.

What have been the effects of this central role of the state? The state has acted to target some groups, particularly when they have opposed the peace process, or have distanced themselves from it, or when crime has simply detonated under the government's feet and has necessitated a response. Alternatively, crime has been downplayed at certain points as a result of decisions about the stability of the peace process. At various points the government has in effect connived in undermining the rule of law to ensure political settlement. This is an empirical observation, not a moral judgement.

With regard to republicans, as detailed in Chapter 2, their criminal activity had to 'go nuclear' before the government took action. Then republicans were subject to concerted policing in the wake of the Northern Bank robbery in 2004 and asset investigations spread to both sides of the border. However, following 2005 and the PIRA's announcement that their war is over, critics say the government is 'at it' again with the NIO (aiming to institutionalise the republicans further) politically driving agreement on restorative justice schemes in republican areas that other actors (PSNI, Policing Board, SDLP) are concerned about.[28] Then in 2006 Hugh Orde (and others) argued that republican movement assets cannot be targeted because they are effectively clean.[29] This remarkable public statement does not fit with the Assets Recovery Agency's stated rationale/ justification that it can target assets gained from unlawful activity which have been hidden in both time and place, and does not fit with its wide capabilities to take action under civil law. The ARA works on case referrals from the police so investigations on the historical structure of republican assets will not be forthcoming, one can presume. Turning to the ARA itself, we do not know the full scale of cases referred but not proceeded with, but as Chapter 7 argues, the Agency has not targeted the throbbing targets of republican and loyalist paramilitarism. Much of its activity appears focused on dissidents, particularly loyalists in the form of the LVF. Now that the ARA has been merged into a much bigger organisation, the Serious and Organised Crime Agency ('Britain's FBI'), asset recovery in Northern Ireland from high profile republican (and loyalist) targets who are adhering to the peace will not be on the agenda.

The argument has oft been made that the state is 'politicising the Provos, criminalising the Prods'. That is, ignoring criminal activity by the PIRA in order to draw the republican movement into the peace process and its institutions while continuing a policy of treating loyalist paramilitaries as common criminals to be subject to law enforcement attention. Care needs to be given here: both sides have been given leeway. Even during the internecine loyalist paramilitary feuds of 2000–2005 much thought was given to effects of de-recognising the ceasefires of loyalist groups and returning UDA leader Johnny Adair to prison. The fact that the UVF and UDA ceasefires remained recognised for so long is evidence of this also, since if organisations were not specified (i.e. officially designated as off ceasefire by the government) it in practice limited the charges that could be brought and gave less space to the police. With regard to law enforcement, as argued in Chapter 3, PSNI policing appears to be part of a process of drawing those loyalist paramilitaries who are open to change into re-engaging with the body monitoring paramilitary activity, the Independent Monitoring Commission (IMC) and the political process generally.

Thus, depending on the context of the peace, the government has oscillated in its relation to paramilitaries. However, overall certain priorities are evident, namely those concerned with the stabilisation of the peace process, and part of this is an understanding that some targets are more equal than others. This could not but fail to affect law enforcement, particularly when linked to the level of state control in Northern Ireland. The police retain operational independence but this does not mean that the Chief Constable and the PSNI are not influenced and pressured by general political movements and specific pressures from government officials. There is an awareness of 'what damages the peace', a miasmic-like high-level consensus which can smother decision making further down, a phenomenon already evident in the 1990s.[30] The PSNI also, of course, makes judgements as to which groups/individuals are the most appropriate targets in the light of police resources.

Overall, few would argue the British government in Northern Ireland has pursued a coherent strategy. Indeed, as Gillespie points out: 'Both security and social issues were inextricably linked with the implementation of the Agreement in respect of which the Government often appeared stagestruck when asked to deal with ongoing paramilitary activity.'[31] This is true of crime.

The institutionalisation of paramilitaries?

The quasi-nationalisation which was evident before the peace process was also evident with regard to anti-state groups and continues as a method of their institutionalisation. The issue of restorative justice schemes is an example. As O'Doherty argues, during the period of conflict, Sinn Féin, through its community 'policing', aimed to usurp state functions, and indeed its position and role could (and can) 'implicate support from rivals and even state institutions'. However, this was always limited in how far it could go and republicans have thus been unavoidably complicit with the state.[32] Indeed well before the peace in terms of its relations with probation and other community services, arguably 'there is no strict separation between a Sinn Féin councillor and community organisations and even statutory bodies'.[33] Thus to some extent the debates in 2006 and 2007 about whether Sinn Féin should join the Policing Board and become institutionalised, and end its parallel policing miss the point. Sinn Féin and the republican movement particularly after the peace process provided effective 'policing and public order' functions in republican areas, and have not been undermining public authority but in effect functioning as a state auxiliary, albeit an irascible and unpredictable one (and one which still sought to protect its own members from local policing and justice, not just in the McCartney case but also other occurrences).[34] Thus at least in this area, the debate is not whether the republican movement becomes institutionalised; it is a debate over the form of its institutionalisation.

With regard to the loyalist paramilitaries much was made in 2005 of their apparent offers to decommission in return for £30 million, or some such figure. This was of course dismissed at the time but since 2005 particularly the flow of public money towards loyalist areas became significant. In mid-2006, £3 million was announced to go toward mural replacement in loyalist areas; £135,000 allocated to the Ulster Political Research Group (UPRG) (the think tank associated with the UDA); and £4 million to clean up major roads in Belfast in loyalist (and republican) areas. This may have been partly behind the UDA South East Antrim brigade's politically misjudged request for £8.5 million of public money to assist in its conversion to a community group over five years, since it had been in discussions with the NIO for some time.[35]

Thus the legacy of state control is central to security, crime, crime control and institutionalisation.

Political transition, politics, paramilitaries and the end of crime

Following the PIRA's historic announcement that it was ceasing military operations in 2005, the issue of the organisation's involvement in crime became even more crucial. Two IMC reports argued that the PIRA was instructing members to desist from crime and closing down criminal operations. Crimes were still being committed but by individuals who had not been sanctioned, and the money was not being transferred up the organisational chain. However, until the 12th IMC report, the question of whether PIRA Volunteers had been paid a 'wage' was left unanswered. The 12th IMC report of October 2006 was impatiently awaited by those wishing to give the republican movement a clean bill of health.[36] These judgements provided the framework within which crime connected to paramilitary groups is now understood.

Other questions persist. PIRA military structure and capacity is being dismantled. The issue of whether money is going to the organisation at all remains open, as do others mentioned in Chapter 2, but there remains the fact that the PIRA financial structure is intact. Overall the test is simple; if the republican movement is no longer involved in crime, those offences associated with it should drop, indeed should already be dropping if the IMCs judgement is accurate. The reduction of PIRA punishment beatings and exiling occurred over the 2003–2006 period. We should also see an end to serious crimes, including fuel smuggling, serious armed robbery and counterfeiting. If they do not drop then the activists have moved into organised crime, or new entrants are evident. If further splits in the republican movement should take place after the decision by Sinn Féin to accept policing structures in Northern Ireland in 2007, crime will occur as these groups gain funds to expand their organisations, although this will of course be at a lower level.

Loyalist paramilitaries appear to be in a genuine process of transition, as a result of the resolution of the long-term destabilisation caused by the formation of the LVF, law enforcement attention and the example of PIRA decommissioning, coupled with an internal critique which was already emerging but had been submerged in internal conflict and crime in the early 2000s. There are many positive signs, including the Progressive Unionist Party (PUP) (the political counterpart to the UVF) and the Ulster Unionist Party working together, and remarkably the PUP and Sinn Féin agreeing to work together on community issues in Londonderry.[37] However, the process is problematic and the self-analysis of transformation is hampered because it concentrates on developments and statements by the leadership or its political supporters and demonstrates denial concerning the persistence of criminality. The naiveté which resulted from this heuristic could be seen with regard to the UDA in the proposal by

'Beyond Conflict', a group backed by the Southeast Antrim UDA that it required £8.5 million to facilitate 'a transformation mechanism' to end paramilitary activity within a 5-year period. If the loyalist groups are making inroads on criminality then similarly offences associated with them should drop from 2007, particularly extortion, drugs and counterfeiting.

This creates an interesting vista: if paramilitaries are desisting from crime we should expect at the least a sharp drop in serious crime figures and other normal offences previously connected to paramilitary groups from 2006. It might be the case that former paramilitaries are already moving into crime. Or it might be that the organised Ordinary Decent Criminal (ODC) crime is on the rise, and Northern Ireland will continue to exhibit an overrepresentation of organised crime in some of its crime patterns.

Conclusion

Crime became an increasingly important factor in the peace process. It was marginalised by the government until occurrences such as the Northern Bank robbery shattered its screen of neglect. Crime became important as a signifier of the transformation of paramilitary organisations, and as such demonstrates the need to integrate it into any comprehensive analysis of paramilitaries. The fact that the PIRA demobilised and decommissioned from 2005 cannot be separated from the way in which the organisation had 'boxed itself in' via the Northern Bank robbery and the murder of Robert McCartney. Its criminal activity became central to judgements over whether it was still active. The same became the case for loyalist paramilitary groups, particularly after their internal violent disputes from 2000 on. These were partly due to the internal split within loyalist groups over how to respond to the peace process. But subsequent overall reform has been measured by their slow desistance from crime.

With regard to policing, the PSNI is more thoroughly 'mainlandised' than at any time in their history. The police have undergone a process of radical organisational and cultural change and modernisation in terms of crime investigation. The structures of accountability in the form of the Police Ombudsman and the Policing Board are more extensive than those on the UK mainland, unless one adopts an unsustainable negativism. Indeed if Gerry Kelly MLA (Sinn Féin's policing and justice spokesman) accepts the extent of change then something important has happened since 1999.

On a wider level, the response to crime via the OCTF and ARA demonstrates similarities with late modern governmental techniques employed elsewhere in terms of governing through crime and extending regulation with an eye to crime control. However, not only are debates about the effectiveness of law enforcement evident, but also the notion of political policing and whether some groups have been disproportionately targeted. The PSNI are policing towards institutionalising paramilitary groups and targeting dissident republican and loyalist groups. The ARA also raises questions concerning such tactics.

Finally, it is clear that over the long term paramilitaries are moving away from crime, but reports of the death of paramilitary crime are exaggerated. It is risky to assert, as the IMC and British government do, that the PIRA is no longer involved in crime, since a number of questions (not least the PIRA financial structure) remain in the air. The UDA and UVF are making efforts to move from criminality, but this is a difficult process, particularly if they and their supporters do not rigorously engage with the issue. It remains early to make pronouncements about the end of paramilitary crime or about the future of organised crime generally. With regard to the latter point, within the general term organised crime, paramilitaries have been involved in crime and are dominant in some areas, and not in others. In many respects in terms of both organised and volume crime Northern Ireland is approximating the rest of the UK, although some interesting contrasts remain (including the area of drugs).

The next chapters deal with the problem of crime related to paramilitaries in Northern Ireland and the practical and symbolic role crime played in their transformation.

Notes

1   Dates vary. Some might identify the beginning as 1966, the year in which a group calling itself the Ulster Volunteer Force appeared. This was just a few years after an active IRA had emerged once more and its 'Border War' had come to an end (1956–1962).
2   There was also talk of a distinct Ulster identity, distinct from Britain, which led to proposals for Ulster independence in the 1970s and 1980s.
3   Two sources of information are Malcolm Sutton's painstaking *An Index of Deaths from the Conflict in Ireland* available in summary at http://cain.ulst.ac.uk/ sutton/index.html and the British Irish Rights Watch site, www.birw.org/.
4   Situational changes refer to changes in the range of physical and social controls which constrain criminal opportunities e.g. national borders, building types and security, access points, social routines in a street or neighbourhood and so forth. Social changes refer to the large-scale political, economic and social developments which may provide the context for crime or its control e.g. unemployment, economic change, state regulation, drugs economies and so forth. For Northern Ireland see J. Moran, 'Paramilitaries, "ordinary decent criminals" and the development of organised crime following the Belfast

Agreement', *International Journal of the Sociology of Law*, 32 (2004), 263–278; also P. Ekblom and N. Tilley, 'Going equipped: criminology, situational crime prevention and the resourceful offender', *British Journal of Criminology*, 40 (2000), 376–398; L. Cohen and M. Felson, 'Social change and crime rate trends: a routine activity approach', *American Sociological Review*, 44:4 (1979), 588–608.

5   J. Brewer (ed.), *Restructuring South Africa* (London: Macmillan, 1994); M. Brogden and C. Shearing, *Policing for a New South Africa* (London: Routledge, 1997); S. Leman-Langlois and C. Shearing, 'Repairing the future: The South African Truth and Reconciliation Commission at work', in G. Gilligan and J. Pratt (eds), *Crime, Truth and Justice. Official Inquiry, Discourse and Knowledge* (Devon: Willan, 2004), pp. 222–242; A. Jackson and A. Lyon, 'Policing after ethnic conflict', *Policing*, 24:4 (2001), 563–585.

6   See Chapter 4.

7   HM Customs and Excise, *The Misuse and Smuggling of Hydrocarbon Oil* (London: The Stationery Office, 2002), pp. 3, 13.

8   RUC, *Annual Report of the Chief Constable 1998/99* (Belfast: RUC, 1999), p. 38.

9   Organised Crime Task Force, *Serious and Organised Crime in Northern Ireland. Threat Assessment and Strategy* (Belfast: OCTF, 2004), p. 27.

10 Figures from CAIN Table NI-SEC 08 *Armed robberies 1969–2001–02*, http://cain.ulst.ac.uk/ni/security.htm (see also Chapter 6). Figures not accounting for inflation.

11 'N. Ireland "tops for business crime"', *UTV News* (8 June 2006), http://u.tv/newsroom/indepth.asp?pt=n&id=74114.

12 J. Horgan and M. Taylor, 'Playing the "green card" – financing the Provisional IRA', *Terrorism and Political Violence*, 11:2 (1999), 2.

13 Political scientists have often neglected crime as a variable, as they often have political violence and its connection to crime. However, detailed historiographical and sociological analyses shows crime, political violence and political development are phenomena which require rigorous study both in terms of state formation, persistence and the development of opposition to state authority. McCamant makes this critique with regard to state violence, which he argues political scientists have neglected in favour of formal modes of explaining political stability or change. J. McCamant, 'Governance without blood: social science's antiseptic view of rule', in M. Stohl and G. Lopez, *The State as Terrorist: The Dynamics of Governmental Violence and Repression* (London: Aldwych, 1984). See C. Tilly (ed.), *The Formation of National States in Western Europe* (Princeton: Princeton University Press, 1975); C. Tilly, 'Urbanisation, criminality and collective violence in nineteenth century France', American Journal of Sociology, 79 (1973), 296–318; C. Tilly, 'War making and state making as organised crime', in P. Evans, D. Rueschemeyer and T. Skocpol (eds), *Bringing the State Back In* (Cambridge: Cambridge University Press, 1985), pp. 169–191. More attention has been given to this topic particularly after the Cold War and the existence of corruption and 'failed states' was framed as an international problem. W. Reno, *Corruption and State Politics in Sierra Leone* (Cambridge: Cambridge University Press, 1995); W.

Reno, 'Clandestine economies, violence and states in Africa', *Journal of International Affairs*, 53:2 (2000), 433–459; A. Doig and R. Theobald (eds), *Corruption and Democratisation* (London, Frank Cass, 1999). With regard to anti-state political organisations, there is nothing remarkable about their being involved in crime, or vice versa, and there is nothing unusual about criminality being a generator of conflict or (in)stability at some points and not others. Italy's political transition following the Second World War was central in the rise of the mafia. See R. Catanzaro, *Men of Respect. A Social History of the Sicilian Mafia* (New York: Free Press, 1992). Crime and politics merged in the anti-colonial Mau Mau movement in Kenya, particularly in urban areas. D. Anderson, *Histories of the Hanged. Britain's Dirty War in Kenya and the End of the Empire* (London: Weidenfeld and Nicholson, 2005), Chapters 1 and 5. The historical links between drugs and insurgency are well established in south-east Asia, as detailed in A. McCoy, *The Politics of Heroin* (USA: Lawrence Hill, 1991) as well as crime and political action in support of national independence. See, for example, R. Cribb, *Gangsters and Revolutionaries. The Jakarta People's Militia and the Indonesian Revolution 1945–49* (Australia: Allen and Unwin, 1991). In 1970s Jamaica the development of competition between rival politicians led to the expansion of political gangs, which connected party politics with street mobilisation. Patron–client relations connected jobs and public works in return for mobilising votes and 'policing' meetings via illegal means. The gangs developed criminal activities in this social and political space. When the gangs had outlived their usefulness government elites officially disowned them but they had already expanded their drugs and serious crime activities. See L. Gunst, *Born Fi Dead* (Edinburgh: Payback Press, 1999). In Colombia the left-wing guerrilla movement, the Revolutionary Armed Forces of Colombia (FARC) was accused of drug trafficking by the United States. This allegation was initially driven by the politics of US foreign policy in the 1980s, but FARC involvement in the drugs economy did later develop as a tactic to raise finance. The organisation began providing protection for drugs transporters, but in the areas it controlled farmers were protected and their crops purchased for fixed prices. The drugs were then transported by the organisation as it moved its participation and control down the supply chain. Ideologically, FARC has little problem with subverting middle-class US drug consumers. International Crisis Group, 'War and drugs in Colombia', *Latin American Report* 11 (2005); F. Thoumi, 'Illegal drugs in Colombia: from illegal economic boom to social crisis', *Annals of the American Academy of Political and Social Science*, 582:1 (2002), 102–116. Links between crime and politics were evident in the late modern urban zones of Los Angeles where, following the disintegration of the Black Panthers, 'The Crips, however perversely, inherited the Panther aura of fearlessness and transmitted the ideology of armed vanguardism.' Mixing 'teen cult and proto Mafia' the gangs represented a distorted political representation of alienated and jobless black youth. M. Davis, *City of Quartz.. Excavating the Future in Los Angeles* (London: Vintage, 1990), p. 299. In this light, crime and politics are not exclusive, merely different facets of an organisation, and to be integrated in any comprehensive analysis of political operation and transformation.

14   For exceptions see J. Cusack and H. McDonald, *UVF* (Dublin: Poolbeg, 2000); H. McDonald and J. Cusack, *UDA* (Dublin: Penguin Ireland, 2004).

15   One of the problems in this area has been that where the link between crime and politically violent groups was examined, it often generated more heat than light. During the Cold War some accounts unconvincingly linked crime to insurgent and other movements opposed by the United States in particular. For example the idea of narco-terrorism linked leftist terrorists to drug trafficking, while the Kremlin was linked to organised crime and terrorism, C. Sterling, *The Terror Network* (New York: Berkley, 1983) in analyses subsequently discredited. See A. Miller and N. Damask, 'How Myths Drive Policy: The Dual Myths of Narco-Terrorism', *Terrorism and Political Violence*, 8:1 (1996), 114–131; P. van Duyne, 'The phantom threat of organised crime', *Crime, Law and Social Change*, 24 (1996), 341–377; M. Levi, 'Perspectives on "organised crime": An overview', *Howard Journal of Criminal Justice*, 37:4 (1998), 335–345; P. van Duyne, 'Money laundering: Pavlov's dog and beyond', *Howard Journal of Criminal Justice*, 37:4 (1998), 359–374 for critiques.

16   English, *Armed Struggle*, pp. 448–449, n. 149. The closest that the PIRA came to holding land was in South Armagh, but no demarcated territory was permanently under their control within which a devolved autonomous political and administrative rule was the norm. No paramilitary group ever came close to waging the quasi-conventional conflict that guerrilla war or insurgency refers to: 'insurgency is violence in support strategically, of a political goal, operationally of a political infrastructure, tactically of local political domination'. T. Marks, *Maoist Insurgency since Vietnam* (London: Frank Cass, 1996), p. 4. Hezbollah approximates such a group even though it is termed terrorist – as does FARC in Colombia. Indeed, FARC's success has been to move from guerrilla war to a quasi-civil war situation, similarly the LTTE ('Tamil Tigers') who control and administer distinct territory in the north of Sri Lanka. On the spectrum from terrorist to insurgent to guerrilla to civil war combatant group, the Northern Ireland organisations including the UVF and UDA are not analytically and empirically comparable to groups such as Hezbollah or the LTTE.

17   P. Hillyard, J. Sim, S. Tombs and D. Whyte, '"Leaving a stain upon the silence": Contemporary criminology and the politics of dissent', *British Journal of Criminology*, 44 (2004), 369–390.

18   It is interesting that in their article on harm Hillyard (*et al.*) focus on the British state but do not address paramilitary crime.

19   S. Poole, *Unspeak* (London: Abacus, 2007), Chapter 2.

20   DUP MP Sammy Wilson, quoted in *Hansard*, 5 July 2006, Col. 253WH.

21   K. Cavanaugh, 'Interpretations of political violence in ethnically divided societies', *Terrorism and Political Violence*, 9:3 (1997), 49, quoted in C. Knox, *An evaluation of the alternative criminal justice system in Northern Ireland*, ESRC research project, L133251003 (2005).

22   P. Shirlow, 'Mapping the spaces of fear: Socio-spatial causes and effects of violence in Northern Ireland', ESRC research project, L133251007 (2001).

23   Northern Ireland Policing Board, 'The life and times of the Northern Ireland Policing Board 4 November 2001–31 March 2006' (NIPB: Belfast, 2006).

24   D. Garland, *The Culture of Control. Crime and Order in Contemporary Society* (Oxford: Oxford University Press, 2001).

25   Author interview, Ian Paisley Jr. DUP, MLA, Belfast, 5 October 2006.

26   D. Anderson and D. Killingray (eds), *Policing and Decolonisation. Nationalism, Politics and the Police 1917–65* (Manchester: Manchester University Press, 1992).

27   T. Geraghty, *The Irish War. The Military History of a Domestic Conflict* (London: Harper Collins, 1998); J. Holland and S. Phoenix, *Phoenix. Policing the Shadows* (London, Hodder and Stoughton, 1997); P. Taylor, *Brits. The War against the IRA* (London: Bloomsbury, 2002); M. Smyth, 'The process of demilitarization and the reversibility of the peace process in Northern Ireland', *Terrorism and Political Violence,* 16:3 (2004), 544–566.

28   Author interview, Alex Attwood SDLP, MLA, Belfast, 6 October 2006.

29   Comment at the meeting of the Policing Board, 5 October 2006.

30   Holland and Phoenix, *Phoenix,* Chapter 9; L. Clarke, 'McGuiness in new spy claims', *Sunday Times* (4 June 2006).

31   G. Gillespie, 'Noises off: loyalists after the Agreement', in M. Cox, A. Guelke, F. Stephen (eds), *A Farewell to Arms? Beyond the Good Friday Agreement* (Manchester: Manchester University Press, 2006), p. 150.

32   M. O'Doherty, *The Trouble with Guns. Republican Strategy and the Provisional IRA* (Belfast: Blackstaff, 1998), p. 145.

33   M. O'Doherty, *The Trouble with Guns,* p. 148.

34   For a trenchant critique see A. McIntyre, 'CRJ – new name for the IRA?' *The Blanket* (December 2005).

35   Representatives of Beyond Conflict had been meeting with the NIO during the year. *BBC Newsline* (2 October 2006); see also L. Clarke, 'Hain offers £1m to disband UDA', *Sunday Times* (24 September 2006) referring to an initial payment of £135,000 to the UPRG to assist in community work.

36   The IMC attributed the killing of UVF paramilitary Mark Haddock to the UVF leadership but the murder of Denis Donaldson, in all likelihood killed by PIRA individuals, remained unattributed.

37   *BBC Digital News Northern Ireland* (18 September 2006).

2

The republican movement: politics, crime and transition

One circle of people will blame the IRA while another will praise them.[a]

The belief in Short Strand is that while the killing of Robert McCartney was in all likelihood the result of a beery brawl, a republican, even a republican who fought the Brits for many years, should have to pay for stabbing somebody to death in a street fight.[b]

No Republican worthy of the name can be involved in criminality of any kind.[c]

There probably is still some localised individual criminality by former and maybe existing Provisional IRA members for their own private gain. What there is not is organised 'from the centre' criminality any more.[d]

[a] Vincent Currie, SDLP councillor in Coalisland after the shooting of an alleged drugs dealer by republicans, quoted in T. Oliver, 'Children see "IRA shoot drugs man"', *Daily Telegraph* (1 September 2001).

[b] Robin Livingstone, editor of *Andersonstown News* in, 'This crisis threatens to halt the advance of Sinn Féin', *Guardian* (19 February 2005).

[c] Sinn Féin President, Gerry Adams, Strabane, February 2005.

[d] Secretary of State for Northern Ireland, Peter Hain quoted in 'IRA has ceased its criminality', *BBC News* (25 July 2006).

Politics, crime and legitimacy

The relationship between the republican movement and criminality is a complex one. However one views republican paramilitary activity it occurs in a complex context. This is particularly true of those assaults which constitute paramilitary justice, but also the organised crimes and financial activities of the republican movement. All these activities have raised important symbolic debates about the role of paramilitaries within their communities, and have played a role in the stability or otherwise of the peace process and the institutionalisation of Sinn Féin and the republican movement in the post-Belfast Agreement universe.

Like many social phenomena in Northern Ireland, crime committed by the republican movement is shot through with multiple meanings and interpretations. Historically, to many in the republican movement, crime was not crime. Since they were struggling against an illegitimate state – the British state ruling Northern Ireland – the laws of that state were null and void. Thus republican prisoners, either on remand or following conviction, sought to attain and maintain special category status whether in HMP Belfast or HMP Maze, viewing themselves as prisoners of war rather than convicted offenders. Conversely, from the mid-1970s the British government sought to criminalise PIRA prisoners, a policy move that eventually led to the hunger strikes of 1980 and 1981.[1] In the end, PIRA and other prisoners effectively attained special category status, ending integrated holding in HMP Belfast through rioting and in the Maze in effect running their own regimes with prison officers limited to small parts of the H Blocks and prisoners out of their cells on a 24-hour basis. Thus the argument is that using the criminal law as an analytical tool with which to understand the Provisional Irish Republican Army (PIRA) is unhelpful. This is a powerful argument, particularly when considering crimes committed against the state, that is, what are normally considered 'terrorist offences', those offences which were in contravention of the Emergency Provisions Act(s), the Prevention of Terrorism Act(s), and following reform of the legislation, the Terrorism Act 2000 and the Anti Terrorism Crime and Security Act 2001. Even critical analyses of the IRA such as English argue that it was a guerrilla organisation and indeed, eschew the term 'terrorism' regarding it as pejorative.[2]

Nevertheless, the situation became more complicated following the 1998 Belfast Agreement. Although the republican movement might not recognise the state, its adherence to the Mitchell Principles and de facto recognition of Northern Ireland institutions created a new legal context even for those wedded to the arguments outlined above. Thus, while Gerry Adams did not endorse the institutions of Northern Ireland he argued that the PIRA Amy Council was not the legitimate government of Ireland.[3]

The same applied with regard to the commission of offences by the republican movement which contravene the 'normal' criminal law, the Theft Act (Northern Ireland) 1969. Following the Belfast Agreement the argument that crimes such as robbery, fraud, extortion and so forth are legitimate because they maintain the capacity for the struggle are inapplicable.

However if we apply the notion of harm to these actions it is clear that they were problematic even before 1998. Critical criminologists argue that if an analysis based on the criminal law is insufficient to characterise the effects of certain actors in society we can substitute the notion of 'harm' i.e. a non-legally constrained definition of the negative effects of distributions of social power and its effects in terms of loss or injury. Much critical criminology has focused on the manner in which some harms caused by states and corporations are not covered by a credible legal framework (not seen as important or trivialised even if reaching some form of formal sanction), or the manner in which the true extent and effects of certain offences classed as crimes in the traditional sense (racist violence) are nevertheless effectively hidden.[4] The way these critics focus on the victims of state and corporate wrongdoing who have been long neglected is particularly important. How does this framework apply to the republican movement (and the loyalist paramilitaries in the next chapter)?

Clearly the PIRA's actions require attention as harms. Crimes committed by the republican movement cause harm in terms of the effects of their actions on victims (such as those injured in robberies), the social cost of fraud and smuggling offences, the intimidation of potential witnesses and complainants, while the current involvement of the PIRA in illegal waste disposal, like that of corporations, presents an environmental threat (for example the chemical processing of illicit fuel produces acid waste). Finally, there is the crucial role of the PIRA in dispensing summary justice in their communities in place of the regular police force which is seen as illegitimate and/or ineffective. Here again, even if one accepts the legitimacy argument, that these actions are supported by some sections of the community, the actual mechanics of paramilitary justice (beatings and shootings) cause disproportionate harm to the victim and his/her family, particularly if, in the absence of due process, an innocent person was attacked.

This chapter will adopt the framework of the normal criminal law in analysing PIRA crime, because, while PIRA crime has this contextual element, the criminal law is a clear framework within which to analyse PIRA actions, within which the notion of harm can be applied, unless one believes that categories such as extortion, theft, attempted murder, robbery and various regulatory offences are completely obfuscatory.

The PIRA's involvement in crime served a number of functions. As the peace process developed, the PIRA's desistance from crime became central to its overall demobilisation, as exemplified by the organisation's two-stage demobilisation: a military one in which in 2005 it announced the war was over and weapons were decommissioned and secondly, from 2005 a closing down of criminality. This process was not predictable, but was the result of the PIRA being in an increasingly tight position. Due to the Northern Bank robbery and Robert McCartney's murder the PIRA had effectively made crime an issue themselves. The British government would in all likelihood have continued to tolerate a level of crime as acceptable, as they generally had in the 1998–2003 period.

The dynamics behind organised crime

Paramilitary organisations are expensive to run. By the time of the peace process the PIRA had built up an impressive structure and capacity. It was estimated that in 2001/2002 the PIRA had estimated running costs of £1.5 million per year but an estimated fundraising capacity of £5–8 million per year.[5] While law enforcement estimates can be subject to critique as they may be affected by ulterior motives,[6] it is clear that the PIRA has a significant fundraising capacity. Thomas 'Slab' Murphy, allegedly a major fundraiser and PIRA chief of staff from the late 1990s had a personal worth estimated at £35–40m.[7] The Northern Bank armed robbery originally netted £26.5 million; the Makro robbery netted £1m; cigarette smuggling, fuel smuggling and counterfeiting net millions per annum as Customs and PSNI seizures reflect. Extortion continued to bring in funds. In one case in 2004, the PIRA were involved in a failed attempt to extort £100,000 from a cigarette smuggler.[8] The PIRA have historically been effective in regulating finance in that funding was and is more centralised, with less chance of 'leakage' on the way up. However, there is a large amount of money flowing through the organisation, and it has recently faced a number of internal frauds.[9]

The PIRA has always been regarded as more multifaceted than Loyalist organisations, in its criminal activities as well as its military operations. The PIRA has displayed innovation, evident from their engineering department which gradually progressed in the development of more sophisticated mortars and explosive devices. To an extent the same can be said of crime.[10] By the time of the peace process the PIRA was active in a number of areas including armed robbery, extortion, smuggling, public and private sector fraud.[11] If it is possible to discern over time a development from more direct methods of raising finance to more sophisticated means, the range of tactics continued to be employed. Thus, although the PIRA moved from bank robbery towards activities which can be encompassed by the term fraud, armed robberies remained a tactic for raising finance, and returned to prominence for a period following the peace process. Further, as with loyalists, extortion (although the tactics increased in subtlety) has remained a significant source of fundraising.

The PIRA's sophistication can not only be traced to its efficient organisational capacity, particularly when compared to the loyalists, but also to the solid basis of its political support, as witnessed by the success of Sinn Féin. The community was, and is, used as a source of funds through black market activities involving taxi firms, drinking clubs, local 'charities', raffles, music evenings and so forth. A number of paper techniques were developed in the 1980s, including frauds, evasion and mechanisms for hiding revenues.[12] Greater attention by the tax and other authorities on clubs, pubs, entertainment and taxi transport forced the PIRA to reorganise or slim down their operations,[13] and by the time of the peace process, paramilitaries' 'access to funds had been diminished' according to one official in the NIO.[14] However, certain areas, such as taxis had not been successfully tackled, and following 1998 fraudulent activities continued and expanded into new areas. The latter expansion was sometimes facilitated by new opportunities in terms of the funds which have been disbursed from various sources for peace and reconciliation, and by the establishment of new local businesses.

As mentioned, armed robbery did not die out as a fundraising tactic. Although it declined relative to other less risky tactics it continued to function as a rapid method of raising large sums. A series of major robberies occurred following the peace process. The Provisional IRA was allegedly responsible for a large theft from the wholesaler Makro at Dunmurry, a large robbery from retailer Iceland and the Northern Bank robbery of December 2004.[15] As argued below, these may have been connected to the amassing of a pension fund for PIRA members (either with or without Army Council full sanction)[16] before the cessation of military activities was announced in 2005.

In terms of extortion, although the PIRA are seen as being overshadowed by loyalist paramilitaries in this area, they are involved, and in the post-1998 period extortion by the organisation rose, as it did with other groups.[17] In a recent study the PIRA was placed above the Loyalist Volunteer Force in terms of numbers of demands.[18] Extortion demands are made under the guise of offering protection and may be conducted via security firms with the proper 'precautions' taken in order to circumvent licensing arrangements (although it must be pointed out that by no means all security companies are paramilitary related).[19] The PIRA is seen as offering a higher quality service in terms of protection, including a proper presence or response to attempted thefts.[20]

Smuggling and counterfeiting activities create media and policy attention and are symbolic of paramilitary crime. Apparently 70 per cent of republican groups are involved in the illegal tobacco trade.[21] Much of the smuggling appears to be organised in South Armagh and the Republic, the materiel arriving via small ports such as Dundalk which is difficult to access due to tidal movements and provides a relatively secure haven for the docking of smuggled cigarettes which are then trucked into the North and distributed across the UK.[22] Counterfeiting provides a major source of revenue, particularly since the range of products which can be counterfeited and marketed (as mainstream products are marketed) had widened with the deskilling of technology and the spread of subcontracting manufacturing across the globe following the collapse of communism. The PIRA organise and distribute a range of counterfeit goods from, sportswear, footwear, CDs, DVDs and washing powder, the latter often taken from over-production in China and put into boxes bearing the logos of major producers such as Daz and Persil,[23] as well as the production of alcohol. This is prevalent on the mainland of the UK, and is another example of the 'mainlandisation' of crime in Northern Ireland, the main difference being the personnel.[24] A major centre of goods distribution is the market at Jonesborough. This market had a long pedigree and had been repeatedly raided by the RUC,[25] but it expanded after 1998. The market was used by mainstream and dissident republicans plus loyalists. Here, 'good commerce drove the groups to break down that structure [of difference]' at least in this area. Policing remained difficult. Republicans put out 'traffic calming' measures to prevent access by police vehicles should they decide to raid. At one point threats in Armagh and Newry District Command Units (DCUs) on investigating police officers were greater than the period before the peace process,[26] and although it was initially decided to disrupt the Jonesborough market,[27] this apparently was unsuccessful and the market was finally closed. Alternatives quickly sprang up[28] in a classic form of crime displacement.

   A number of techniques have been used in the area of what might be regarded as traditional public sector fraud. Regarding frauds involving farming and fuel subsidies (often including cross-border fraud in the Republic), these activities had been targeted for a long period through a series of financial investigation initiatives by the NIO and police criminal investigation by specialised units in the RUC CID,[29] but large-scale oils, petrol and agricultural frauds worsened after 1998[30] and included the 'classic' fraud which was investigated by the South Armagh Deception over Deceased Livestock Enquiry (Operation SADDLE). However, opportunity also arose following the Belfast Agreement with the influx of funds into Northern Ireland from various sources: the EU, Peace 1 and Peace 2, the Lottery, the Sports Council, the Department of Education (via Individual Learning Accounts) and so forth. The disbursement of these funds was often not rigorously scrutinised in terms of expenditure or audit,[31] presumably for political reasons. This 'peace money' presented – and presents – a fraud risk for crime generally (discussed in Chapter 4) and it should be noted that paramilitary groups such as the PIRA have played a very minor role. Many of these frauds are identical to those conducted on the mainland, and should be seen in context, facilitated by opportunity and lack of control. Indeed, carousel VAT frauds have been employed, and such frauds are a clear problem in the UK.[32]

In terms of the drug situation, the republican movement remains publicly strongly opposed to personal drug use or widespread importation and distribution. Since the mid-1990s a number of individuals identified as drug dealers have been murdered by the PIRA under the guise of Direct Action Against Drugs (DAAD). The PIRA are not directly involved in drugs. This is an activity dominated by ODCs and loyalist groups. However, the movement apparently receives money from licensing dealers.[33]

Illegal waste disposal was identified as an emerging area by 2004.[34] The use and disposal of both business and private waste has become lucrative both due to the increasing amounts of the latter and the expanding restrictions on disposal due to European and British environmental and health and safety regulations. A 'grey market'[35] has opened up in which legitimate organisations contract out to organisations which then dispose of the waste illegally. Waste appears to be brought into Northern Ireland for illegal dumping from the Republic and the United Kingdom.[36] The republican movement has been identified as being involved in illegal waste dumping involving household and other waste, employing threats against those who object. Again this is a form of crime that has expanded in the UK and the Republic of Ireland, and represents the rise of illicit markets in response to regulation and incentives.[37]

Geographically, South Armagh is over-represented in republican crime. This continues a historical pattern which developed in the early 1980s when the republican leadership turned to the South Armagh PIRA, which had been financing itself, to play a bigger role in funding the movement as a whole.[38] In terms of financial gain, the major areas are smuggling and counterfeiting activities.[39]

The leadership has recently made efforts to control and eliminate criminal activity, but the organisation is not 'flat' and some of the PIRA cell structure is moving into crime. There is a practical issue of the methodology by which the organisation is deemed to have stopped involvement in crime, particularly in certain geographical regions, South Armagh being an example. The issue of PIRA desistance from crime is controversial and is explored in more detail in the rest of this chapter.

Money laundering/business infrastructure

The republican movement built up an infrastructure for disguising and investing their proceeds of crime in the 1980s. The PIRA used and uses taxis, pubs, clubs and collections, where the true level of income can be hidden. These businesses can also be used to sell or distribute smuggled goods.[40] Businesses may be paramilitary 'fronts' i.e. run under licence by 'clean' individuals who in practice represent the PIRA, or they may be intimidated into cooperating with paramilitaries.[41] Operating a taxi business does not require a licence (although driving a taxi does). Taxi firms may be controlled by paramilitaries and individual drivers encouraged to perform duties such as distributing counterfeit goods.[42] Paramilitaries can hide large amounts of money in taxi firms but recently this has changed, and with more taxi firms now owned by independent operators, they have resisted paramilitary involvement.[43] Security companies can be another conduit for raising finance (see extortion) but also disguising and transferring it. By no means all security companies are paramilitary related. Some small charities may function as an effective conduit for raising funds and laundering funds.[44] The charity sector is under-regulated compared to the mainland, and there is no Charities Commissioner. But again the charity sector is not dominated by paramilitaries or used by them to raise large amounts,[45] although both British and Irish governments were proposing reform in 2005.[46] Other small businesses which were relatively under regulated and which were used for money laundering include bureaux de change. Some small bureaux in isolated areas were handling vast amounts of money.[47]

More sophisticated long-term methods emerged in the 1990s centring on forms of investment. Much attention has focused on properties in the UK. The investigation into the Northern Bank robbery saw PSNI and Garda money laundering investigations and charges of IRA membership laid against individuals. The raids have apparently uncovered a portfolio of properties, including 300 alone in the north-west of England allegedly owned by Thomas 'Slab' Murphy, identified as a major PIRA fundraiser.[48] By early 2007 the Assets Recovery Agency had frozen a second tranche of 77 properties estimated at over £12 million.[49] However the contemporary dynamic is international. Properties in Spain, Cyprus, Turkey and Eastern Europe have been used to launder funds. Properties in England are being superseded to an extent because of the tighter regulations introduced by the Financial Services Authority, buttressed by legislation culminating in the Proceeds of Crime Act 2002. As well as property, a number of money laundering mechanisms can be used to hide large sums, including insurance policies, trust funds, or using companies to purchase shares.[50]

The PIRA is a sophisticated organisation where crime is concerned, although care must be taken to avoid phantasmagorical notions of complex organised crime networks with an octopus-like reach.[51] It appears that the PIRA has developed a multifaceted strategy for putting the finance gained from crime into physical and liquid assets but the organisation has weaknesses and a capacity limit like any other. The PIRA made a mistake in terms of the Northern Bank robbery. They did not have the structure to launder the money, and lost a considerable amount as a result of rash manoeuvres.[52] Subsequently Gardai and PSNI seizures reduced this further and the Northern Bank's reissuing of new notes further reduced the capacity for laundering the proceeds.

Paramilitary 'justice'

The PIRA developed a politically informed strategy in the mid-1970s. Although one of the ideas involved, the building of alternative structures of government 'had virtually disappeared',[53] the PIRA had become deeply embedded in areas such as West Belfast, Derry and South Armagh in this period. Furthermore, the 'Administrative IRA' leg of these alternative structures did persist and develop into a policing role: 'With the Troubles now nearly a decade old, law and order had broken down in many nationalist districts and established value systems had been upturned. Crime, vandalism and joyriding were endemic and there was a demand for a policing system.'[54] The demand for policing was particularly evident since formal policing via the RUC had been rejected following the period of the early 1970s. Once the PIRA moved to establish local 'policing' this set up a self-replicating structural pattern. The security risks to police meant that they did not venture into republican areas for more than brief periods. When they did they were often criticised as being more concerned with recruiting informants.[55] Thus was the PIRA role as the effective policing authority confirmed. The number of punishment shootings was substantial in the early 1970s[56] as the system developed. This policing system continued, but has long formed a complex, multifaceted phenomenon.[57] A number of motivations lie behind punishment attacks, particularly since 1998, and they have a number of intended and unintended effects.

Firstly, as the Moloney quote above signified, there is a genuine demand for summary justice; not dissimilar to the mainland where sympathy for vigilantism is evident. In the 1990s there was a move towards this in urban areas in England and Wales, both at formal level in the form of privately contracted street patrols (which were characterised by a lack of regulation and accusations of unaccountable coercion) and informal, self-appointed groups attacking those identified as undesirables (car thieves, drug dealers, paedophiles). Volume crime rose in Northern Ireland following the peace process, and families were experiencing an increase in car crime. Thus punishment beatings held and hold a clear measure of public support in republican areas where the police are ineffective and/ or viewed as illegitimate and the demand is to 'do something' about local criminals.[58] Of course, the legitimacy of this is also questioned. Kennedy terms the attacks 'paramilitary child abuse' when young victims are selected, in a clear attempt to wrest legitimacy from the perpetrators.[59]

Secondly, such actions could also serve a strategic military and political purpose within the armed wing of republicanism, being an important area where capacity and training could continue. Thus, when the first ceasefire was declared in 1994 the IRA's '"policing" functions in nationalist areas' were maintained.[60] In 1995 at a sensitive political moment the PIRA under the cover name Direct Action Against Drugs shot dead a drug dealer. The rank and file 'gained some reassurance from this brief return to the use of firearms'[61] and in the subsequent Christmas period five drug dealers were shot in areas in which discontent was evident with Sinn Féin leader Gerry Adams's political strategy, discontent which in South Armagh eventually resulted in the Canary Wharf bomb.[62] The killings petered out, flaring again as Brendan Campbell was murdered in February 1998. Following the Belfast Agreement, more individuals labelled as drug dealers were killed, including Paul Downey in 1999. Patrick 'Donkey' Quinn, a close associate of Brendan Campbell was shot allegedly by DAAD in 2000 as well as three others so identified.[63] The PIRA's anti-drugs stance thus satisfied those who genuinely opposed the drugs trade, wished to keep the military capability fine-tuned, met demands for community justice and also sent out a signal to the community that the PIRA continued to set the bounds of acceptable behaviour.

Punishment attacks demonstrate a high degree of organisation. From January 1998 to May 2004 republicans carried out 613 punishment beatings compared to 1083 by loyalists. Periods of few or no PIRA-administered beatings in September 1998, November 1999 and November 2003 have, according to PSNI Chief Constable Hugh Orde, coincided with two key Sinn Féin statements and the Assembly election.[64] Republican attacks have dropped markedly recently. Between January 2003 and February 2006 republicans shot 89 individuals and loyalists 273; in terms of assaults between January 2003 and February 2006 republicans committed 119 and loyalists 245,[69] but if the period February 2005 to February 2006 is examined republicans shot 11 individuals, loyalists 83. This is reflective of two processes. The first, short-term one reflects the low level of activity following the Northern Bank robbery and Robert McCartney murder: both shootings and beatings show a sharp drop from February 2005. The second reflects the demobilisation of the PIRA in terms of traditional military activities: visceral punishment attacks have been replaced by other tactics such as exiling and the development of effective community restorative justice schemes, 14 of which operate in republican areas. Attacks further declined to zero in late 2006.[66]

Whatever the dynamic behind these attacks, thirdly, the overall effect is to maintain paramilitary authority and legitimacy, although there are important exceptions, mentioned below. The active support (or acquiescence) for locally administered punishment strengthens the general position of the PIRA as the chief actor in the 'community justice system' and its decisions with regard to what punishments for what offences and to whom are meted out. Indeed, punishment shootings and intimidation demonstrate continuing PIRA/Sinn Féin authority and control, including the authority of single figures. Crossing a senior republican can be seen as a 'crime' which can lead to retribution: 'Mr. B, who had a public altercation with a well known IRA leader, was shot in the legs and left to bleed to death after the killers ripped out telephone lines, rendering medical assistance impossible.'[67] This is where paramilitary authority and legitimacy may clearly conflict. And it is the authority of single figures of the republican movement to which the next section turns.

Crime, legitimacy and social control: the Robert McCartney murder

Much crime is symbolic. Certain forms of crime function as signifiers for societal concerns, or may even produce and reproduce such concerns. Crime functions in this manner particularly in modern societies which have been characterised as risk societies.[68] However, crime also engendered feelings of anxiety within certain social classes or even mass society well before the idea of risk became prevalent.[69] Certain single offences may engender feelings of social dislocation or even push political change. Individual violent or sexual offences have been instrumental in engendering organisational, legal and even social change. In the UK such offences might include the racist murder of Stephen Lawrence in London in 1993, the murder of two-year-old James Bulger by two ten-year-old boys also in 1993, the murders of schoolchildren committed by Thomas Hamilton with firearms at Dunblane, and the Soham murders of two ten-year-old girls committed by school caretaker Ian Huntley.[70]

Following the Belfast Agreement crimes unsurprisingly function in a specific political context. The Omagh bombing of 1998 in which the Real IRA killed 29 people appears to have receded in the public consciousness (certainly on the mainland) and may have been more significant in the Republic in terms of the resulting legal change and anti-terrorist policing actions by the Gardai. Even murders such as that of Denis Donaldson, the Sinn Féin official who admitted to being a long-term British agent, have evaporated as an issue almost as soon as they were committed. Both the Irish and British governments reacted with what might be termed unseemly haste to assert that Donaldson's murder would not affect the peace process. However, if a crime occurs or re-emerges as an issue *in a certain context*, it can create a political effect within paramilitary, party, media and government circles. Crime in Northern Ireland has been important during the peace process both in general and as a single issue, particularly when it cannot be embedded and resolved/neutralised within the evolving political process.

The McCartney murder achieved even global importance, albeit briefly, particularly as it could not be controlled as an issue within the peace process. Robert McCartney was murdered after he and a companion had 'insulted' a senior republican in a bar in the centre of Belfast. His friend Brendan Devine was also attacked. Following the killing the bar was cleaned by republican supporters to reduce the amount of forensic evidence and 'messages' were sent out to the community that witnesses should not speak about the incident. There were over 70 people in the bar,[71] including two Sinn Féin candidates, one local, one Assembly. A Sinn Féin councillor in the bar did not speak to the police. It should be noted that this was not the first murder to be connected to a personal dispute with republicans,[72] and a number of other killings had taken place allegedly by republicans which had not engendered a political crisis for various reasons.[73]

The McCartney case metamorphosed into a major issue for a number of connected issues. Again this is similar to other crimes.[74] The McCartney family, who were/are Sinn Féin supporters and whose family had been based in the Short Strand area for decades immediately conducted a high profile media campaign to raise awareness and effectively flush the killers out in the open. Further, Sinn Féin and the republican movement made a series of tactical blunders. They could not control or neutralise the rapid development of the murder as an issue, and once this was the case they were in a strategic bind. Clearly the crime could not be politically framed. A cover up would reduce the breadth of Sinn Féin's support, which had shown a pattern in which those middle-class and ex-SDLP voters who supported Sinn Féin over various issues (beginning with the hunger strikes) fell away when PIRA military activity (bombings and shootings) resumed.[75]

Sinn Féin was in a difficult position. The Party had to be seen to be cooperating but had still not signed up to the post-Patten policing arrangements or recognised the legitimacy of the PSNI, since the police still effectively constituted a six county police under British control.[76] The issue of policing retained a powerful symbolic and practical power –

policing is, to republicans, the still glowing core of 'the Orange State'[77] and Sinn Féin could not be seen to be accepting policing arrangements without proper guarantees. Despite the nature of the murder, early and overt cooperation might have given further proof to those who already believed Sinn Féin's participation in devolved institutions effectively represented an acceptance of Northern Ireland's status and a betrayal of the republican movement's core principles. Thus Sinn Féin suspended seven members who had been in the bar, and this later rose to twelve. Some suspensions were rescinded following the cooperation by these individuals with the relevant authorities. The Party set down a motion in Belfast City Council to 'encourage anyone with information or evidence to go to the organisation of their choice'. Sinn Féin recommended individuals with information should contact their solicitor or the Police Ombudsman for Northern Ireland (PONI). This was not passed, and the SDLP motion encouraging anyone with information to go to the PSNI was passed, with Sinn Féin abstaining.[78] The PIRA eventually argued that those with knowledge of the killing should report to the appropriate authorities i.e. the PSNI.

These attempts to prevent the murder escaping the republican universe failed. The PIRA gave three detailed statements over the murder, arguing that McCartney was murdered by four people, two of whom were PIRA members, but according to one statement, 'the IRA knows the identity of all these men'. The organisation then offered to shoot the killers, a media disaster.[79] Sinn Féin remained under pressure from the UK government, the Republic's government, and supporters in the USA with figures such as Edward Kennedy and the White House supporting the McCartneys; indeed, they were received at the White House while Adams was excluded. As momentum built, Sinn Féin attempted further control measures. Martin McGuinness warned the McCartney sisters, 'The McCartneys need to be very careful. To step over that line, which is a very important line, into the world of party political politics, can do a huge disservice to their campaign', after one of them had mooted standing for election.[80]

The turbulence around the murder bent back into republican areas, disturbing some existing community concerns about the position and activities of the PIRA. This case demonstrated the limits to which the community was prepared to continue implicitly sanctioning the PIRA as the legitimate authority if its control of violence was clearly being employed illegitimately. This expanded into general criticism of PIRA activity as increasingly overstepping the boundaries between legitimate anti-state activity and self-interested racketeering, engendering tropes about 'the boys not being what they were'. According to one republican:

> In the old days IRA men didn't go around drinking; they didn't get involved in silly public fights that left somebody dying in an alleyway. People are getting sick

of it. Ordinary people living here are now saying this gang is now more menacing, more oppressive to the community, than the Brits ever were.[81]

As the author of the article pointed out, this is an understanding similar to those which apply to 'old style' British villains such as the Krays who committed acts of extreme violence in the 1960s but were seen as adhering to established codes of honour, such as applying violence only to opponents or those who clearly 'deserved it'. The quote above implies that the problem lies with, perhaps, just this gang. Furthermore, support for the republican movement remained high and the McCartney incident did not affect Sinn Féin's performance in elections in the Republic of Ireland or in Northern Ireland in 2005. The extent to which the PIRA still maintained the support of sections of the community could be seen in the comments about 'what really happened', which circulated in republican areas. Indeed, all the McCartneys have now moved from the Short Strand area after facing alleged intimidation. During the year they faced a threat of arson from unidentified sources and McCartney's friend and a relative of his fiancée were beaten up during disturbances in which loyalists had attacked the Short Strand enclave and republicans were present to organise defence if necessary.[82]

The issue died down: one man was charged in connection with the murder, and one in connection with the attack on Brendan Devine. During the trials the issue might flare up again, but this is unlikely as the political context has changed: the PIRA has since made its historic statement and has been deemed by the government as being no longer an organisation involved in crime. However, in a specific context, a nighttime murder in a city centre bar flared like magnesium brightly illuminating a series of connected and complex issues concerning crime, the republican movement and the peace process. Crime is thus not a phenomenon to be encapsulated by reference to tight legal notions, but is intimately connected with politics, ideology, symbolism and legitimacy and social control.

Politics, crime and peace: the institutionalisation of Sinn Féin and the republican movement?

Crime as a problem has a complex context, both in relation to the political consolidation of the peace process and the institutionalisation of the republican movement in that process. Crime was linked to the continuing capacity of the republican movement to return to 'war'. Certain crimes prevented the return of devolved government. Other crime has been absorbed in a way that did not threaten the peace process. Finally, desistance from crime by the PIRA became an important factor in estimating whether the republican movement was/is demobilising.

In the 1970s in response to the successful recruitment of informants by British military intelligence or the RUC, the IRA set up an internal security unit, termed the 'nutting squad'. As Moloney argues, this 'proved to be a double edged weapon, however' since 'The security department's members knew many of the IRA's most intimate secrets, including the identity of key gunmen and bombers, and a double agent placed within their ranks could cause havoc. The years since the department was set up have been characterised by persistent suggestions that this is just what happened.'[83] The suggestion was correct. A high-level agent, known as 'Stakeknife', did exist exposed as – allegedly – Freddie Scapaticci in 2003.[84] Scapaticci has not, so far, been murdered, and Martin McGartland, revealed as an RUC Special Branch agent, was shot six times in 1999 but survived.[85] Denis Donaldson, Sinn Féin administrator had been one of the three arrested in 2002 as part of the PSNI probe into an alleged spy ring at Stormont. He admitted to being a British and police agent to Sinn Féin in 2005 shortly after the prosecution of the 'spy ring three' at Stormont was discontinued on public interest grounds. Donaldson was murdered in 2006 apparently by PIRA members. Donaldson may have been killed by PIRA elements in South Armagh concerned that he was the third informant to be given an amnesty by Sinn Féin.[86] The republican movement has been particularly exercised over the issue of informants since the 1970s because they (particularly those working for British military intelligence) stand as such an affront to the principles of republicanism. Other individuals faced murder for 'crimes' other than informing. Eamon Collins was murdered in 1999. He was not an informer, although he had made a statement to the RUC under interrogation which he later withdrew, a common practice for many PIRA men. However, he had written a highly critical book on the PIRA which was published in 1998, and had also testified against Thomas 'Slab' Murphy in a libel trial.[87] Murphy had lost the case and Collins was preparing to testify in another libel case involving Murphy's brother. In addition he had made a number of outspoken criticisms of the South Armagh PIRA, which appeared to turn the balance against him.[88] Finally in addition the Provisional IRA has also taken action against dissident republicans such as the Real IRA, one important tactic in preventing a serious split in the movement. This has included one murder. This 'policing' function was beneficial to the peace process (see Chapter 8).

Thus there has been a mixture of actions conducted by the 'military men' against informers and dissidents before any final stages of demobilisation. This demonstrates the extent to which an individual crime can or cannot be fused into the political process (for example, the murder of Robert McCartney compared to others). Following the death of Denis

Donaldson British and Irish government spokesmen condemned the murder but in the same breath announced that it would not derail the peace process.[89] Now this may be partly because the identity of the perpetrators is unknown, but that is insufficient. The murder occurred in a context in which it could be contained within existing frameworks of discourse, unlike the McCartney murder and the Northern Bank raid, to which the next section turns.

The Northern Bank robbery and law enforcement

A third act of PIRA decommissioning had been completed in 2003 but issues of verification had become mired in claim and counter claim, and this was one area which allowed the Democratic Unionist Party (DUP) to overhaul the UUP in the Assembly elections of that year. The Ulster Unionists under David Trimble were seen as too weak to secure full PIRA decommissioning. The DUP under Dr Ian Paisley promised a harder line. During this period of stalemate the Independent Monitoring Commission had been established to report on paramilitary activity and security normalisation. The IMC had been opposed by Sinn Féin, treasured project as it was of David Trimble.[90] The IMC began reports in 2004 on continuing paramilitary activity: murders, shootings, beatings and also criminal activity, relating these to the respective political leaderships. The PIRA and the UDA were identified as being involved in a particularly wide range of criminal activities. However, by the end of 2004 negotiations were proceeding in which there was a realistic prospect of the PIRA decommissioning the rest of its weapons and an agreement between Sinn Féin and the DUP.

The branch of the Northern Bank which was targeted stands in the centre of Belfast. The robbery involved over 30 individuals. The families of bank workers were held hostage while the bank workers were taken to the branch to organise the withdrawal of the cash and its transfer into a waiting van. The estimated haul was over £26 million.

The robbery clearly raised the issue of crime and paramilitarism – as the Robert McCartney murder did shortly afterwards – and the relationship of Sinn Féin to the PIRA and the motivations for criminality. The issue of sanctioning was central: could the Northern Bank robbery have taken place without the knowledge of the republican leadership both political and military? According to the IMC – with which Sinn Féin and the PIRA do not cooperate – the robbery was 'carried out with the prior knowledge and authorisation of the leadership of PIRA'.[91] While also placing responsibility at the feet of Sinn Féin, since its personnel are also in the PIRA, the IMC also accepted that the Party was 'not in a position actually to determine what policies or operational strategies the PIRA will adopt'.[92] This raises the question of whether – if as alleged, Sinn Féin politicians Gerry Adams, Martin McGuinness and Martin Ferris (an SF member of parliament in the Republic of Ireland) were on the Army Council – they were overruled or some members of the Army Council ordered it without telling those relevant Sinn Féin members. Following the raid Gerry Adams, rarely a man to let words slip unconsidered from his lips mentioned, 'I may be wrong', with regard to his assertion that the robbery was not a PIRA operation.[93] Whatever the case, the possible motivation behind the robbery is interesting. One interpretation might see in the raid a last gasp of 'military-style' actions taken by the PIRA (as the IMC points out it came at the end of a series of lucrative robberies elsewhere) to secure 'pension funds' for those who had contributed to the PIRA campaign. The struggle is such a potent symbolic and empirical representation of republican politics and has been absolutely central to arguments for and against the political route pursued by republicanism since the 1980s. In this respect actions like the Northern Bank robbery can be seen in historical context with regard to the difficult process of ending the 'war'.[94]

Whatever the case, the politics of the event were deeply connected to the prospects for political development. Within two weeks, the PSNI attributed responsibility for the robbery to the PIRA. However, the political fallout from the robbery drifted according to the 'laws' of how this would affect the prospects of decommissioning and a return to devolution. Unionists called for immediate sanctions on Sinn Féin. The British government asked the IMC for a report but once this had attributed responsibility, the political structure of the situation could not be rejigged. The British government and Irish government attributed responsibility to the PIRA. Northern Ireland Secretary of State Paul Murphy fined Sinn Féin and continued the withdrawal of its Assembly grant (introduced after the abduction of Bobby Tohill).[95] The Republic's government took a strong public line with Justice Minister Michael McDowell, a hardline critic of Sinn Féin, accusing Sinn Féin members of being on the PIRA Army Council.

How does this relate to institutionalisation? First, crime illustrated the extent to which the political process is stable. After being blamed for the Northern Bank robbery, the PIRA stated: 'We do not intend to remain quiescent within this unacceptable and unstable situation. It has tried our patience to the limit', but interestingly actors from Hugh Orde to Government dismissed the prospect of a return to violence, following which another IRA statement appeared: 'Do not underestimate the seriousness of the situation. The two governments are trying to play down the importance of our statement because they are making a mess of the peace process.'[96] The robbery had illuminated the contours of the peace process, and the extent to which such statements had lost the force of similar

PIRA statements aimed at inducing pressure made in the 2001 period.

A further factor contributing to stability was the calming statements of Gerry Adams concerning the irreversibility of the peace process. This was bolstered by the fact that electorally the raid did not have a major effect, as some had predicted. As the then editor of *Andersonstown News* argued: 'Thanks to the robbery, Sinn Féin may well simply hold on to its existing vote come election time rather than continue its steady expansion ... Electoral meltdown of the kind experienced by the SDLP in recent years is unlikely. The McCartney affair is potentially more dangerous for Sinn Féin.' The author argued that the robbery of the Northern Bank would be met with indifference by most republican voters, particularly since banks generally arouse little sympathy amongst the public.[97] Indeed, Sinn Féin candidate Joe Reilly increased his vote from 9 per cent to 12 per cent in the Meath by-election in the Republic[98] and Sinn Féin performed well (although slightly below expectations) in the 2005 UK general election. The robbery in the end was stabilised as an issue but served as a factor placing pressure on Sinn Féin and encouraging the push for a final historic statement from the PIRA.

In terms of law enforcement, the British government had been warned by the SDLP that a large-scale cigarette robbery in Belfast carried out by republicans in October 2004 had been a test of its response to crime[99] but the government displayed a studied refusal to engage with the evidence. The Northern Bank robbery followed. However following this, law enforcement operations did target the PIRA's financial structure. By September 2005 there had been a series of raids, arrests and document seizures as part of money laundering investigations on both sides of the border, much of it centring on Thomas 'Slab' Murphy. Murphy has long been a target for police on both sides of the border. Allegedly, he was IRA Chief of Staff and a major fundraiser for the republican movement.

If the argument is accepted that the recent activity in the republican movement has been to stabilise an investment portfolio which will fund the republican movement and politics in the long term[100] and individual criminality has been used to garner 'pension funds' for the 'military men', then the prospect of aggressive law enforcement activity – particularly centring on the asset seizure and recovery powers by the Criminal Assets Bureau (CAB) in the Republic and the ARA in Northern Ireland – threatens this. The example of Murphy shows how rapidly even substantial assets can be stripped away.

However, the targeting of Slab Murphy, although sending out a warning shot, raises questions. Although his fundraising capacities are allegedly prodigious, he has long been a critic of the peace process and recently lost his place on the Army Council. Indeed, since he could be characterised as an obstacle to republican political strategy and progress his removal is not a great blow. He is a high profile target and sends out a signal, but not enough to destabilise the process.[101] In November 2007 after an operation by the Garda and the Criminal Assets Bureau, Murphy was arrested and charged with nine counts of failing to file tax returns involving an alleged 2.5 million euros.

This raises the issue of the extent to which criminal investigation has been employed to 'move' republicans along in the same way as it has with loyalists (see Chapter 3). The policing in the 2005 period appeared to constitute a gentle screw-tightening, and it is interesting to speculate what would have been the case if the Northern Bank raid had not occurred. Investigations like that into 'Slab' Murphy may take a long time to plan, but it appeared the government and the police were pushed into the investigation. The pendulum then swung back. Following the PIRA's statement ending its war in 2005, progress in ending criminality and progress towards restoring devolution, Hugh Orde stated in the October 2006 meeting of the Policing Board that republican movement assets were effectively beyond reach.

Finally, a crucial variable in institutionalisation is the tension as republicanism moves deeper into constitutional politics and becomes involved in the administration of law and order. Sinn Féin wants to be involved in policing and justice but in a devolved administration. They do not wish to effectively 'administer British rule' in Northern Ireland (as their dissident republican critics claim they do). This was particularly evident over the Robert McCartney murder, where the republican movement and Sinn Féin could not countenance publicly calling for cooperation with the PSNI, particularly as Sinn Féin had not joined the Policing Board. This is also evident in terms of the plans for restorative justice. Republicans had not signed up to the government guidelines for restorative justice in 2006 because these state that all cases must be referred to the PSNI, and have an 'unambiguous and appropriate relationship with the police'. Community Restorative Justice Northern Ireland which operates 14 schemes in republican areas stated, 'We will not be able to actually implement agreed arrangements until there is an overall settlement on policing.'[102] The schemes continued to run, as they had since 1999. In July 2006 the government introduced new guidelines, publicly recognising that the previous ones were inappropriate (i.e. unacceptable to Sinn Féin). They still insisted that the police must be involved; that is non-negotiable, but in other respects the schemes were allowed to maintain a clear distance from the PSNI. Other schemes, in areas such as South Armagh have been running independently of the police with little or no intention of cooperation. Alternatively, the PIRA have been involved in defusing public order flashpoints, including ordering young republicans off the streets, and Sinn Féin also provided effective stewarding at Orange marches in republican and nationalist areas in 2006. Thus while eschewing formal involvement, the republican movement and Sinn Féin were engaging in the equivalent of cooperative parallel policing before they finally accepted the PSNI and joined the Police Board.[103]

The end of crime?

The 2004–2007 period is interesting in terms of the relationship examined throughout this chapter between the republican movement, Sinn Féin, crime and political institutionalisation. The Northern Bank robbery, the McCartney murder, the consequent pressure on the republican movement, the historic statement of 2005, followed by large-scale money laundering investigations into republicans by law enforcement on both sides of the border, has been followed by another seismic change in terms of official judgements on PIRA criminality.

Following the PIRA's statement ending its armed campaign, the IMC was tasked to produce a report on PIRA criminality. The British government clearly hoped that this report would provide the PIRA with a clean bill of health on the crime front, particularly since, as mentioned, the issue of crime could easily detonate under the feet of the British and Irish governments, in a sense replacing previous political landmines of the peace period, notably PIRA military actions such as intelligence gathering on law enforcement officers and politicians, and the arrest of the 'Colombia Three' (republicans convicted of assisting the guerrilla movement the Revolutionary Armed Forces of Colombia). The report duly noted the clear evidence of the PIRA to pursue a political path, and the follow up in April 2006 was even more direct. A clear analytical distinction was made between the PIRA as an organisation and individuals:

> There are indications that some members, including some senior ones (as distinct from the organisation itself) are still involved in crime, including offences such as fuel laundering, money laundering, extortion, tax evasion and smuggling. Some of these activities are deeply embedded in the culture of a number of communities, not least in the border areas, and increasing proportions of the proceeds may now be going to individuals rather than to the organisation. We have no reason to amend our earlier view that money is a strategic asset and that the organisation will look to the long term exploitation of discreetly laundered assets which were previously gained illegally.[104]

The IMC stated that the PIRA 'continues to seek to stop criminal activity by its members and to prevent them from engaging in it' and that certain PIRA units were closing down criminal operations.[105] The 2006 Organised Crime Task Force report was careful to repeat the judgement of the IMC that the PIRA is reducing criminality and that which does persist is connected to individuals, albeit including senior ones:

> evidence suggests that since their statement of 28 July 2005 announcing a cessation of all illegal activities the leadership has actively sought to prevent criminal activities being carried out by its members ... the IMC has made a clear distinction between the activities of members and those of the PIRA as an organisation.[106]

The political representatives of the British government were clear on the IMC report. Following a meeting with the Irish government on cross-border crime, Peter Hain argued an 'absolute state of perfection' from the IRA was not realistic: 'There probably is still some localised individual criminality by former and maybe existing Provisional IRA members for their own private gain. What there is not is organised "from the centre" criminality any more.'[107] The Republic's Justice Minister Michael McDowell, an implacable critic of Sinn Féin and the republican movement, agreed. Unionists responded predictably. Peter Hain was 'living in fantasy land' according to Democratic Unionist Party MP Nigel Dodds,[108] although the DUP had leaped to agree with previous IMC reports which criticised the PIRA. A further and eagerly awaited IMC report in late 2006 confirmed the trend: the PIRA was closing down criminal operations and instructing members to desist from crime.

Crime and transition

There is no doubt that the PIRA is ending its large-scale involvement in crime. There are nevertheless issues of the appropriateness of judgements concerning the end of crime linked to the PIRA. Is it credible that the PIRA's organisational criminality should, if not melt into air, at the least rapidly shrink in effect overnight? Police on the ground might disagree with recent statements, particularly detectives investigating financial and other issues with clear links to the PIRA; indeed, there are a number of money laundering and other related financial investigations still extant. Indeed, differing interpretations were evident at all previous stages of discussion about PIRA crime. At the high level, Chief Constable Hugh Orde had stated in 2005 shortly before the 8th IMC Report into PIRA and other criminality: 'we are keeping a close eye on criminal activity' by the PIRA and 'I'd be surprised to see any paramilitary organisation stop overnight.'[109] Indeed, a short time later, while Security Minister Shaun Woodward was arguing the PIRA was not involved in crime, PSNI Assistant Chief Constable Sam Kinkaid was briefing the Policing Board on continuing PIRA criminality.[110] The contemporaneous Northern Ireland Affairs Committee report on organised crime argued all paramilitary groups were involved, although the report itself was coy on attributing responsibility to individual groups.[111]

The contents of the IMC Reports showed much ambiguity. It appears that groups are engaged in criminal acts such as major robberies and smuggling and money is going into long-term investment portfolios but the IMC cannot estimate what amount of money is going to personal uses and what to the organisation.[112] Further, it appears that the leadership may still be tolerating some low-level criminality by volunteers as a stabilising measure during the transition. Finally, although Sinn Féin has made consistent and clear statements against criminality in 2005 and 2006, the IMC was circumspect on any links between PIRA fundraising/investment and Sinn Féin. It remains the case that an allegedly unlawfully acquired asset portfolio may fund republican politics for the foreseeable future.

In this transition period, if it is the case that organised crime in some sectors is at the same 'serious' level or even worse in others (as the Northern Ireland Affairs Committee argues), but it is not now attributable to paramilitary organisations, then their members may be involved in organised crime. This may be the case in Armagh. Of the 19 fuel laundering plants identified as having been broken up in 2002/2003, 15 were in Tyrone and Armagh. Of the 18 fuel laundering plants broken up in 2004/ 2005, 14 were in Tyrone and Armagh.[113] In 2004 a cross-border operation covering Armagh and Monaghan was aimed at a fuel fraud estimated at £5 million.[114] In 2005/2006, 35 million cigarettes were seized in Northern Ireland, 15 million of them in South Armagh in a multiagency operation.[115] Armagh is either overrepresented in police operations or constitutes a focus of smuggling. In the same period £9.9 million value of counterfeit goods were seized by PSNI, £2.2 million of this in South Armagh in late 2005 at Jonesborough market.[116] Some of this is linked to dissidents and ODCs, but it provides an idea of the scale of activity which was connected to the republican movement. Although figures are not available for the period following the PIRA's historic announcement, it is unlikely that a) these operations were/are unconnected to the PIRA and b) this activity has reduced to zero.

The situation is complex, and fundamental change is evident. But it would be plausible to argue that, for some years yet, the PIRA will continue as a virtual organisation, retaining presence, capacity and a detached membership. Even on a stripped down analysis this is likely to be the case to manage or confront the continuing activity of dissident republican groups (even though the PIRA might term the Real IRA (RIRA) and the Continuity IRA (CIRA) 'micro-organisations') or those like the Irish National Liberation Army (INLA) politically opposed to the Belfast Agreement. Furthermore, the loyalists show few signs of decommissioning.

In short, fundamental change has been evident but political judgements ran ahead of analytical and empirical judgements to accelerate political change and restore devolution in the 2005–2007 period. This is to be expected. The important feature in political terms appears to be the fact that if murders and crimes should be committed they will now be 'understood' within the new framework as the work of individuals within the PIRA but unconnected to the organisation as a whole.[117] The issue of paramilitary crime is being managed away by the state. Whatever one's views on PIRA crime and its relation to the peace process and institutionalisation, the process has been markedly different to loyalist institutionalisation, as Chapter 3 demonstrates.

Notes

1 H. Patterson, *The Politics of Illusion. A Political History of the IRA* (London: Serif, 1997); P. Taylor, *Provos. The IRA and Sinn Féin* (London: Bloomsbury, 1998); R. English, *Armed Struggle. The History of the IRA* (London: Pan, 2004).

2 English, *Armed Struggle*, p. 381, pp. 448–449, n.149.

3 M. Devenport, 'Key questions remain for Sinn Féin', *BBC News Northern Ireland* (7 March 2005) http://news.bbc.co.uk/1/hi/northern_ireland/4324747.stm.

4 J. Muncie, 'Decriminalising criminology', *British Criminology Conference: Selected Proceedings*, Vol. 3 (2000), http://lboro.ac.uk/departments/ss/bsc/bccsp/vol03/muncie.html> D. Kauzlarich, R. Matthews, W. Miller, 'Towards a victimology of state crime', *Critical Criminology*, 10 (2001), 173–194; S. Tombs and D. Whyte, *Unmasking the Powerful: Scrutinising States and Corporations* (New York: Peter Lang, 2003).

5 Northern Ireland Affairs Committee, *The Financing of Terrorism in Northern Ireland*, Vol. 1 HC 978-1 (London: The Stationery Office, 2001–02), para 33.

6 P. van Duyne, 'The phantom threat of organised crime', *Crime, Law and Social Change*, 24 (1996), 341–377; P. van Duyne, 'Money laundering: Pavlov's dog and beyond', *Howard Journal of Criminal Justice*, 37:4 (1998), 359–374.

7 J. Sturcke (*et al.*), 'Police raids target alleged IRA chief', *Guardian* (9 March 2006).

8 'Man jailed over blackmail plot', *UTV News* (28 June 2006).

9 Author interview, Detective Chief Superintendent, PSNI attached to the OCTF, Stormont House Annexe, 25 July 2003.

10 Loyalists often had to rely on 'information slippage' for organisational development. Author interview, Detective Chief Superintendent, PSNI, attached to the OCTF, at Stormont House Annexe, 25 July 2003.

11 J. Horgan and M. Taylor, 'Playing the "Green Card" – financing the Provisional IRA Part 2', *Terrorism and Political Violence*, 15:2 (2003), 1–60.

12 Author interview, Detective Chief Superintendent, PSNI attached to the OCTF, Stormont House Annexe, 25 July 2003.

13 P. Norman, 'The Terrorist Finance Unit and the Joint Action Group on Organised Crime: New organisational models and investigative strategies to counter "organised crime" in the UK', *Howard Journal of Criminal Justice*, 37:4 (1998), 375–392.

14 Author interview, Member of the NIO dealing with financial matters,

Stormont House Annexe, 25 July 2003.

15 IMC, *Fourth Report of the Independent Monitoring Commission* (London: The Stationery Office, 2005), pp. 5–6.

16 Certainly the IMC argued it would be remarkable if these major attacks were not sanctioned at the top level. See IMC, *4th Report*.

17 Author interviews, Detective Chief Inspector [a] and Detective Inspector [b], PSNI, Belfast, 24 July 2003 and 24 February 2004.

18 E. Adair, 'To pay or not to pay. The extent of paramilitary extortion within the construction industry', M.Sc. dissertation, Leicester University, 2005, pp. 88–89.

19 IMC, *Fifth Report of the Independent Monitoring Commission* (London: The Stationery Office, 2005), p. 33.

20 Author interview, Detective Constable, PSNI, Belfast, 22 July 2003.

21 This includes dissidents. Organised Crime Task Force, *Serious and Organised Crime in Northern Ireland. Threat Assessment and Strategy 2004* (OCTF, 2004), p. 10.

22 BBC, 'Organised Crime', *File on Four* (broadcast on BBC Radio Four, 15 March 2005).

23 Author interview, Detective Chief Inspector [a], PSNI, Belfast, 10 November 2005.

24 I am grateful to DC Simon Almond, Essex Police for this information, author interview, 25 May 2006.

25 Author interview, Detective Constable, PSNI, Belfast, 22 July 2003.

26 Author interview, Detective Chief Superintendent, PSNI attached to the OCTF, Stormont House Annexe, 25 July 2003.

27 Author interview, Detective Chief Superintendent, PSNI attached to the OCTF, Stormont House Annexe, 25 July 2003.

28 Northern Ireland Affairs Committee, *Organised Crime in Northern Ireland, Third Report of Session 2005 015006*, Vol. 1 HC-886-II (London: The Stationery Office, 2006), para 45.

29 Norman, 'The Terrorist Finance Unit', 378–379.

30 See the publications of the OCTF generally. Deliveries of legitimate road fuel into Northern Ireland did not increase in Northern Ireland from 1996–2000. Organised Crime Task Force, *Strategic Response: Serious and Organised Crime in Northern Ireland* (OCTF, 2003), p. 12.

31 Author interviews, Detective Chief Inspector, PSNI, Belfast, 22 July 2003; member of the NIO dealing with financial matters, Stormont House Annexe, 25 July 2003; Detective Chief Superintendent, PSNI, Belfast, 25 July 2003. For SADDLE see also T. Harnden, *Bandit Country. The IRA and South Armagh* (London: Hodder and Stoughton, 2000), pp. 452–453.

32 Author interview, Detective Chief Inspector, PSNI, Belfast, 22 July 2003.

33 Author interview, Detective Chief Inspector [a], PSNI, Belfast, 10 November 2005.

34 Organised Crime Task Force, *Confronting the Threat. Threat Assessment and Strategy 2004* (Belfast: OCTF, 2004), p. 13.

35 For the development of grey markets and the links between economies, regulation and crime opportunities see V. Ruggerio, 'War Markets: Corporate

and organised criminals in Europe', *Social and Legal Studies,* 5 (1996), 5–20; V. Ruggerio, *Crime and Markets. Essays in Anti-Criminology* (Oxford/Clarendon: Oxford University Press, 2001).

36 Northern Ireland Affairs Committee, 'Organised Crime in Northern Ireland', paras 47–48.

37 See note 35 and for example, H. Griffiths, 'Smoking guns: European cigarette smuggling in the 1990s', *Global Crime,* 6:2 (2004), 185–200; P. van Duyne, 'Organising cigarette smuggling and policy making: ending up in smoke', *Crime, Law and Social Change,* 39:3 (2003), 285–317.

38 Harnden, *Bandit Country,* pp. 249–250.

39 Author interview, Detective Inspector, PSNI, 11 November 2005.

40 Author interview, member of the NIO dealing with financial matters, Stormont House Annexe, 25 July 2003.

41 IMC, *5th Report,* pp. 32–33.

42 IMC, *5th Report,* p. 34.

43 Detective Inspector, PSNI, interviewed by the author, Belfast, 11 November 2005.

44 IMC, *5th Report,* pp. 37–38.

45 Author interviews, Detective Chief Inspector, PSNI, Belfast, 22 July 2003; Detective Inspector, PSNI, Belfast, 11 November 2005.

46 IMC, *5th Report,* p. 38.

47 Author interview, Detective Inspector, PSNI, Belfast, 11 November 2005.

48 See A. Chrisafis, 'Sinn Féin in crisis following laundering arrests', *Guardian* (19 February 2005); D. McKittrick, 'Police raid IRA's £30m "property portfolio"', *Independent* (7 October 2005); H. McDonald, 'Bomber owns flat behind Harrods', *Observer* (26 March 2006).

49 *BBC News* (18 January 2007).

50 Author interview, Detective Inspector, PSNI, Belfast, 11 November 2005.

51 M. Levi, 'Perspectives on "Organised Crime": An Overview', *Howard Journal of Criminal Justice,* 37:4 (1998), 335–345; P. van Duyne, 'Organised crime, corruption and power', *Crime, Law and Social Change,* 26 (1997), 201–238.

52 Author interview, Detective Chief Inspector [a], PSNI, Belfast, 10 November 2005.

53 E. Moloney, *A Secret History of the IRA* (London: Penguin, 2002), p. 152.

54 Moloney, *A Secret History,* p. 153.

55 R. Gilmour, *Dead Ground. Infiltrating the IRA* (London: Little Brown, 1998); C. Knox, 'See no evil. Hear no evil: Insidious paramilitary violence in Northern Ireland', *British Journal of Criminology,* 42:1 (2002), 176.

56 A. Silke, 'Rebel's dilemma: the changing relationship between the IRA, Sinn Féin and paramilitary vigilantism in Northern Ireland', *Terrorism and Political Violence,* 11:1 (1999), 55–93; Knox, 'See no evil. Hear no evil', fig. 1, p. 175.

57 R. Munck, 'Repression, insurgency and popular justice', *Crime and Social Justice,* 21/22 (1984), 81–94; P. Hillyard, 'Popular justice in Northern Ireland', in S. Spitzer and A. Scull (eds), *Research on Law, Deviance and Social Control* (Greenwich: Jai, 1985).

58 K. McEvoy and H. Mika, 'Restorative justice and the critique of informalism in Northern Ireland', *British Journal of Criminology* (42) 2002, 536; Knox, 'See

no evil. Hear no evil', 168. 'The person who does not necessarily support Sinn Féin or the IRA may be driven by exasperation to ask for the movement's help against burglars or car thieves or drug dealers.' O'Doherty, *The Trouble with Guns*, p. 145.

59 L. Kennedy, 'They Shoot Children Don't They? An Analysis of the Age and Gender of Victims of Paramilitary Punishments in Northern Ireland', *Report prepared for the Northern Ireland Committee Against Terror and the Northern Ireland Affairs Committee*, http://cain.ulst.ac.uk/issues/violence/docs/kennedy01.htm.

60 H. Patterson, *The Politics of Illusion. A Political History of the IRA* (London: Serif, 1997), p. 285.

61 Moloney, *A Secret History*, p. 437.

62 Moloney, *A Secret History*, pp. 440–441; see also English, *Armed Struggle*, p. 322.

63 Edmund McCoy, a drug dealer had been threatened by the PIRA prior to his murder and was shot in 2000. Bobby McGuigan, involved in criminality, possibly drugs, was shot dead in 2001 in Lurgan by the PIRA. Christopher O'Kane, a Derry 'drugs baron' was shot possibly by DAAD but he was a police informer and had also been subject to threats from the UVF and UDA. Also in 2001 Paul Daly, allegedly involved in drugs, was shot dead. See British Irish Rights Watch, *Conflict Related Deaths 2000*, www.birw.org/Deaths%20since%20ceasefire/deaths%2000.html; Paul Daly's estate was subsequently targeted for civil recovery in 2005 by the Assets Recovery Agency as being the proceeds of unlawful activity.

64 Hugh Orde, answer to a question from the DUP to the Police Board, quoted in *BBC News* (12 May 2004).

65 IMC, *Tenth Report of the Independent Monitoring Commission* (London: The Stationery Office, 2006), see p. 23 for assaults, p. 22 for shootings.

66 IMC, *Thirteenth Report of the Independent Monitoring Commission* (London: Stationery Office, 2007), p. 10.

67 Knox, 'See no evil. Hear no evil', 174.

68 U. Beck, *The Risk Society* (London: Sage, 1992); F. Furedi, *The Culture of Fear. Risk Taking and the Morality of Low Expectations* (Continuum, 2002).

69 G. Pearson, *Hooligan. A History of Respectable Fears* (London: Macmillan, 1983).

70 *The Stephen Lawrence Inquiry: Report of an Inquiry by Sir William Macpherson* Cm 4262 I (London: The Stationery Office, 1999); *The Bichard Inquiry Report* (London: The Stationery Office, 2004).

71 A. Chrisafis, 'IRA offers to shoot McCartney killers', *Guardian* (9 March 2005).

72 Matthew Burns was shot dead in early 2002. According to police, he was shot dead as part of a personal vendetta with a group of Republicans and not as part of any action against drugs distribution. Sinn Féin stated that there was no mainstream republican involvement in the killing after the PIRA was blamed. Later in the same year Brian McDonald was killed. The Red Hand Defenders claimed responsibility but the McDonald family had had a history of feuding with the IRA which had just accelerated, McDonald having been involved in a fight with an IRA individual. See British Irish Rights Watch, *Conflict Related Deaths 2002*, www.birw.org/Deaths%20since%20ceasefire/deaths%2002.html.

73 Gareth O'Connor disappeared in May 2003 after being charged with terror-
    ist membership in the Republic. He had been linked to the real IRA but he
    was also allegedly a police informer, and during the trial of four men on
    terrorist charges his name emerged and apparently was connected to the
    application for a public interest immunity certificate by the Crown. His fam-
    ily and the police accused the PIRA of killing him but they denied this. BBC,
    'Missing man "was police agent"', *BBC News Northern Ireland* (6 January 2004).
    The IMC have not attributed responsibility other than to a republican group.
    Such murders have too complex a framing to produce controversy, particu-
    larly as they are effectively sidelined by governments interested in sustaining
    the peace process. The killing was not 'unique', http://news.bbc.co.uk/1/hi/
    northern_ireland/3372381.stm; BBC, 'Adams silent on IRA murder claim',
    BBC News Northern Ireland (14 June 2005). http://news.bbc.co.uk/1/hi/
    northern_ireland/4091762.stm.
74 For studies of the social, cultural and political context to crimes see G. Pearson,
    Hooligan; R. Reiner, 'Media made criminality: the representation of crime in
    the mass media', in M. Maguire, R. Morgan and R. Reiner (eds), *The Oxford
    Handbook of Criminology* (Oxford: Oxford University Press, 1997), pp. 189–
    231.
75 Patterson, *The Politics of Illusion,* Chapter 7; G. Murray and J. Tonge, *Sinn Féin
    and the SDLP. From Alienation to Participation* (Dublin: O'Brien, 2005).
76 Murray and Tonge, *Sinn Féin and the SDLP*, pp. 216–217.
77 M. Farrell, *Northern Ireland. The Orange State* (London: Pluto, 1976).
78 BBC, 'Sinn Féin reject McCartney police motion', *BBC News Northern Ireland*
    (3 February 2005), http://news.bbc.co.uk/go/pr/fr/-/1/hi/northern_ireland/
    4310553.stm.
79 Chrisafis, 'IRA offers to shoot McCartney killers'.
80 D. Teather and A. Chrisafis, 'McCartneys warned by Sinn Féin not to "cross
    line"', *Guardian* (15 March 2005); D. McKittrick, 'McCartney sisters wel-
    comed as Sinn Féin leader gets cold shoulder in US', *Independent* (15 March
    2005).
81 Quoted in C. Moreton, 'They're not republicans. They are just a gang of
    scumbags', *Independent on Sunday* (13 March 2005).
82 R. Cowan, 'Ministers reassure McCartney family after threat of arson', *Guard-
    ian* (14 May 2005); A. Chrisafis, 'Family of murdered man accuse IRA of
    attack on best friend', *Guardian* (14 September 2005).
83 Moloney, *Secret History*, pp. 155–156.
84 M. Ingram and G. Harkin, *Stakeknife* (Dublin: O'Brien, 2004).
85 In July 2006 Martin McGartland's sister was informed by the PSNI that she
    was under threat from (unspecified) republican paramilitaries. McGartland
    stated they were PIRA.
86 H. McDonald, 'Donaldson murder sparked IRA emergency summit', *Ob-
    server* (9 April 2006).
87 E. Collins, *Killing Rage* (London: Granta, 1998); Harden, *Bandit Country*, 443–
    447.
88 I am grateful to Liam Clarke for full background on the Collins case.
89 BBC, 'Agent's death "won't stall peace"' *BBC News Northern Ireland* (5 April

2006), http://news.bbc.co.uk/1/hi/northern_ireland/4877944.stm.

90 D. Godson, *Himself Alone. David Trimble and the Ordeal of Unionism* (London: Harper Perennial, 2004), Chapter 13.

91 IMC, *4th Report*, p. 6.

92 IMC, *4th Report*, p. 7.

93 'Adams "might be wrong" on robbery', *BBC News* (16 February 2005), http://news.bbc.co.uk/1/hi/northern_ireland/4271971.stm.

94 In effect the raid can be understood as a type of crime equivalent of the Canary Wharf bomb which broke the ceasefire in 1996. This was undertaken by the South Armagh IRA, backed by the Army Council without – apparently – telling Adams until the last minute. The short-term reason for this was rooted in PIRA exasperation at ceasefire since 1994 producing nothing for the movement in terms of political negotiations (English, *Armed Struggle*, pp. 289–290) but a return to violence had been on the cards for some time, reflecting the tensions between different strategic views of the role of military action (Moloney, *Secret History*, 436–443) or because of it represented a necessary mechanism to keep the movement together (for discussion see Patterson, *The Politics of Illusion*, pp. 281–285). If we use this as a template to read off the Northern Bank robbery then part of the motivation may have been a raid to keep the movement together in terms of providing financial security.

95 D. McKittrick, 'McGuinness and Adams on IRA Army Council, says Dublin', *Independent* (21 February 2005). Bobby Tohill was a dissident republican who had been abducted in the centre of Belfast by Provisional IRA members according to the police.

96 T. Harding and G. Jones, 'Fears of IRA return to violence discounted', *Daily Telegraph* (4 February 2005).

97 R. Livingstone, 'This crisis threatens to halt the advance of Sinn Féin', *Guardian* (19 February 2005).

98 M. Devenport, 'Will events affect Sinn Féin's fortunes?' *BBC News Northern Ireland* (13 March 2005), http://news.bbc.co.uk/go/pr/fr/-/1/hi/northern_ireland/4344759.stm.

99 Author interview, Alex Attwood, SDLP MLA and Policing Board member, Belfast, 6 October 2006.

100 IMC, *Eighth Report of the Independent Monitoring Commission* (London: Stationery Office, 2006), p. 19.

101 Indeed one theory argues that Murphy was betrayed by PIRA because he was considering defecting to the dissident republicans. Information was provided to the CAB in the Republic with regard to Murphy's assets. See 'Slab shafted by IRA', *Sunday Life* (16 October 2005). This is unlikely to have been the cause of the raid, since the authorities on both sides of the border already had sufficient evidence against Murphy and had been investigating him for some time (at least in the latest stage – Murphy has been under investigation for decades). However, it is interesting in terms of highlighting Murphy's position as an acceptable target, since after having been an Adams supporter he later criticised republican political strategy and the military inactivity of the republican movement.

102 C. Thornton, 'Stalemate feared over restorative justice plan', *Belfast Telegraph* (6 December 2005).

103 For an early and coruscating view of de facto republican cooperation with the police see A. McIntyre, 'Out of the ashes of armed struggle arose the Stormonistas. And they fought ... Ardoyne youth', *The Blanket* (5 September 2002).

104 IMC, *10th Report*, p. 14.

105 See respectively, IMC, *10th Report*, p. 13, p. 12.

106 Organised Crime Task Force, *Annual Report and Threat Assessment* (Belfast: OCTF, 2006), p. 29.

107 Quoted in BBC News, 'IRA has ceased its criminality', *BBC News Northern Ireland* (25 July 2006).

108 Quoted in BBC, 'IRA has ceased its criminality'.

109 Orde quoted in front of the Select Committee on Northern Ireland Affairs, *BBC Parliament* (9 November 2005).

110 M. Devenport, 'Minister "in hole" over IRA remarks', *BBC News Northern Ireland* (22 January 2006), http://news.bbc.co.uk/1/hi/northern_ireland/4636528.stm.

111 Northern Ireland Affairs Committee, 'Organised Crime in Northern Ireland', *Third Report of Session 2005–06* Vol. 1 HC 886-II (London: The Stationery Office, 2006).

112 IMC, *8th Report*, p. 19; IMC, *10th Report*, p. 14. The reports argue that acts are unsanctioned but this raises a further set of questions.

113 See respectively, Organised Crime Task Force, *Serious and Organised Crime in Northern Ireland. Threat Assessment and Strategy* (Belfast: OCTF, 2004), p. 61; Organised Crime Task Force, *Annual Report and Threat Assessment 2006*, p. 13.

114 Organised Crime Task Force, *Confronting the Threat. Serious and Organised Crime in Northern Ireland* (Belfast: OCTF, 2005), p. 12.

115 Organised Crime Task Force, *Annual Report and Threat Assessment 2006*, p. 7, p. 14.

116 Organised Crime Task Force, *Annual Report and Threat Assessment 2006*, p. 7, p. 10.

117 See, for example, IMC, *10th Report.*

3

Loyalist paramilitaries: violence, crime and legitimacy

They (the loyalist paramilitaries) were set up to protect one side and fight against the other. Well that's done. We've got peace now. They're big business. They're hiding behind this paramilitary protection of communities, but really all they are is big business and extortionists into fraud and drugs. There's no place for them.[a]

We are trying to fix ourselves from within. We've lost (the support) of part of our community by some of the activities of individuals – and I'm not just talking about the UDA side. A lot of people have committed crimes against our own community. We want to get our community back.[b]

Are they all drug dealers? Are they all extortionists?[c]

I grow weary of people being murdered just because someone puts a title on them.[d]

Pure criminality.[e]

[a]   Focus group interview in Loyalist area of Belfast, quoted in C. Knox, 'See no evil. Hear no evil. Insidious paramilitary violence in Northern Ireland', *British Journal of Criminology*, 42:1 (2002), 164–185, 177.

[b]   UDA Brigadier, quoted in 'Loyalist ceasefire ten years on', *BBC News* (13 October 2004) http://news.bbc.co.uk/go/pr/fr/-/hi/northern_ireland/3738146.stm.

[c]   PUP leader David Ervine discussing the UVF, quoted on BBC Radio Ulster (6 September 2006).

[d]   DS Roy McComb, quoted in 'Six arrested over loyalist feud', *BBC News* (4 August 2005), http://news.bbc.co.uk/1/hi/northern_ireland/4745541.stm.

[e]   Author interview, Detective Chief Inspector, PSNI, on the North Belfast UDA leadership, Belfast, 10 November 2005.

Introduction

If the relationship between criminal activity, politics and ideology is controversial with regard to the republican movement, it is particularly troublesome with regard to loyalist paramilitaries. Many would argue that contemporary loyalist paramilitarism is almost entirely driven by criminality. The phrase 'For God, Ulster and my back pocket' appears to have been reduced to the 'back pocket' alone.

This chapter will argue that this is an overstatement. Ideology and politics remain vital to paramilitary organisation and development. For example, the feuding within loyalism which took place in the 1996–2005 period was influenced by a substantial organisational component (who would dominate a possible new pan-Loyalist paramilitary front) and an ideological component (differing views of the peace process). By 2005 the feud appeared to have been resolved. The Loyalist Volunteer Force (LVF), which had been at the centre of the feud, stood down. The UVF was in internal debate about its future and its political counterpart, the Progressive Unionist Party (PUP) continued political innovation and pushed progressive politics. By 2006 the UDA was developing a long-term political programme for its conversion to a exclusively political path, albeit one marked by a characteristic political misjudgement as its East Antrim brigade called for £8.5 million of public funds to assist it in this.

Having made this point, the argument that criminality is not an important variable in loyalist paramilitarism is difficult to sustain either analytically or empirically. Whatever its sympathisers might argue, the Ulster Defence Association of the new millennium is not the UDA of the 1970s. Then, the organisation underpinned the 1974 Ulster Workers Council strike which brought an end to power sharing, developed an innovative political programme and displayed a marked level of organisation under Andy Tyrie. By the year 2000, parts of the UDA were importing and distributing large amounts of ecstasy and cocaine and were politically shambolic. Similarly, the newest major loyalist paramilitary organisation, the Loyalist Volunteer Force, shortly after its formation and the deaths of its main leaders engaged in an impressive level of drug importation and distribution while eschewing any credible political programme. A number of murders within the loyalist feuds were related to criminal activities. Such activities should not be marginalised or overdetermined by formal political analyses; they require integration into any analysis of the loyalist paramilitaries.

These overlapping factors which helped to generate the conflicts within loyalist paramilitarism have in fact been identified by seasoned observers. Progressive Unionist Party leader David Ervine identified three reasons behind the 'internecine outbreak of violence' between the UVF and the UDA in 2001: firstly, the perceived advances of Sinn Féin following the peace process gave weight to anti-agreement figures who responded with violence; secondly, 'A degree of gangsterism has always existed within Loyalism and some wanted to demolish restraints against drug dealing, extortion and lawlessness'; and thirdly, 'someone wanted to destroy the Combined Loyalist Military Command' to prevent the advance of Loyalist political thinking and cooperation.[1] This model provides a useful template for examining the links between public policy, politics, security and crime in Loyalism after the Belfast Agreement.

Loyalism after the Agreement

In terms of Ervine's first point, up to and including the Belfast Agreement, loyalist representatives from the Ulster Democratic Party (the political wing of the UDA) and the Progressive Unionist Party (known as the political wing of the UVF) displayed political imagination and acumen. However, following the Agreement the response of Loyalism to the developing peace process has been marked by disorganisation and reorganisation with groups and factions within groups being pro- and anti-agreement and at times seemingly both at once. Underlying this has been the structural fault-line which had already opened up with the formation of the anti-Agreement Loyalist Volunteer Force in 1996. The ramifications of this split took over a decade to work themselves out.

The development of a stable peace process was logically bound to have a green tinge since it had to warm up the 'cold house' which Northern Ireland had been to Catholics since 1921.[2] The depth of the shading would remained contested, but at times the developing architecture of the Belfast Agreement appeared such a vivid green that it at various points disconcerted even the SDLP. On the macro level, Godson's detailed analysis illustrates that the balance of forces on the diplomatic level was towards securing an agreement, institutionalising that agreement and ensuring Sinn Féin remained within the peace process. Reforms in the areas of demilitarisation, security, policing, decommissioning and the symbolic neutralisation of the province saw Unionism and Loyalism on the back foot ideologically and culturally.[3]

Meanwhile, in the period following the Agreement, Sinn Féin's electoral success eclipsed the SDLP. Within Unionism, the strong vote in 2005 for Ian Paisley's Democratic Unionist Party and the decimation of the Ulster Unionist Party in the UK general election signalled that this part of the electorate had lost patience with what came to be regarded as Trimble's acceptance of concessions to Nationalist opinion and to the republican movement in particular.[4] Ironically, the rise to dominance of the hardline DUP coupled with that of Sinn Féin represented a more coherent platform on which to restore devolution, since the previous process had compromised the UUP in the eyes of unionists and unsettled the SDLP.

Now if Sinn Féin and the DUP have become the 'big beasts' of the Northern Irish political jungle, particularly following the 2007 Northern Ireland Assembly elections, this shows how adept republican paramilitarism has been in consolidating its political position after the Agreement.[5] In contrast, loyalist paramilitaries and their political representatives appeared disorganised and dazzled by the evolving political process. Loyalists have always had less room for political growth and manoeuvre than Republicans for a number of reasons.[6] However, the period following the Belfast Agreement saw Loyalism appear to be in meltdown in terms of its limited mainstream political representation and internecine conflict between its paramilitary organisations. Thus, the UDP had ceased to exist as a political party by 2001 and the PUP's vote, while holding up better, remained limited. However, a major – and debilitating – development within loyalist paramilitarism was the violent internal conflict between the major groups and within the groups (largely the UDA) about the response to the peace process and the issue of which groups would play the leading role within Loyalism. The genesis of this conflict lies in the period after the first ceasefire by paramilitaries, declared in 1994, which already signalled that major ructions within Loyalism would result from any credible peace process. At the centre of the dispute was the emergence of the Loyalist Volunteer Force.

The Loyalist Volunteer Force was formed from the Mid Ulster brigade of the UVF that operated from Portadown. This unit had been particularly prolific in murdering Catholics, particularly those it believed were connected to the republican movement. The brigade was apparently sceptical of the 1994 ceasefire, believing it frustrated them just as they were 'taking the war' to the republicans in an area in which the Provisional IRA's East Tyrone Brigade had been particularly active.[7] The Mid Ulster UVF did generally support the ceasefires but its members displayed increasing opposition to the manner in which the Framework Agreement agreed by Dublin and London appeared to be 'selling out' the Union in favour of a creeping system of joint rule by the UK and the Republic of Ireland. Local UVF figure Billy Wright had already taken a lead in voicing criticism of the developing peace process. Wright was influenced by religion but also disliked the socialism evident in the PUP–UVF's political direction. Drumcree, a high point of the Protestant marching season, became the catalyst for the formation of the Loyalist Volunteer Force. An intense dispute arose in 1996 concerning whether the Orange Order marchers would be permitted to travel down the nationalist Garvaghy

Road. During this, as thousands of mainstream unionists gathered at Drumcree church, elements of loyalist paramilitarism voiced their opposition to the general political evolution of Northern Ireland by causing violence.[8] The murder of Michael McGoldrick, a Catholic taxi-driver, during the dispute was attributed to the UVF, but was in fact an effective rebuff to the pro-peace UVF leadership by elements of the Mid Ulster brigade now firmly opposed to political developments.[9] The Combined Loyalist Military Command ordered that the Mid Ulster brigade be stood down and that Wright should leave Northern Ireland. Wright refused and the LVF was established from elements of the UVF. The new organisation rapidly killed a number of Catholics, although Wright was imprisoned for witness intimidation in relation to a case in 1995. Wright never left prison, being murdered by the INLA in HMP Maze in 1997. Following a spate of murders of Catholics in response to this, the LVF supported the peace process and in 1998 decommissioned (ancient) weapons, the first loyalist or republican group to do so. However, Wright's death destabilised the organisation and illuminated the dynamics between politics and crime in loyalist paramilitarism. One observer of Wright and the LVF argues, 'From 1999–2001 the Loyalist Volunteer Force appeared to lose direction'[10] and in 2002 the man who had replaced Wright, Mark 'Swinger' Fulton committed suicide. In the absence of this original leadership the balance towards criminality tilted. However, the main political issue was the developing links between the LVF and that part of the UDA/UFF centred on C-Company led by Johnny Adair.

From as early as 1997–1998, elements in the LVF wished to move into alliance with the UDA as part of a developing loyalist front but also as a shield against the Ulster Volunteer Force. Following Wright's murder Johnny Adair 'was instrumental in having the remaining LVF prisoners accommodated with the UDA's H block. This increasing alliance between the UFF and the LVF was clearly seen as a threat to the UVF, as perhaps it was intended'.[11] Adair and the LVF developed links behind the back of the UDA Inner Council,[12] as the dynamic of the LVF leadership switched from Mid Ulster to Belfast.

In 2000 a feud between the LVF and the UVF saw Adair involved. Richard Jameson, a UVF Mid Ulster commander was shot dead, following which two young men, Andrew Robb and David McIlwaine, said to be on the fringes of the LVF were murdered.[13] Adair went to Robb's funeral and was spotted elsewhere socialising with the LVF. At the Protestant day of culture centred on the Shankhill, at which guarantees had been given to the UVF by the UDA that the Loyalist Volunteer Force would not be present, an LVF flag was nevertheless unfurled outside the UVF-linked Rex bar. UVF supporters attacked the LVF group.[14] C-Company supporters came to the aid of the LVF resulting in serious violence for which a number of convictions eventually resulted. Two hundred families identified as being associated with the UVF were then forced from the Shankhill by Adair. The UVF retaliated by killing UDA figure Jackie Coulter, and Bobby Mahood. Adair was recalled to prison by then Secretary of State for Northern Ireland Peter Mandleson but C-Company and the UVF continued to attack each other. Between August and October seven people were murdered.[15] Adair was released in 2002 and continued to destabilise the UDA by his manoeuvres. Following the suicide of LVF leader Mark 'Swinger' Fulton, Adair forged closer links to the organisation to the extent that he 'viewed the mid Ulster LVF as an extension of his paramilitary empire'.[16] This was occurring at a time when the UDA was already riven by differing approaches to the peace process. Many UDA representatives declared their opposition, arguing that there had been too many concessions to republicans. John White, Adair's political adviser was pro-peace but making little headway since he and Adair were at the centre of the feud. The UDA's ceasefire had been de-recognised in 2001 by then Secretary of State John Reid on the basis of the violence involved in the dispute.

In 2002 after Stephen Warnock of the LVF was shot dead, rumours circulated that the UDA was responsible. When UDA figure Jim Gray paid his respects at Warnock's brother's house, Gray was the subject of an attempted murder by the LVF. Adair was present at this attack, apparently the last straw for the Ulster Defence Association. Adair was publicly dismissed as West Belfast brigadier by the UDA, and elements of the UDA in East Belfast attacked those with LVF links.[17] The LVF's alliance with Johnny Adair proved unstable however: 'The LVF as a whole had little relish for an alignment with Adair which would involve it in a major confrontation with the mainstream UDA'[18] and following a final pair of tit for tat killings the LVF eventually called a truce with UDA, publicly accepting that the East Belfast UDA had had no part in Warnock's murder. In fact Warnock had been killed by the UVF/Red Hand Commando, apparently as part of a dispute over drug money.

Adair became increasingly isolated as elements of the UDA formerly close to him could see the balance of forces was against them. Adair's closest supporter Andre Shoukri sided with the UDA, as did later Mo Courtney, a long time ally, while Adair also forced out old allies such as Winkie Dodds.[19] Adair's C Company attacked those linked with the mainstream UDA even as Adair's licence was revoked again in January 2003 and he was returned to prison.[20] The final act occurred shortly afterwards when Adair authorised C Company's murder of UDA Brigadier John Gregg, shot in his car when returning from a Glasgow Rangers match. The Ulster Defence Association leadership made clear that Adair's supporters would be forced out of the Shankhill but offered amnesty to those who disowned him.[21] Adair's wife and family and some supporters fled to Scotland, then settled in Bolton. There they were the subject of some attention from the Greater Manchester Police until Adair's son and others were convicted of drugs offences. Adair himself was released in January 2005. After a brief stay in Bolton in the north-west of England (during which he was convicted of violence towards his wife) he moved back to Scotland. Other associates remain scattered over England and Scotland.[22]

The ousting of Adair represented a movement to restore control and coherence to the UDA, reflecting the fact that despite the fact that it was an 'Association' it required a basic functional level of organisational and political coherence. Jackie McDonald, the oldest serving UDA brigadier, is credited with restoring order, having played a role in bringing down Adair.[23] Moves were made to stabilise the UDA and control public disorder by young loyalists more tightly. The organisation reannounced its ceasefire in early 2004, which the government recognised later in the year. McDonald took further action to consolidate UDA stability and enhance his position by engineering the dismissal of Jim Gray, a figure seen as more criminal than useful. Gray was ousted from the UDA in April 2005. He had been under pressure for some time from a law enforcement investigation into his assets, which had seen him sell off a number of business concerns.[24] Following his expulsion he was arrested for money laundering offences. Other UDA figures were apparently concerned that he would become a police informant, not merely concerning contemporary UDA activities, but also allegedly with regard to the murders of Geordie Legge (2001) and John McIver (1992).[25] Gray was protected by the police from this potential UDA threat after his release on bail, but he was shot dead in November 2005.[26]

McDonald had publicly stated that there should be no more leadership styles akin to Jim Gray's in future,[27] and in what appears to be the final phase of stabilisation, Andre and Ihab Shoukri, brigadiers formerly associated with Adair and seen as being involved in excessive criminality and opposed to the political direction of the UDA, were expelled from the Association in 2006. When Shoukri supporters attempted a 'coup' to regain control of the North Belfast leadership it was rebuffed by a show of strength by the UDA Inner Council.

Other internecine loyalist conflict continued in parallel with these developments: the original blood feud between the UVF and the LVF accelerated once more. Individuals linked to Warnock's family had murdered Red Hand Commando leader Jim Johnston in 2003 in revenge for his role in the killing of Stephen Warnock.[28] However, an intense period of violence was sparked by the murder of Brian Stewart by the UVF in mid-2004. In the year following there were 4 more murders and 17 attempted murders, most of these attributable to the UVF.[29] The IMC's perspective on this was clear: 'the UVF leadership has decided now is the right time to finish off the LVF'.[30] However, crime played a role; the UVF had been in receipt of complaints from the local community concerning the level of LVF criminality, particularly drug dealing in Belfast.[31] The LVF stated it would have stood down in 2004 had the DUP and Sinn Féin agreed a deal and the PIRA ended activities and decommissioned[32] but this masked the fact that the LVF was fizzling out as an organisation of influence. In addition to attack from the UVF, the LVF was also being targeted by the Police Service of Northern Ireland and the Assets Recovery Agency. The Loyalist Volunteer Force stood down its members in 2005 but has not decommissioned.

What is to be made of these internecine inter- and intra-loyalist conflicts? They have a long pedigree. The UDA and UVF have feuded before. Sporadic disputes have been the visible peaks in an often antagonistic relationship, which has also been marked by periods of accommodation and mechanisms for regular consultation and dispute resolution. However, the contemporary conflicts appear qualitatively different. From a structural perspective, the long-term feuds that characterised Loyalism from the mid-1990s may be seen as a working out of the instability caused by the formation of the LVF. This structural reorganisation had a number of dynamics, to which the quote from Ervine at the start of this chapter testifies. Each organisation had its own problems as a result of the formation of the LVF and the changing panorama of the peace process.

Loyalism, politics and crime

'Loyalism involves a complex set of political and social expressions, including militarism, sectarianism, community, regional and class based dynamics. All of these may find some expression and outlet within loyalist paramilitary organisations.'[33] The forms of expression range from formal politics to violence to community work. It may appear a harsh judgement but following the peace process, dynamic loyalist political evolution in the formal political process almost completely halted. At a time when republican politics was at a high point (1998–2002) Loyalist political groups could not produce a response of equal quality. Spokesmen for the groups appeared to support both peace and opposition to the peace process at once. This is not new in politics, but within Loyalism these fractures and inconsistencies were more than a republican-style product of tensions between the armed and the political wing. They represented a loss of coherence within the paramilitary organisations themselves.

By the turn of the twenty-first century the UDA had lost political direction as reflected in its political wing the Ulster Democratic Party: 'Although UDP leader Gary McMichael had threatened to resign as party leader in January (2001) if the UDA withdrew its support for the Agreement his position was undermined both by the activities of the UDA and by the Party's own ineptitude in failing to register as a political party ... leading to only three UDP members being returned as independent councillors.'[34] By the following year, 'The Ulster Democratic Party had, for all practical purposes, ceased to exist. It had held no area or constituency meetings for nearly two years and had failed to contest any seats as a party in the most recent council elections.'[35] The Ulster Political Research Group emerged as the public political face of the UDA but often initially to little effect; no surprise considering the internal instability outlined above. Thus, at least measured by formal political participation (and this is an important variable) UDA politics had withered on the peace process vine.

In the area of informal politics, in terms of violence based activities, continued operations were evident. In addition to those mentioned above as part of feuds, sectarian murders continued after the peace process. These were at a lower level, and some could be connected to the low intensity ethnic conflict which has characterised Belfast (and other areas), which in some cases worsened after 1998 and which has seen both sides engage in intimidation, sporadic and organised attacks and other forms of disorder.[36] It is commonly stated that while the major peace walls in Belfast were unsecured following peace, elsewhere more walls have been established. An estimated 92.5 per cent of public housing in Northern Ireland is divided along religious lines, rising to 98 per cent in Belfast.[37] When any shifts are attempted they tend to be total rather than towards an area becoming mixed. In this environment the UDA has played a role in attempting to 'draw the line' at the advance of Catholic settlement in what were previously Protestant areas, to attack Catholic areas via pipe bombs, and respond to attacks by republican activists on Protestant homes, a constant along the dividing lines between communities.[38] Pipe bomb attacks increased in 2001 and 2002[39] and in 2003 the individual identified as the new North Belfast brigadier 'Bonzer' Borland allegedly ordered attacks on Catholic houses in Deerpark Road.[40] Violence was employed in other areas. In 2005 the Whiterock riots were orchestrated and then controlled by the UDA and UVF in response to the re-routing of an Orange parade from a nationalist area. This clearly demonstrated paramilitary 'political' and social capacity: during three days of rioting loyalists threw 167 blast bombs, over 1,000 petrol bombs and discharged live ammunition. The UDA continued capacity building, including increased recruitment and PSNI arrests uncovered submachine guns, ammunition and pipe bombs. The UDA stated it would not decommission as long as tension continues along interface areas,[41] a position maintained in 2007.

The UDA continued its deep involvement in mainstream community action and support, in which it has a long tradition. UDA community work is evident in a number of areas: community forums, restorative justice and rehabilitation (including drugs counselling) and prisoners' aid and welfare. The Ulster Political Research Group lobbied the NIO over investment and public infrastructure provision.

Thus in a number of ways, the UDA 'represents' the community groups who are under pressure and have no one to speak for them in the sense of the working class having been left behind by the Agreement and marginalised by mainstream politicians. The dispute at Holy Cross Girls Primary School sparked from pre-existing tensions at an interface area over the placing of loyalist symbols, which were removed by nationalists. The dispute escalated and saw protestors throwing stones at Catholic children on their way to and from school. This intimidation was a clear own goal but the contemporary comments by Protestants illuminated the extent to which Loyalist communities felt they had been under siege since the Belfast Agreement and that the media would not give them a fair hearing,[42] a fatalism already evident in the late 1980s and early 1990s before the peace process but similarly based on the Loyalist assumption that the tide of history was turning against the community.[43]

However, if these activities often represented Shirlow's conceptualisation of the community areas as 'sanctuary' the punishment beatings which continued and indeed increased, oscillated these territories to 'prison'.[44] Further, the crime issue was becoming a problem in terms of political and social legitimacy. As the conflict died off the urban community, which perceived itself losing out in the peace process, saw senior UDA figures making large sums of money and moving to the green slopes of North Down and elsewhere. Also, the intimidation of those who spoke out about crime was evident.[45] Following the expulsion of Adair the UDA leadership stated that it would control criminality, but then, for example, was under pressure to end a spate of low-level thuggery and extortion which belied this.[46] The Inner Council became concerned at the level of (overt) criminality in east Belfast. Apparently Jim Gray was a source of criticism by other members of the Inner Council and was expelled by UDA in 2005.[47] Andre Shoukri's overt criminality and excessive gambling was also seen as a problem, and in any case the North Belfast UDA leadership had begun to face a welter of charges including blackmail, terrorist and murder charges from late 2005. In June 2006 Andre and Ihab Shoukri were expelled from the UDA. A final counter-move to this from Shoukri supporters was faced down by the UDA leadership, with the expulsions being carried out without violence. This may signal the UDA regaining coherence and reducing criminality. There are senior individuals who are opposed to crime, and the UPRG has adopted a more prominent role since early 2006. In 2006 it held a series of consultations with the NIO and was developing business cases for community funding. By September 2006 this had borne fruit with £135,000 being provided for community work in various areas.[48]

With regard to the UVF it has not had the mass movement, community front style approach of the UDA. 'The modern UVF straddles two worlds – sectarianism and political innovation.'[49] The UVF has been the loyalist group most committed to the peace process, and has supported progressive politics: the UVF has removed members for racism. The UVF performs community support and rehabilitation roles. The restorative justice scheme Greater Shankhill Alternatives was endorsed by the UVF/RHC and received referrals from them as well as other statutory agencies. They promote cooperation with the Probation Board and police.[50] Crime appears less of an issue with regard to UVF legitimacy, and the UVF is relatively more opposed to the drugs trade. However, the UVF had its ceasefire (and that of the Red Hand Commando) declared void in 2005 on the back of the murders its members had committed in their feud with the LVF (and the PUP had its Assembly allowances withdrawn). The UVF has also been involved in sectarian murders and attacks and punishment beatings, and like the UDA has organised public disorder.

The UVF's formal political development has been more effective than the UDA's. Its political wing, the Progressive Unionist Party (PUP) gained two seats in the first Assembly elections in 1999 and still retained one of them in 2003, an election in which the DUP did particularly well at the expense of those political parties, including the PUP which had supported the Belfast Agreement. The PUP displayed more acumen but at times appeared sand-trapped by the UVF feuds with the LVF and UDA and generally could not match republican political tactics, even accepting that the political context was more propitious for Sinn Féin. The PUP continues to display political innovation, for example in its relationship with the UUP (or is it political desperation on the part of the UUP?) and its announced community cooperation with Sinn Féin in Londonderry in 2006. The PUP has expressed support for ethnic minority community members and gay and lesbian rights. It retains limited electoral support, however, and its relationship with the paramilitary organisation remains problematic. The death of PUP leader David Ervine in 2007 was a severe blow for the Party's future development.

The UVF's relationship to the PUP has been held to be more stable and credible because the PUP has ex-paramilitaries in it,[51] but UVF activities showed that the organisation repeatedly diverged from the PUP's political statements, although it should be noted that this has been par for the course with regard to the PIRA and Sinn Féin, (particularly in the comparable 1994–1998 period). The PUP has, Sinn Féin-like, publicly distanced itself from the UVF, but the connections fade in and out as necessary. David Ervine and others issued opaque statements about politics and paramilitarism, arguing that the PUP could not influence the UVF but then warned of what the UVF might do in certain circumstances. This is part of the PUP's strategy to transform paramilitarism and it has argued that criticism of paramilitary activity is unhelpful:

> it is easy to complain about ongoing paramilitary activity and to both theorise about and prescribe methods of addressing such activity. It is not so easy to put such theories and prescriptions into practice. Conflict transformation is a process in which we seek to move from violent responses to non-violent responses. It is about working to transform the nature of the conflict from violent encounter to democratic exchange.[52]

This represents (like the South East Antrim UDA's call for funding to convert to politics) a fundamentally problematic political discourse. The argument above is representative of PUP strategy generally: concerns over violence and criminality should be subsumed within the argument that the process of change is difficult. However this represents a difficulty in engendering wider legitimacy, particularly when issues of UVF activity become public. The Police Ombudsman's report into the criminal activities of UVF members while they were police informants requires engagement rather than marginalisation, as reflected in the PUP statement on the matter. For if the PUP seeks to encourage 'non violent responses' in the UVF, it is central to the 'democratic exchange' to highlight those problems which might actually characterise the extent of change.[53]

Political activity by both organisations and their political representatives has aimed at rectifying the perceived imbalance in the peace process. The UDA/UPRG and the PUP have urged the Government to direct assistance to loyalist areas in terms of health, education, housing and employment.[54] David Hanson, the Political Development Minister stated that developing assistance to disadvantaged loyalist communities was a response to a report that argued NIO policy was not impacting on working-class Protestant areas,[55] politics-speak for the Government's acknowledgement that Protestants felt they were losing out on a number of fronts following the Belfast Agreement. The appointment of Bertha McDougall as the Victims Commissioner in 2005 continued the series of low-level confidence building measures with the Unionist community;[56] and this stretched to loyalist working-class areas. In 2005 the NIO invested £500,000 in the Kilcooley estate in Bangor, and the following year Hanson announced that a £10 million regeneration plan would be implemented, and explicitly linked this to assisting loyalist paramilitaries in 'moving on'.[57] In addition over £3 million was announced to fund the replacement of paramilitary murals with more neutral images, followed rapidly by £135,000 to the UPRG for community work, and £4.1 million to redevelop major roads in republican and loyalist areas in Belfast, including the Shankhill.[58] Pressure from loyalist groups' political representatives as well as the rise of the DUP has been central here but it would be naive to think that the public order problems in loyalist areas, culminating in events such as Whiterock and the continuing activities of paramilitary groups had nothing to do with this. Cynics argued the state was effectively 'buying off' the loyalist paramilitaries and that such funds were part of the famed £30 million which they had demanded to disband. This is too sweeping, since it came along with a policing strategy which aimed to 'bring the paramilitaries in'.

The previous sections in this chapter have attempted to provide a political and organisational context for the actions of loyalist paramilitary organisations. Within this, the issue of crime has often emerged, since it so clearly links with politics and legitimacy. Thus the next section deals directly with this issue.

Loyalist paramilitaries and crime

Bruce argues that there are 'three strands of paramilitary activity: politics, terror and corruption' and that the three coexist in a complex relationship. 'Only politics and terror could be publicly defended', since few if any are prepared to openly advocate corruption, although it might be seen as a necessary evil tolerated by the community if the overall causes of Loyalism and community protection are advanced.[59] These variables may not be in conflict but 'time and effort put into one thing reduces the time and effort available for others. Further the conditions required for one may not be fertile for the others.'[60] Terror on the scale of the early 1990s assumed a lesser role as the peace process developed following the first ceasefire in 1994. Politics became vital in the run up to the Belfast Agreement. But, as mentioned, following this the internal power struggles detailed above (which were of course themselves political), left little time for a coherent formal politics. If terror and formal politics had declined as central variables, it appeared that crime had relatively increased in importance. As Bruce points out in a later analysis, 'The rewards of contemporary terrorism, and hence the intensity of rivalry over their control, are far greater than they were at the start of the Troubles.'[61] This was bolstered by a structural aspect: as argued in the introduction, the 'room' provided for republicans and loyalists by the British government also had an effect on space for crime.

The organisation which has excited most interest in terms of the relationship between loyalist paramilitarism and crime is the UDA. It is possible to trace an increase in criminality both just before and following the first ceasefire in 1994. Particularly after 1994, money which had been channelled into the organisation and setting up of more professional attacks which targeted Sinn Féin and PIRA activists, was now channelled into personal and network activities which we would associate with Ordinary Decent Criminals i.e. leisure, 'play' and consumption. Elements of the UDA appear to have moved into drug importation and dealing, particularly ecstasy, in the early 1990s.[62] However, this appeared particularly evident in Johnny Adair's C Company, where,

> It was widely held that Adair had become involved in drug dealing, extortion, money laundering and prostitution. While the mainstream UDA did not have an unblemished record in many of these areas, the organisation's involvement in prostitution was widely regarded as a step too far. The claim that there was no contradiction between being a drug dealer and a patriot was also called into question by the political and non-criminal elements of both C Company and the UDA, who clearly viewed these claims as mutually exclusive.[63]

This development was intertwined with Adair's developing closeness to elements of the LVF.[64] Drugs were initially imported from the mainland, including Manchester but then gained more directly from Spain and the Netherlands.[65] Drug dealing remains an important practical and symbolic trope of the 'proper behaviour' expected of paramilitaries, who stand as community defenders. Brigadier Jackie McDonald's attempts to control the drug trade in his bailiwick in contrast to other areas were evidence of this, as was the criticism of local drug dealing,[66] often in the form of graffiti, the ubiquitous community noticeboards of Belfast.

Like most paramilitary organisations, the UDA has a long pedigree in terms of extortion. It developed as a means of raising revenue early on in the organisation's existence as a more stable tactic to be employed compared to other methods such as bank robbery, which many groups undertook over the decades of conflict but which were seen as relatively risky (however certain forms of armed robbery returned to prominence following the peace process). Extortion has worsened since 1998. Loyalist groups accounted for 80 per cent of reported extortion cases in 2002,[67] one recent study demonstrating that the UDA is predominant, either as the Association itself, the UFF or Loyalist Prisoners Aid.[68]

The decentralised nature of extortion in loyalist areas remains an important feature of the practice, a function of the relative autonomy of UDA Brigade areas. Funds are extorted through subtle arrangements such as donations, security payments and so forth. Loyalists operate security companies through which 'negotiations' for protection take place and payments are made.[69] Experienced paramilitaries are engaged deeply in this practice, and many have previous convictions.[70] The building industry, small businesses and wealthy individuals are particular targets for extortion.[71] The average extortion payment is approximately £1000, but payments on large building sites may amount to £20–30,000 and above. In terms of protecting these expanded criminal activities, should extortion be reported, the intimidation of witnesses is evident, dealt with in Chapter 6.[72]

There seems to be a consensus that the loyalists are becoming more involved in 'white collar' activities. Some of this is an expansion of previous patterns of activity. Before 1998 loyalists were using smuggled cigarettes and stolen alcohol in their clubs.[73] Members of the UDA are involved in counterfeiting, particularly the distribution of goods via the Nutts Corner market in Antrim. This is an area, as with drug distribution, in which the UDA is internationally linked in its criminal operations e.g. with south-east Asia, including Thailand and Malaysia.[74] The UDA (and other loyalist groups) and republicans are cooperating in counterfeit markets, distributing each other's goods for a 'cut' and buying off each other. Cooperation is also evident in drugs and cigarette smuggling.[75] Long practised frauds are evident, including fraudulent tax avoidance certificates, rife in the construction industry (£50 million overall according to one estimate), facilitated by weekly cash payments. This is an area where the UDA copied the PIRA in the late 1980s.[76]

Much funding goes towards running the organisations and personal consumption. According to PSNI estimates, the UDA cost £500,000 per year to run in 2001–2002 and had a fundraising capacity of up to £1 million.[77] Recruitment expanded following this, raising costs, but income from extortion also increased. The surplus funds which are not immediately expended have to be invested unless they are held in cash 'under the bed'. The UDA's Jim Gray was allegedly planning to invest in the redevelopment of the Titanic docks and other areas of the construction industry.[78] Loyalists, including the UDA are hiding funds with more skill and employing solicitors, financial advisors and accountants. Under anti-money-laundering law, these individuals are now classed as 'responsible officers' for the purposes of Knowing Your Customer and are legally bound to report suspicious activity. They are not employed officially but provide 'off the books' advice. The advice covers the depositing, conversion, transfer and investment of funds.

When discussing criminality, as implied, a distinction has to be made between UDA brigade areas, with some brigadiers being seen as anti-drugs, for example. But there are also, of course, distinctions within areas. Each brigade contains individuals who are opposed to criminality and can agitate against it (although this can be a distinctly risky practice and was in certain areas of North Belfast in the early 2000s). The criminal networks that do exist can be fluid, with individuals networking with Ordinary Decent Criminals and the nature of the network changing. Jim

Gray's 'gang' was an example of this.[79] Nevertheless this does not mean attribution is impossible. It is also the case that networks are still operating within the organisation, using it as authority and as an intimidatory mechanism. Further, the public pronouncements of a number of leaders do not match private actions, and, simply, the organisation annually requires substantial funds to operate which are not gained legally. The moves by some UDA areas to reduce criminality from 2005 were and are patchy and represent these features. If we cannot attribute crime to the UDA because it is a fissiparous organisation, then, logically, neither can we attribute much else to it.

The Ulster Volunteer Force is generally viewed as the more sophisticated and disciplined of the loyalist groups, eschewing the decentralised brigadier system of the UDA for a more centralised structure, which was developed by the UVF in prison under its leader Gusty Spence as well as on the outside.[80] Of course the UVF has had problems with 'independent' elements. As with other loyalist groups in the early years, the UVF stole weapons from the police and army during the 1970s and committed bank robberies to raise funds. Extortion became a staple fundraiser.[81] With regard to contemporary criminal activities the UVF are seen as being more similar to the PIRA than the UDA in that criminal activities have a closer relationship in underpinning organisational development and capacity and ideology, that is, in the contemporary period there has been relatively less 'leakage' into personal coffers.

The UVF has a tradition of being relatively free from the drugs trade.[82] The UVF received complaints from individuals and community groups about LVF drug dealing and was requested to deal with this; the LVF was heavily involved in drugs and these complaints built on the already developing feud between the two groups.[83] However, the UVF's public anti-drugs stance is relative and increasingly open to question. In the 1990s, UVF figures were subject to accusations of drug taking and dealing, particularly in connection with a grotesque sectarian murder,[84] and elements of the UVF and the associated group Red Hand Commando were involved in the drugs trade. Jim Johnston of the UVF/RHC, who was shot dead in 2003 was a millionaire who had gained substantial sums from racketeering and drug dealing.[85] Of the 72 crimes that police 'Informant 1' in the Mount Vernon UVF was alleged to be implicated in between 1992 and 2003, the greatest number, 17, were drugs related.[86] Recent claims refer to UVF drug dealing in east Belfast, and its 'licensing' of dealers.[87]

The UVF is deeply involved in extortion and was prominent in a recent study of the practice.[88] The UVF, as with other paramilitary groups, operates via subtle demands but of course employs coercion. The UVF has been involved in intimidation which has been classed as racist but

has in fact been part of extortion demands. Some ethnic minority businesses were subject to demands and on refusing to pay their families were
then targets of intimidation, which had a racist element but ended following payments. This does not diminish its significance but it does highlight, as other cases highlighted in this chapter the complex threads and
perceptions with regard to paramilitary activity. Like the UDA, the UVF
is also adept at rapidly organising public order problems to counter PSNI
criminal investigation or police disruption tactics such as search/seizures
and arrests.

The LVF lost a great deal of coherence with the death of Billy Wright
and Mark Fulton but from its inception was surrounded by accusations of
crime. Apparently, 'Wright never drank or smoked and did not allow his
men to take drugs around him (though in later years he was happy to
benefit from the LVF's drugs empire)',[89] although others argue Wright
did deal in drugs.[90] The LVF were involved in drugs and extortion rackets in mid Ulster[91] and a number of figures in this relatively small
organisation have convictions for drug dealing. The LVF imports drugs
from the Netherlands, Spain and Malta. Accusations of drug dealing have
affected the organisation, particularly constant police allegations that the
organisation is controlling drugs shipments, and in 2003 the LVF took
the remarkable step of offering to shoot a drug dealer who had been
publicly linked with the group but who they claimed was not.[92] However,
in 2001 the LVF had murdered Martin O'Hagan, a journalist who amongst
other lines of investigation had focused on their drug dealing activities.
LVF figures practised extortion, and the organisation was allegedly involved in other areas such as alcohol manufacture and counterfeit cur-
rency.[93] The LVF purchased weapons from Eastern Europe with money
gained from drug dealing, and apparently has a quite modern and substantial arsenal.[94] Although the organisation stood down in 2005 it is unlikely the individuals have stopped.

While the political and organisational context of the loyalist feuds has
been detailed in previous sections, the lucrative elements of criminal activity cannot be discounted as a generator in these conflicts. If Johnny
Adair wanted to create a pan-Loyalist front, was it merely for politics or
did he envisage some sort of reward accruing from his control? Similarly,
when the LVF supported the UDA did its members never have any con-
sideration as to the rewards which might flow from it effectively increasing its territory?[95] Does the control of territory and the use of social power
by paramilitaries have no substantial relationship to crime and revenue
generation?

Finally as a coda for those interested in examining the links between
paramilitaries and crime, rich evidence for sociological analysis has taken
place over recent years, with the physical displacement of paramilitaries

from all three groups who have moved to those areas of Bangor and associated zones not previously known for a paramilitary presence as a result of feuds or the classic 'moving up and out' often evident in urban organised criminals. A number of murders attributed to the UVF–LVF split have occurred, such as Warnock's and Johnston's. Further, there has been a (relative) rise in crimes significant of paramilitary presence (beatings and shootings) and according to the chairman of the North Down District Policing Partnership, 'There's also the drugs situation. Some people have been displaced from east Belfast because of paramilitary activity, and they've been allocated homes in the area by the Housing Executive, and they've brought their activities with them.'[96] The same is true of the faction linked to Adair, who, within a fairly short space of time of moving to Bolton in the north-west of England were convicted of offences related to violence and drug dealing.

Politics, policing, crime and the British state

Ervine's latter identification of the shadowy influence of the British state or 'establishment interests' as fuelling loyalist disorganisation is familiar to that symbolic explanation used by republicans to interpret some political events. The latter tend to conjure up the ghostly network of 'the securocrats', a coterie of establishment and security figures acting to undermine republicans and destabilise the peace process. For Loyalism, establishment interests are also manifested in the workings of the security elements of the British state, a state they have never been able to trust since it has no stomach for a sustained war against the PIRA and which further infiltrates loyalist organisations and uses them for its own purposes.

Certainly the security services have played a deep role inside loyalist organisations. The revelations of informers which have followed the peace process raise important questions about the operation of RUC Special Branch. One set of questions relates to the protection of loyalist informants by the Branch when they were engaged in serious criminal activity. These questions have been the subject of calls for public and police inquiries, most notably over the murder of Patrick Finucane.[97] Following the Stevens Inquiries, criminal charges were laid against UFF individuals involved in the murder. However, other equally serious allegations continue to surface. The Police Ombudsman investigated issues surrounding the alleged protection of UVF members of the Mount Vernon unit while they were Special Branch informers with regard to the 1997 murder of Raymond McCord, nine other murders and ten attempted murders. But there were other cases of UVF informants engaged in serious criminality including murders[98] and this extends beyond the peace.

Indeed, some of the violence within loyalist paramilitary groups following the Belfast Agreement was not just a result of factionalism and differing responses to the peace process; it was also a result of the exposure of informants. Some paramilitaries engaging in criminal acts were no longer protected by their roles as informers when they were brought up on criminal charges, for a number of reasons. Either informants were simply 'let go' by Special Branch or the police since they had outlived their usefulness (even as Special Branch was picking up new informants elsewhere), or secondly (as the example of the Sinn Féin spy ring demonstrates), even if the charges were dropped the identities of informants leaked. Or figures were seen as possible informants. Thus UDA Quartermaster William Stobie, already suspected of being a Special Branch informer was charged as a result of the Finucane investigation. Although the case collapsed Stobie supported calls for 'a proper inquiry' into Finucane's murder and shortly afterwards was murdered by the UDA.[99] The risk of informing may have been behind Jim Gray's murder in 2005. With regard to the UVF the unmasking of Mark Haddock, leader of the Mount Vernon unit, as an informer was followed by a murder attempt on him in 2006 sanctioned by the UVF leadership.[100] As more leaks and revelations occur, more old scores are being settled. Indeed, as the unmaskings continue – and if they are to be believed in the hall of mirrors which is Northern Ireland's political discourse – it appears that republican and loyalist paramilitary organisations were jammed so full with informants that the British state may have been effectively fighting a war with itself.

Another set of questions relates to the argument that in the late 1990s the British state was using informants to destabilise Loyalism. For example, the theorists would have it that the British state was behind Billy Wright's formation of the LVF as a splitting operation to destabilise a putative pan-Loyalist paramilitary front, and was also later behind the death of Billy Wright in the Maze prison because he was too dangerous to have around, since his charisma might unite loyalist anti-agreement paramilitarism. This fits with arguments that British intelligence was generally disrupting Loyalism by encouraging hardliners to oppose the developing peace negotiations because a disorganised and dispirited Loyalism would make a deal with republicans easier.[101] Following the exposure (for the umpteenth time) of Jim Spence as an alleged informant, one account from a former member of military intelligence, Force Research Unit (FRU) stated that his actions in the UDA had been to sow dissent. During the feud within the UDA this involved him backing Adair and John White in their pro-peace stance against other UDA brigadiers.

However, these accounts tend to overemphasise those areas where the state has acted to destabilise loyalists rather than stabilise and institutionalise some sort of engagement. Even in the dark days of the 1970s, Special Branch – in addition to sowing black propaganda to destabilise loyalist groups – was attempting to encourage the development of political thinking in such groups. At other times the establishment has attempted to draw loyalists in, as it did with the PIRA.[102] If the state has been acting to disorganise loyalist paramilitary organisations by encouraging anti-agreement forces it has also adopted the reverse strategy i.e. measures to create the conditions for a wind-down and stabilisation of loyalist groups; recent evidence if anything points to the British state adopting this tactic. Whatever the case, a more rigorous methodology is required to deconstruct these accounts, since they are at risk of the charge of functionalism.[103]

How does the trickery of British police and military intelligence relate to crime? The relationship varies in emphasis. On one hand, if some of these men were informants they have been permitted to commit serious offences including murder and also develop substantial sums via criminal activity and the toleration of their criminal activities. On the other, the British state's attempt to incapacitate loyalists or draw them in has influenced strategies of criminal investigation and analysis. Some groups have faced sustained law enforcement activity. The LVF suffered not only from its feuding with other loyalist paramilitary organisations but also from concentrated police and Assets Recovery Agency activity. A number of LVF members were convicted of serious offences, including violence and drugs.[104] With regard to the UVF this has been an area where loyalist groups developed and stabilised links. In September 2005 then PSNI Assistant Chief Constable Sam Kinkaid and a senior member of the Policing Board (in his role as community representative rather than Policing Board figure) met David Ervine to press the UVF to stop the paramilitary feud with the LVF then in progress. These meetings continued, with seven taking place by early 2006. The meetings covered several issues, including the prevention of paramilitary violence on the forthcoming Love Ulster Day in Dublin. But they also covered general issues, centrally the idea of moving the UVF away from organised crime. The PSNI provided the PUP with an assessment of what types of organised crime the UVF was involved in. In the past, local religious and community leaders had engaged with loyalist paramilitary groups but did not possess the detailed context of the groups' operations and were not in a position to evaluate the groups' claims concerning crime and other issues. The information which the PSNI possessed was employed as a 'benchmark' for change.[105] No information was shared which would interfere with current investigations; indeed UVF members were arrested as the talks continued. However this opened up a valuable line of communication since the UVF had stopped talking to the International Monitoring Commission[106] following the IMC's report recommending sanctions against the PUP as a result of the UVF's continuing paramilitary violence.[107] The PUP organised a series of meetings with UVF/RHC officials throughout the province, as this had chimed in with a process of internal discussion over the future of the UVF. This had been given impetus by the statement from the PIRA that their military strategy had ended. Those who focus almost solely on an internal political analysis of developments within loyalist groups as the driver for change would presumably reject the idea that policing provided a lever for change.

With regard to the Ulster Defence Association it is clear that intensified activity by the PSNI (and ARA) undermined the UDA. The then Secretary of State Paul Murphy recognised the UDA's ceasefire in late 2004 but the UDA was subjected to continuing law enforcement attention. The North Belfast UDA leadership effectively took a broadside from the criminal justice process via arrests and disruption from the Assets Recovery Agency. Informants were used in one case against six men charged with membership and/or drugs offences, the first time this had been used as a tactic for some time.[108] UDA leader Andre Shoukri was charged with blackmail in late 2005. Some North Belfast UDA figures attempted to derail this by apparently arguing to the UDA leadership that this might hamper the developing peace process, since loyalists including Shoukri were due to meet General de Chastelain (the individual responsible for monitoring the decommissioning of republican and loyalist weaponry) to discuss decommissioning.[109] However, Ihab Shoukri, Andre Shoukri and 'Bonzer' Borland were all facing prosecution by the end of 2005 for terrorist and other offences. At this time, news of the UVF meetings mentioned above leaked out to the UDA, and in December 2005 the UDA requested a meeting with Assistant Chief Constable Kinkaid and the senior Policing Board member mentioned above on the possibility of establishing similar lines of communications with the PSNI.[110]

This police-led disruption has two possible motives. It removed the elements of the *ancien régime* which destabilised the UDA and made it easier for Jackie McDonald to retain control and move towards a downturn in UDA activity (this is if one adopts the theory that state strategic actions at the level of high politics govern law enforcement relations with loyalists); alternatively in more general terms (i.e. law enforcement operating within a context in which they are aware of politics but not directed in operational matters), it is sending out a signal to the UDA that without political normalisation their organisation may be undermined by intensive law enforcement activity. Thus this is in effect political policing (has

the policing of paramilitaries ever been otherwise?) but not at the close
direction of the British state.

Crime and transition

In the 2005–2006 period there was significant change. Both the UDA
and the UVF contain individuals committed to stopping criminal activity
in 'their' organisations.[111] The UDA was closing down criminality in certain areas such as Tiger's Bay. Both organisations were taking internal
measures to reduce crime by early 2007. Punishment attacks by both
organisations are on the decline. But the charges about the end of crime
are premature, and should be subject to the caveats applied to the republicans in Chapter 2.

First, the level of change should not be overestimated, something the
UDA and UVF admit. In addition, there is a lack of political depth in the
organisations and their political representatives in engaging with the issue of crime. As mentioned in Chapter 2, crime is framed in a certain
way, particularly by the PUP, as effectively unsanctioned and not representative of the 'true' nature of the organisation and its leadership, and
something which 'gets in the way' of the 'real issues'. Thus while the
discourse of loyalists and their sympathisers is one of political change and
engagement, this takes place within a very specific frame of understanding in which 'the political' is given heuristic status. This is unsustainable
as a methodology of change, and such a self-referential focus was responsible for the South East Antrim UDA's ill-judged public announcement
that its political and community strategy for demobilisation required £8.5
million.

Secondly, in terms of organisational change, similar questions can be
raised to those aired in Chapter 2 on republicans. What is the likelihood
that the UVF and UDA fade away and become an Ulster Volunteer Force
or a British Legion? The South East Antrim UDA's offer to move into a
peaceful and political path was costed at over £8 million and taking five
years. This is presumably the best case scenario presented by this
organisation. It illuminates the monumental bulk of such a task. This would
be dependent on organisational instability. (It also illustrates the point
made in the introduction, that the state is once again, at the centre,
'nationalising' the paramilitary–community issue, whether via investment
or law enforcement and is seen as such by the participants). Some would
argue that the organisations are by nature unstable, and predicted more
feuding within a short space of time.[112] This raises the further question of
whether some parts of these organisations break away, as elements in
North Belfast attempted to do in 2005–2006.[113] The tension was evident
throughout 2007 as the UDA continued to experience instability particularly over attitudes to peace and crime. The South East Antrim UDA

refused to accept the existing UDA leadership and allegedly attempted to murder UDA leader Jackie McDonald, an incident in which a police officer was shot. The UDA was involved in orchestrating anti-police rioting, and continued to face allegations of involvement in drug dealing even as UDA figures meted out a punishment attack on an alleged drug dealer in Belfast in September. This activity resulted in the devolved government taking stronger action than would have been the case under the NIO: the funding it had in effect been awarded to the UDA by the NIO was withdrawn by SDLP Social Development Minister Margaret Ritchie. Shortly afterwards, in November 2007 the UDA announced that the UFF was standing down but was not decommissioning its arms. The UVF has retained more stability and announced it was ceasing to exist as a paramilitary organisation in May 2007, the culmination, it stated, of three years internal debate. It may be the case that, just as it is apparently effective for the PIRA to continue to oversee its own demobilisation and prevent the emergence of other splinter groups, then it will be strategically appropriate that the UVF and UDA continue to prevent any splits.

Conclusion

This chapter has argued that crime has been a constant variable in loyalist paramilitary organisations and that it should not be depoliticised and marginalised in any analysis of the operations of paramilitary groups. Alternatively, as argued at the start of the chapter, it should not be seen as overdetermining all other factors. Instead it should be integrated into any analysis of paramilitary groups. Thus, following the Belfast Agreement, crime of course continued in the 'classic' manner as a means to garner financial resources to support prisoners, ex-prisoners and their families, other welfare activities, and purchase arms and other equipment to underpin the capacity to return to violence if necessary. However, loyalist groups appeared to expand their criminal activities following the first peace process in 1994, and this accelerated after 1998. Since 1998, crime has been an issue in the internal disorganisation and conflicts within loyalist paramilitaries, an issue in terms of their legitimacy and an issue in terms of British security policy and policing.

Taking the first, the formation of the LVF destabilised Loyalism, a process which continued after the peace process was instituted. In the formal political sphere, loyalist groups struggled to maintain the impetus of the pre-1998 period. They continued traditional political activities such as attacks and public order problems along interface areas, and their mainstream community advocacy and support activities.

As politics and terror declined, crime and legitimacy became an issue.

The UDA's involvement in crime became an issue with regard to its local legitimacy and the battle for stability in the Inner Council. The ouster of Adair, Gray and the Shoukris was connected to stability, particularly as the criminal activities of these senior individuals were seen as de-legitimising the organisation. The LVF, following the deaths of Billy Wright and Mark Fulton became deeply involved in criminal activity, and disputes concerning the control of criminal enterprises cannot be divorced from its feuds with the UVF and UDA. The UVF is more stable than these groups, but has itself been repeatedly targeted by accusations of criminality.

One other element to the dynamic is that criminality is in effect partly a bargaining tool between the British state and the loyalist paramilitaries. Informants have been allowed to get away with murder (literally it seems in some cases) due to their position; the British state's definition of ceasefire allowed paramilitary groups a valuable breathing space within which to expand criminal activities, something reflected in official crime statistics and the qualitative analysis of paramilitary groups. Alternatively, the state and law enforcement adopted a harder line to organised crime to effectively draw loyalists into a republican-style path, particularly following the IRA's historic 2005 statement. This has occurred while the government recognised the UDA's ceasefire in 2004 and announced large-scale investment in working-class areas. This process of engagement by the state following a decline in the intensity of the inter- and intra-loyalist paramilitary feuds might be termed 'low institutionalisation'. The interesting variable for policing is the evolving mixture of carrot and stick in this process. For example, the issue in future is whether the UDA and UVF can control 'excessive criminality' (the strange but potent methodology by which crime is viewed as illegitimate or legitimate) as many in the organisation seek to do, and pursue a path of gradual demobilisation, and whether crime might decline as figures associated with the war secure their 'livelihoods'. This would require the Assets Recovery Agency not taking their 'nest eggs' away from them, creating the incentive for further criminality. It would be surprising if the PSNI/ARA began to target those senior members of the UDA and UVF and others who are moving towards institutionalisation.

The test in terms of crime is simple: those offences associated with paramilitaries should decline. Key here would be extortion and drug economies in certain areas of Belfast. If these offences do not decline, then either new entrants have appeared or individuals and networks have moved into crime.

Notes

1 H. Sinnerton, *David Ervine* (Dublin: Brandon, 2002), p. 230, see also H. McDonald and J. Cusack, *UDA* (Dublin: Penguin Ireland, 2004), Chapter 18. The Combined Loyalist Military Command was the unified umbrella organisation which covered the UDA, Ulster Volunteer Force and Red Hand Commando and announced the 1994 Loyalist paramilitary ceasefires.

2 The term 'a cold house for Catholics' had been used by David Trimble in his Nobel Prize acceptance speech in 1998.

3 D. Godson, *Himself Alone. David Trimble and the Ordeal of Unionism* (London, Harper Perennial, 2005), Chapters 27 onwards particularly.

4 A. Aughey, 'The 1998 Agreement: three unionist anxieties', in M. Cox, A. Guelke and F. Stephen (eds), *A Farewell to Arms? Beyond the Good Friday Agreeement* (Manchester: Manchester University Press, 2nd edn, 2006), pp. 89–108.

5 For an overview of such adeptness see L. Clarke and K. Johnston, *Martin McGuinness: From Guns to Government* (Edinburgh, Mainstream, 2001); R. English, *Armed Struggle: The History of the IRA* (London: Pan, 2004); G. Murray and J. Tonge, *Sinn Féin and the SDLP. From Alienation to Participation* (Dublin: O'Brien, 2005).

6 S. Bruce, *The Red Hand: Protestant Paramilitaries in Northern Ireland* (Oxford: Oxford University Press, 1992); S. Bruce, 'Turf war and peace: Loyalist paramilitaries since 1994', *Terrorism and Political Violence*, 16:3 (2004), 501–521; 509; J. McAuley, '"Just fighting to survive": Loyalist paramilitary politics and the Progressive Unionist Party', *Terrorism and Political Violence*, 16:3 (2004), 522–543; 523–524.

7 For an analysis of the UVF's role in effectively neutralising the PIRA in Tyrone see E. Moloney, *A Secret History of the IRA* (London, Penguin, 2002), Chapter 11; see also M. Urban, *Big Boys' Rules* (London: Faber, 1992), Chapters 23 and 24.

8 C. Ryder and V. Kearney, *Drumcree* (London: Methuen, 2001).

9 J. Cusack and H. McDonald, *UVF* (Dublin: Poolbeg, 2000), p. 346.

10 C. Anderson, *The Billy Boy* (Edinburgh: Mainstream, 2002), p. 73.

11 C. Crawford, *Inside the UDA. Volunteers and Violence* (London: Pluto Ireland, 2003), p. 213.

12 McDonald and Cusack, *UDA*, p. 314.

13 D. Lister and H. Jordan, *Mad Dog. The Rise and Fall of Johnny Adair and 'C Company'* (Edinburgh: Mainstream, 2003), pp. 223–224.

14 Lister and Jordan, *Mad Dog*, pp. 223–224, p. 294; Cusack and McDonald, *UVF*, p. 394.

15 Lister and Jordan, *Mad Dog*, p. 230.

16 Lister and Jordan, *Mad Dog*, pp. 244–245.

17 Geoffrey Gray was shot dead as he walked home. He 'may have unwisely voiced LVF sympathies in the Bunch of Grapes pub'. I. S. Wood, *Crimes of Loyalty. A History of the UDA* (Edinburgh: Edinburgh University Press, 2006), p. 284.

18 Wood, *Crimes of Loyalty*, p. 285.

19 Lister and Jordan, *Mad Dog*, p. 251; Wood, *Crimes of Loyalty* p. 283.
20 Lister and Jordan, *Mad Dog*, pp. 252–253.
21 Wood, *Crimes of Loyalty*, p. 291.
22 One Adair supporter, Alan McCullough, who returned to Belfast in 2003 was murdered. Wood, *Crimes of Loyalty*, p. 302.
23 Cusack and McDonald, *UDA*, p. 395; Wood, *Crimes of Loyalty*, Chapter 11.
24 S. Breen, 'Gray's canary revenge fears' *Sunday Life* (4 September 2005); Wood, *Crimes of Loyalty*, p. 300; 'Gray day for sunny Jim', *Sunday Life* (12 September 2004).
25 Breen, 'Gray's canary revenge fears'.
26 The Legge murder is an example of the intertwining of the various issues involved in this chapter. Jim Gray had Geordie Legge tortured and murdered. Legge had been involved in drug dealing and expelled from the UDA, but the reason for his killing has been identified as his standing in the way of drug dealing by Jim Gray's son. Another is that following his expulsion from the UDA Legge was relatively unprotected and revenge could be taken for his role in the 1992 murder of UDA figure Ned McCreery, who himself had been implicated in corruption and drug dealing and had been a possible RUC informant. H. McDonald and J. Cusack, *UDA*, p. 226; Wood, *Crimes of Loyalty*, p. 264, p. 299; 'No flood of grief at death of the bling bling brigadier', *Sunday Life* (9 October 2005); S. Breen, 'I was prepared to shoot Gray: Stone', *Sunday Life* (1 May 2005).
27 S. Breen and A. Murray, 'We will stay in business – UDA', *Sunday Life* (12 June 2005).
28 Which, as mentioned above, the LVF had originally blamed on the UDA and which had been one spark for the Adair-centred feud.
29 IMC, *Sixth Report of the Independent Monitoring Commission* (London: HMSO, 2005), pp. 5–6.
30 IMC, *6th Report*, p. 8
31 Author interview, Detective Chief Inspector [a], PSNI, Belfast, 10 November 2005.
32 *BBC Digital News Northern Ireland* (19 November 2005).
33 McAuley, '"Just fighting to survive"', 523–524.
34 G. Gillespie, 'Noises off: loyalists after the Agreement', in M. Cox, A. Guelke and F. Stephen (eds), *A Farewell to Arms? Beyond the Good Friday Agreeement* (Manchester: Manchester University Press, 2nd edn, 2006), p. 145.
35 Wood, *Crimes of Loyalty*, p. 278.
36 For example, the murder of Catholic postman Daniel McColgan, attributed to the UDA was in revenge for the death of Protestant Thomas McDonald who had been run down by Alison McKeown. McDonald and Cusack, *UDA*, p. 358.
37 M. O'Hara, 'Plans to end segregated public housing in Belfast are doomed', *Guardian Society* (14 April 2004).
38 McDonald and Cusack, *UDA*, pp. 353–354; Gillespie, 'Noises off', p. 139, p. 143, p. 148.
39 Gillespie, 'Noises Off', p. 147; McDonald and Cusack, *UDA*, pp. 345–347.
40 McDonald and Cusack, *UDA*, p. 396.

41 See Jackie McDonald quoted in, 'UDA is holding on to its guns', *Sunday Life* (5 February 2006).

42 See Gillespie, 'Noises Off'.

43 See S. Bruce, *The Edge of the Union. The Ulster Loyalist Political Vision* (Oxford: Oxford University Press, 1994).

44 P. Shirlow, 'Mapping the spaces of fear. Socio-spatial causes and effects of violence in Northern Ireland' (ESRC Grant No. L133251007, 2001).

45 Independent Labour councillor Mark Langhammer, a controversial figure and a regular critic of UDA crime sought a local police presence in Rathcoole and faced repeated attacks organised by East Antrim Brigadier John Gregg. Wood, *Crimes of Loyalty*, p. 269; McDonald and Cusack, *UDA*, pp. 349–350. It would be disingenuous at best to view these attacks as primarily politically motivated and apologists for the UDA who downplay its criminal activities have to explain this sort of intimidation. With regard to the intimidation of former Ulster Democratic Party member Davy Adams see A. McIntyre, 'Intimidation of a Writer', *The Blanket* (26 September 2004). Other intimidation was directed at playwright Gary Mitchell in 2005.

46 Following a series of attacks on local businesses, the UDA said they had not been 'sanctioned'. S. Breen, 'Terror boss faces leadership crisis', *Sunday Life* (9 January 2005).

47 A. Murray, 'I won't be put in the shade', *Sunday Life* (3 April 2005).

48 L. Clarke, 'Hain offers £1m in bid to disband UDA', *Sunday Times* (24 September 2006).

49 Cusack and McDonald, *UVF*, p. 274.

50 C. Knox and B. Dickson, *An Evaluation of the Alternative Criminal Justice System in Northern Ireland*, ESRC research project L133251007 (2001), p. 12.

51 S. Bruce, 'Turf war and peace', pp. 504–505.

52 Progressive Unionist Party, *Rebuttal of the First Report of the International Monitoring Commission* (April 2004), p. 2.

53 The Ombudsman's report on UVF members who were also police informants shows a continuity of activity in the Mount Vernon unit before and after the peace. The unit was engaged in bank robbery, drugs, punishment attacks and intimidation. The unit might have been unique (this is debatable) but if it was not, and this is a reasonable 'dip sample', it highlights the involvement of the UVF in crime. PONI, *Statement by the Police Ombudsman for Northern Ireland on her Investigation into the Circumstances Surrounding the Death of Raymond McCord Junior and Related Matters* (Belfast: PONI, 2007), pp. 30–31.

54 BBC, 'Loyalists fear being left behind', *BBC News Northern Ireland* (11 February 2004) http://news.bbc.co.uk/go/pr/fr/-/1/hi/northern_ireland/3974671.stm.

55 *BBC Digital News Northern Ireland* (18 October 2005).

56 *BBC Digital News Northern Ireland* (24 October 2005). In his judicial review of the appointment, Mr Justice Girvan stated that while the question of McDougall's suitability for the post was not an issue, the manner in which Secretary of State Peter Hain made the appointment was improper and was coloured by its purpose as a confidence building measure towards Unionists.

Girvan listed a number of questions that required investigation. T. Peterkin, 'Inquiry into "misleading" Hain letter', *Daily Telegraph* (22 November 2006).

57 BBC Loyalists are 'part of the process' *BBC News Northern Ireland* (6 July 2006) http://bbc.co.uk/1/hi/northern_ireland/5154750.stm.

58 L. Clarke, 'Hain offers £1m in bid to disband UDA', *Sunday Times* (September 24 2006); BBC TV Northern Ireland *Newsline* 10 July 2006; BBC TV Northern Ireland *Newsline* 2 October 2006.

59 S. Bruce 'Loyalists in Northern Ireland: Further thoughts on pro state terror', *Terrorism and Political Violence*, 5:4 (1993), 256.

60 Bruce, 'Loyalists in Northern Ireland', 257.

61 S. Bruce, 'Turf war and peace', 509.

62 McDonald and Cusack, *UDA*, pp. 217–218; Lister and Jordan, *Mad Dog*, p. 210, p. 222.

63 Crawford, *Inside the UDA*, p. 215.

64 'We believe he bought into the LVF dealing as a wholesale buyer. This inevitably brought him close to that organisation and it also made him a lot more money.' RUC drugs squad officer, quoted in Lister and Jordan, *Mad Dog*, p. 208.

65 Jordan and Lister, *Mad Dog*, p. 209, p. 222.

66 See Wood, *Crimes of Loyalty*, p. 240, Chapters 10 and 11 and pp. 307–310.

67 OCTF, *Threat Assessment. Serious and Organised Crime in Northern Ireland 2003* (Belfast: OCTF, 2003), p. 3.

68 E. Adair, 'To pay or not to pay. The extent of paramilitary extortion within the construction industry', M.Sc. dissertation, University of Leicester, 2005, p. 88, p. 108.

69 Author interview, Detective Chief Inspector [a] and Detective Inspector [b], PSNI, Belfast, 24 July 2003.

70 Author interview, Detective Chief Inspector [a] and Detective Inspector [b], PSNI, Belfast, 24 July 2003.

71 The percentage of organised crime groups active in extortion rose from 34 per cent in 2002 to 40 per cent in 2003. OCTF, *Threat Assessment 2003*, p. 2.

72 J. Moran, 'Paramilitaries, "ordinary decent criminals" and the development of organised crime following the Belfast Agreement', *International Journal of the Sociology of Law*, 32 (2004), 263–278.

73 Author interview, Detective Constable, PSNI (formerly in CI3), Belfast, 23 July 2003.

74 Author interviews, Official at the NIO attached to the OCTF, Stormont House annexe, 25 February 2003; NIO official involved in financial matters, Stormont House annexe, 25 July 2003; Detective Chief Inspector [a] and Detective Inspector [b], PSNI, Belfast, 24 July 2003.

75 Author interview, Detective Chief Superintendent, PSNI attached to the OCTF, Stormont House annexe, 25 July 2003.

76 Author interview, Detective Chief Superintendent, PSNI, Belfast, 24 July 2003.

77 Northern Ireland Affairs Committee, *The Financing of Terrorism in Northern Ireland* Vol. 1 HC 978-1 (London: The Stationery Office, 2001–02), para 33.

78 A. Murray, 'Death of a crime lord', *Sunday Life* (9 October 2005).

79 Author interview, Chief Officer [c], PSNI, Belfast, 13 April 2005.
80 Gusty Spence was an original member of the UVF, which formed in the 1960s. He was convicted of murdering a Catholic barman and sentenced to life imprisonment. He left the UVF and joined its political wing, the PUP, after he became committed to political development, critiquing existing elitist Unionism, and promoting community work. Having been released in the 1980s, he was chosen to read out the statement of ceasefire by all loyalist paramilitary groups in 1994.
81 Bruce, *The Red Hand*; Cusack and McDonald, *UVF*; A. Silke, 'In defense of the realm: Financing Loyalist terrorism in Northern Ireland: Part one', *Studies in Conflict and Terrorism* (21:4) 1998, 331–361; A. Silke, 'Drink, Drugs and Rock 'n' Roll: Financing loyalist terrorism in Northern Ireland: Part two', *Studies in Conflict and Terrorism*, 23:2 (2000), 107–127.
82 Author interviews, Detective Chief Superintendent, PSNI attached to the OCTF, Stormont House annexe, 25 July 2003; Detective Chief Inspector [a], PSNI, Belfast, 10 November 2005. This was a view expressed by a number of officers in informal conversation with the author.
83 Author interview, Detective Chief Inspector, PSNI, Belfast, 10 November 2005.
84 Cusack and McDonald, *UVF*, p. 303.
85 Billy Elliot, shot in 1995, also of the RHC had been a drug dealer. Cusack and McDonald, *UVF*, p. 328; A. Murray, 'UVF repeats call for LVF to disband', *Sunday Life* (22 February 2004).
86 PONI, *Statement by the Police Ombudsman for Northern Ireland on her Investigation into the Circumstances Surrounding the Death of Raymond McCord Junior*, p. 31.
87 A. Murray and S. Breen, 'Loyalist links sealed fate', *Sunday Life* (6 June 2004). See also the accounts of 'Informant 1' to his police handlers: 'in August 1994 Informant 1 told his handlers that the North Belfast UVF had taken control of drug dealing in the hotel [in Larne]. He stated that the UVF were allowing local dealers to sell drugs on their behalf, and that Man O [a senior UVF figure] allowed this practice to continue on a trial basis, as long as UVF members were not directly seen to be involved in drug dealing themselves.' PONI, *Statement by the Police Ombudsman for Northern Ireland on her investigation into the circumstances surrounding the death of Raymond McCord Junior*, p. 112.
88 Adair, 'To pay or not to pay', pp. 88–89.
89 Lister and Jordan, *Mad Dog*, p. 207.
90 Bruce, 'Turf war and peace', 511–512.
91 Author interviews, Detective Chief Inspector [a] and Detective Inspector [b], PSNI, Belfast, 24 July 2003.
92 A. Murray, 'LVF's kill threat to coke accused', *Sunday Life* (2 November 2003).
93 See the allegations made by the ARA, 'Assets Recovery Agency freezes £300,000 worth of assets in Portadown' (18 March 2005).
94 A. Murray, 'LVF rejects UVF peace talks', *Sunday Life* (15 February 2004); 'UDA is holding on to its guns', *Sunday Life* (5 February 2006).
95 A number of murders in Belfast and Down, while also part of the UVF–LVF feud, were also linked to problems regarding drugs (such as Stephen Warnock).

Wood, *Crimes of Loyalty,* p. 282.

96 A. Murray, 'Muscling in', *Sunday Life* (25 July 2004); 'Ihab Shoukri sets up home in Bangor', *Sunday Life* (5 September 2004).

97 For a measured discussion of the issue of 'collusion' between the state and loyalist paramilitary groups see Wood, *Crimes of Loyalty,* pp. 311–322.

98 PONI, *Statement by the Police Ombudsman for Northern Ireland on her investigation into the circumstances surrounding the death of Raymond McCord Junior.* On the links between Special Branch and the UVF in a number of areas see J. Brown, *Into the Dark. 30 Years in the RUC* (Dublin: Gill and Macmillan, 2005).

99 Lister and Jordan, *Mad Dog,* p. 233.

100 Haddock was labelled a Special Branch agent by TD Pat Rabitte in the Dáil in 2005; IMC, *Twelfth Report of the International Monitoring Commission* (London: The Stationery Office, 2006), p. 15.

101 McDonald and Cusack, *UDA,* Chapter 18, p. 283; Cusack and McDonald *UVF,* pp. 380–388.

102 E. Moloney, *A Secret History of the IRA.*

103 There are a number of methodological problems with the idea that the security services are manipulating paramilitary developments: a) these things may be true, but the state would need to be nimble and subtle to arrange such affairs, for example with regard to the formation of the LVF, 'creating' Wright and then terminating him. If pursued, the destabilisation strategy appeared an incredibly risky strategy if it was aimed at demoralising Loyalists to allow a clear field for a deal with the republican movement. Thus there is a risk that stressing the role of Government, security and police in these events implicitly accepts that the British state displayed a degree of organisation and foresight which in the light of other analyses on Northern Ireland alone is difficult to sustain (see Moloney, *Secret History;* Godson, *Himself Alone.*) Introducing such *deux et machina* at least as a major explanatory device is not especially helpful in analysing Loyalist (or Republican) paramilitarism and politics. See S. Bruce, 'Loyalist assassinations and police collusion in Northern Ireland: An extended critique of Sean McPhilemy's *The Committee*', *Studies in Conflict and Terrorism,* 31:1 (2000), 61–80. It is probably more appropriate to accept that the British state is not a unitary or coherent entity. See English, *Armed Struggle,* p. 358; Peter Gill, *Policing Politics. Security, Intelligence and the Liberal Democratic State* (London: Frank Cass, 1994). Although the area where the state does achieve its greatest level of coherence is in the field of security, it is nevertheless still appropriate to situate it within the context of British security and public policy. The British state in Northern Ireland was no more coherent or omniscient than it is through the workings of the NHS or Treasury. The destabilisation in Loyalism was no doubt connected to some British security and police service operations. But it is also evident that paramilitary groups have displayed self-generating reasons for violent internal disputes; b) there are problems with handling agents, they may get out of control so that not everything can be explained by the shadowy hand of the British state, unless we see *all* the actions of informants being explained by the fact that they are informants, a functionalist argument; c) connected to point a) renegade elements in the state ('securocrats') might be operating

alone, but this contrasts with those views of the British state which see it as a malign but generally coherent conductor or puppeteer. These renegade elements clearly lack the 'joined up thinking' which characterises republican and loyalist accounts of 'the British state', and fails to specify their concrete effects, especially as their level of power and direction is never specified.

104 William Fulton, a leading LVF figure was jailed in early 2007 for a minimum of 25 years for the murder of Elizabeth O'Neil in 1999 and over 40 terrorist offences.

105 Author interview, Chief Officer [c], PSNI, Belfast, 26 January 2006.

106 Author interview, Chief Officer [c], PSNI, Belfast, 26 January 2006.

107 Progressive Unionist Party, *Rebuttal of the First Report of the International Monitoring Commission* (April 2004), p. 2.

108 BBC News, 'Informers to be used in UDA case', *BBC News Northern Ireland* (27 April 2005), http://news.bbc.co.uk/1/hi/northern_ireland/4489771.stm.

109 A. Murray, 'Arrest may scupper arms move', *Sunday Life* (13 November 2005).

110 Author interview, Chief Officer [c], PSNI, Belfast, 26 January 2006.

111 Author interview, Chief Officer [c], PSNI, Belfast, 26 January 2006.

112 Author interview, Ian Paisley Jr., DUP MLA and Policing Board member, Belfast, 5 October 2006.

113 Elsewhere Billy Leonard, a Sinn Féin councillor on Coleraine Borough Council argued that loyalism in the area, 'has declared its own version of independence from other loyalists who are trying to move on', *BBC Digital News* (25 November 2006).

4

'Ordinary decent' organised and volume crime

Normalisation has brought with it the contemporary problems of normal societies: drunken yobbery on a Saturday night, anti-social behaviour, joy-riding, car crime and so on.[a]

Crime in Northern Ireland

One of the oft-cited facts about crime in Northern Ireland is that it has been historically low compared to the rest of the UK. This lower level was confirmed as methods of recording crime improved. During the 1980s the British Crime Surveys were introduced, and throughout the 1980s and 1990s UK government and civil society campaigns encouraged the reporting of crimes which had previously been underreported, such as those with a racial or homophobic motivation, child physical and sexual abuse, domestic violence and sexual assault. In Northern Ireland the introduction of victim surveys (firstly as part of Office of National Statistics household surveys and then via the specific Northern Ireland Crime Survey) still showed crime as lower than the mainland. Indeed, they showed Northern Ireland had a higher crime reporting rate than the mainland.[1] However, this position must be viewed with a number of caveats.[2] The crime which was not reported was important. Crime was historically underreported in republican areas for obvious reasons, and although individuals in nationalist areas may have been relatively less antagonistic

[a] Peter Hain, Secretary of State for Northern Ireland quoted in 'Hain urges SF to aid policing plans', *UTV News* (17 July 2006).

to the RUC they still lacked trust in the police. In addition, a measure of crime was kept down by paramilitary authority and if necessary, punishment attacks.[3] Although these paramilitary attacks appeared in RUC statistics, many punishments were not reported to the police; more so in the case of intimidation. Finally, bare statistics can erase the visceral and disproportionate effects of conflict related crime. Punishment attacks, arson attacks and intimidation resulted in harm in the sense outlined in Chapter 2.

Since the peace process crime has risen. Official accounts argue that the marked upsurge in crime can be attributed to the changes in crime recording in 1998 and 2002: 'much of the large increase in recorded crime between 2000/01 and 2002/03 has been attributed to technical changes, such as a new National Crime Recording Standard'.[4] This new change meant that more incidents which came to the notice of the police would be recorded as crimes whether individuals reported them to police or not, and where previously the police might have decided not to take official action and thus no record of a crime would have been made. However, even using old counting rules there would have been a marked increase, and not all offences were equally affected by the changes in recording; less serious offences were likely to see inflated increases; serious offences were not.[5] The NIO itself said that 'there is some evidence to indicate that crime in Northern Ireland is on the increase'.[6] Victimisation surveys demonstrated crime was rising in 1998 then dropping and rising again: the findings of NICS 2003/04 'appear to indicate that a real, but not substantial increase in crime also occurred'.[7] Thus while it is true that changes in recording have led to an apparent increase in crime, the underlying trend is of a real increase in crime. By 2005, crime had dropped from a high point in 2002 and 2003 but remained higher than in the 1990s.[8] Furthermore, other indicators show that serious offences or those associated with organised crime rose following the peace process, or remained disproportionate, as evidenced by other indicators such as seizures of drugs, counterfeit goods, oils and the closures of laundering plants, reports of extortion and so forth mentioned in detail in previous chapters.

The International Monitoring Commission is perhaps the latest organisation to adopt the position that many observers do: crime is still lower than in England and Wales.[9] This is obviously important: comparative analysis can highlight social patterns and trends, differing opportunity structures and constraints on various forms of criminality, and this chapter also makes comparisons with the rest of the UK. However, this analysis overlooks the vital task of measuring and explaining crime with regard to Northern Ireland. If one jurisdiction, Area A, has a crime rate of 10 offences per 100,000 people and another jurisdiction, Area B, has a crime rate of 40 offences per 100,000 people but over a period of 2 years the crime rate in Area A rises to 25 offences per 100,000, the rise in Area A requires explanation.

The rise in crime raises a number of issues. The problem of crime related to paramilitaries has been addressed in previous chapters. This chapter addresses crimes committed by Ordinary Decent Criminals, offenders unconnected or only tangentially connected to paramilitary groups whose crimes have no political motivation.[10] These 'ordinary' crimes may be committed by professional/organised criminals. Professional crime denotes crime which requires some form of skill, such as cash-in-transit robbery or certain types of fraud, and which offenders undertake as a career. Organised crime simply denotes crime which requires a level of cooperation and organisation by offenders,[11] and may be separated into two types: organised *crime* groups who engage in a variety of offences as part of a tight or loose network, and organised *crimes* (a crime requiring planning and 'management' committed by one person or a group coming together to commit a fraud, for example, but not as part of a 'criminal career' as with professional and organised crime). Finally this chapter also deals with volume crime, common crimes mainly concerned with property (car crime, burglary and so forth). This crime may be connected to organised criminals (e.g. cars stolen to order) but most of it is not.

Symbolic representations of 'ordinary crime'

'ODC' crime raises a number of issues: symbolically it raises the question of how crime is conceptualised. In terms of professional crime, the ODC label can be a positive nomenclature, a 'rogue' going about his daily business unconnected to sectarianism and political violence; this is a crime trope similar to those occurring on the mainland. This is a cultural frame that has been mooted by professional criminals themselves: 'there is a noticeable tendency to hark back to a golden age of predictability, stoicism, honour and reliability. Aged villains in particular are predisposed to nostalgia, yearning for stability and a mythical age … that stands in stark relief to the amorphous nature of contemporary crime.'[12] Linked, professional criminals and organised crime groups may be representative of an independent entrepreneurial culture which seeks to evade state controls in a quasi-freemarket way, maintaining a culture of independence.[13] Even where violence is evident they may be framed in popular discourse and private imagination as dominant, ruthless figures who nevertheless bring order to an area (for example the 1960s London gangsters the Krays).[14] Single events can also provoke popular reactions of respect and even admiration. Thus the Northern Bank robbery and the Securitas £53 million robbery in Kent, England in 2006 produced comments with a hint of 'respect' from media and *vox populi*, and – with regard to the Kent robbery – even at police press conferences. These events can also produce alternative readings: many cash-in-transit robberies in Northern Ireland are in fact seen as signifying a breakdown of order, as is the large-scale importation of drugs, where PSNI seizures of massive stocks of ecstasy tablets do not produce reactions of 'respect'. This is often the case in terms of volume crime. Here, away from large-scale dramatic bank robberies, the label ODC signifies more general concerns. Car crime, burglary and petty theft may be seen as representing the breakdown of social order (as in the series of burglaries of old age pensioners and robberies of isolated farmhouses which took place in Northern Ireland around the 2005 period) or as by-products of other societal ills such as drug use. Here the 'decent' part of the label may be excised, leaving merely the symbolic (perhaps hooded) ordinary criminal.

Crime 'in practice'

Beyond the popular representation of the 'ordinary decent criminal' is the emprical nature of crime in Northern Ireland. Crime has been facilitated by the physical and social changes to the province, and in the economic and social development which has taken place in Northern Ireland following 1994 the province is beginning to resemble the mainland, or more generally may be experiencing crime as experienced by late modern economically developing societies generally.[15] This is evident in offences such as car crime, low level armed robberies and some evidence of a rise in 'normal' violent crime. Drugs remain an exception although it appears that change is evident.

(Dis)connections between ODCs and paramilitaries

One important development in terms of the peace process appears to be the increased activity of 'ordinary' organised criminal groupings who are not connected to paramilitary groups. Of 78 organised crime groups identified by the Organised Crime Task Force in 2001, 35 had no paramilitary connections, although this 44 per cent later declined to 33 per cent in 2003.[16] There are links which exist between ODCs and the paramilitaries, which operate at a number of levels. At a more oblique level, to an extent there has been a skills transfer from paramilitaries to ODCs. The past experience of paramilitary organisations and their previous experience of terrorist and other court cases has provided a reservoir of knowledge concerning law enforcement investigative measures. This 'common sense' has seeped out to major criminals who inhabit the same areas and frequent the same clubs as paramilitaries, and also has passed down to low level criminals and their operations. In more concrete terms, links may range from paramilitaries who may 'sanction' criminal activities in their 'territory' in return for a 'cut'. This may be evident in armed robbery and drugs. Operations such as cigarette smuggling in South Armagh may be carried on by ODCs and 'sanctioned', since it is highly unlikely that they could operate without PIRA approval.[17] Finally, there may be evident practical links: 'counterfeiting is one of the areas where there is a demonstrable link between the paramilitaries and a vast network of other criminals'.[18] Generally, ODCs may pay paramilitaries for protection by associating themselves with them in return for a 'cut'; ODCs might also buy weapons from paramilitaries,[19] although some of the evidence cited publicly for these links may be overstated.[20] There are many organised criminals evidently operating with little or no contact with paramilitaries, and depending on the crime areas and the point of the chain of manufacture, supply or distribution of illicit goods and services, ODCs may be the majority or only participants. Also there seem to be areas in which ODCs will resist and oppose paramilitaries, and this has resulted in violence. These are important areas of change following the peace process and ones which require more analysis. The subsequent sections deal with some areas of crime in which ODCs play a marked role, and in which they may have more or less contact with paramilitaries.

Drugs

Dealers

Drug dealing is an area not dominated by paramilitaries in the manner that, for example, extortion is. Statistics showed that 56 per cent of those investigated by the PSNI drugs unit had paramilitary links, and 44 per cent did not.[21] Although other estimates 'on the ground' from detectives also show a rough 50/50 split, this varies depending on area. The economy of drug importation and distribution leaves ample scope for 'ordinary' individuals and paramilitaries to take up positions. Despite various media dramatisations of hideously rich drug kingpins, profit remains restricted to certain roles and measures of control. At the high level, in terms of control or influence over local markets, the economy of drug dealing can lead to differing power dynamics and thus volatility. This is evident from the mainland where in major cities (London, Birmingham, Manchester) and provincial urban areas (Nottingham) disputes over drug distribution (turf, profits and so forth) result in sporadic violence (shootings, beatings). In the Northern Ireland case, this has been one variable in intra-paramilitary violence as mentioned in Chapter 3. Although the killing was bound up with the LVF–UVF feud, the proximate cause of the murder of Stephen Warnock was an unpaid drugs debt. In terms of mid-level dealers, tension might also arise if paramilitaries effectively 'license' dealing in their area, and then the licensees fail to pay for the 'franchise'. Similarly, the operation of drug dealers in areas where they have not made such an arrangement or areas where there is simply political opposition to drug dealing may see violence result. Thus Direct Action Against Drugs (DAAD), the pseudonym for the Provisional IRA has murdered a number of alleged drug dealers since the mid-1990s, allegedly for the various reasons outlined above, and in certain areas the UDA and UVF have carried out punishment beatings of suspected drug dealers.[22] In 2006 UDA supporters beat a man to death whom they suspected was a drug dealer, an unsanctioned attack. There has also been tension between paramilitaries and ordinary dealers, some of them former paramilitaries with access to their own weapons and less likely to be intimidated. Further down the drugs economy profits are marginal. Cocaine and ecstasy dealing at the lower level, away from bulk import shipments is through decentralised networks. The heroin users in Ballymena apear to follow the classic mainland pattern of users becoming dealers to fund their own addiction.[23]

Users

Northern Ireland missed out on the spread of heroin use across the rest of the UK in the 1980s in which heroin use (particularly via injecting) appeared in Edinburgh, Glasgow and London and spread from nodal points there to provincial cities such as Bristol and Leeds in the 1990s. Heroin is still a problem in the UK. Although it receives less media coverage, as the street price has dropped heroin use has surfaced in North Wales, spread down the narrow South Wales valleys and clustered in towns and villages in less populated parts of the mainland such as the semi-rural north-east of England. Heroin use in Northern Ireland approximates such pockets, in Ballymena as mentioned, south Belfast, and North Down.[24] The community in Ballymena is a long-term presence and most of the problem users have been identified.[25] This accuracy is not replicated across the rest of Northern Ireland as the Ballymena area has its own specific characteristics, but the problem is low overall. The number of registered heroin addicts in Northern Ireland fluctuates around the 210 mark[26] although, as on the mainland, this does not represent the true figure: a later more comprehensive study identified 1,395 opiate users nationally, with the figure of 3,330 for opiate and/or problem cocaine users[27] Northern Ireland might in future see more heroin-using clusters appear, as the street price of heroin has fallen[28] but the prevalence of problem opiate use 'is less than a tenth' of the rate of England, Ireland and Scotland.[29]

There is a growing cocaine market[30] but again its use is relatively restricted. Crack cocaine is not the problem it is on the mainland, although care should be taken since official estimates (e.g. PSNI) conflict with those of community workers who see its use as more prevalent,[31] though still relatively constricted.

Cannabis, ecstasy and amphetamines are the main drugs consumed, and use is associated with younger groups (those aged 16–34), a long-term pattern.[32] From 2000–2003 the street price of cannabis dropped from £120 to £80 an ounce.[33] In terms of supply-side theory as with any commodity, cheapness and availability facilitate more individuals experimenting. However, this cannot be abstracted from demand-side factors: cannabis is clearly a drug that spreads through networks of users and contexts in which the drug is recommended; as with many drugs there is a high end demand (e.g. use is employed in urban, professional contexts) and use associated with socio-economic deprivation (e.g. on the massive housing estates that ring Belfast, by unemployed or underemployed youth). In terms of ecstasy, it arrived in quantity in the early 1990s[34] and rose in popularity, fuelled in urban areas by loyalist and other dealers (see Chapter 3). Much use of cannabis and ecstasy is recreational, similar to the mainland, in which users reject any description of their use as other than being dependent on choice and context.[35] There has been some comment about Northern Ireland being characterised as a multidrug using population. There appears to be increasing misuse of prescription drugs with an effective black market in operation of tranquilisers such as diazepam and temazepam. But overall Northern Ireland's multidrug users are a restricted group. Those who do use more than one drug are likely to combine ecstasy with cannabis and/or alcohol.[36]

Although there is much debate about the drugs–crime nexus,[37] there are knock-on effects from drug use, particularly problem drugs use. It seems that a number of the low-level armed robberies in Northern Ireland (those aimed at petrol stations, off-licences, convenience stores and so forth) are aimed at gaining quick money to fund drugs purchases. In addition, 'a recent study showed that a significant number of the most prolific burglars are heroin addicts',[38] replicating studies elsewhere.[39]

Overview

Perhaps the main point to make is the extent to which nine years after the peace process (13 years after the first ceasefire), while other forms of crime which can be associated with economic and consumer opportunities and 'play'[40] such as smuggling and counterfeiting have risen, hard drug use has not to the same extent. Northern Ireland's main problem remains cannabis. However, indications are that ecstasy and cocaine and crack cocaine use is increasing, and increased police seizures of these narcotics reflect the increased supply into Northern Ireland. Drugs offences did buck the trend of decreasing crime in Northern Ireland in the 2003–2004 period and were still rising in 2006.[41]

What might explain this pattern of use and relative restriction? Although unlucky in experiencing conflict, Northern Ireland was 'lucky' in that it was bypassed by the expansion of drug demand and supply in England, Wales and Scotland during the 1980s. This may have restricted the expansion of drug use in terms of numbers and successive generations that occurred in the rest of the UK:[42] the British Crime Survey shows higher levels of lifetime use at more advanced ages than the Northern Ireland studies.[43] In terms of individual drugs, as mentioned, cocaine use in Northern Ireland is restricted to areas and groups such as the urban middle class, as in the UK mainland but in Northern Ireland it is small. Overall, Northern Ireland might be more 'European' in respect of drug consumption.[44]

Although the drugs trade may have been prevented by the general environment in the form of the security infrastructure of Northern Ireland from the 1970s to 1998[45] its growth has not been prevented by specific criminal justice action. The number of prosecutions for drugs offences fell markedly from 2000–2003 onwards, which fits in with the period of police disorganisation and demoralisation discussed in Chapter 5 and PSNI charging for cannabis, cocaine and crack cocaine offences remained static or dropped from 2003–2006.[46]

As mentioned, drugs importation and distribution is not dominated by paramilitary organisations. However, paramilitary organisations do play a significant direct and indirect role in the development or constriction of the trade. Certain UDA brigade areas are known to be anti-drugs, and this also applies to certain UVF areas. This may result in punishment attacks on dealers. The PIRA license dealers but do not sell drugs themselves and this restricts its development. Further, the PIRA have taken action as DAAD in shooting drug dealers. The LVF (before its standing down) was deeply involved in drugs and the INLA oscillates (it has shut down some operations in its areas but also faces accusations of dealing in the Republic of Ireland). This 'second tier' social control is also buttressed by paramilitary and political party backed community work. The role of restorative justice in this area is also an important variable. Other second tier social control is reflected in attitudes to drugs in Northern Ireland, which at the moment differ from the UK mainland. One result of the dissolving of paramilitaries – or their putative conversion into criminals – may be the spread of drug use.

Armed robbery

In 2002, 'the Northern Ireland figures for armed robbery and hijacking [were] significantly higher than the United Kingdom average'[47] They have declined but still remain disproportionate (see Chapter 6). In previous decades armed robbery was more deeply connected to paramilitaries; this has not been the case following the peace process.[48] When different types of armed robbery are disaggregated, overall Northern Ireland appears to be resembling the mainland. This section concentrates on high-level targets (banks, cash-in-transit, warehouses and deliveries for large takes of goods or cash) and low-level (small commercial establishments and individuals for small value goods or cash). The term armed robbery includes attacks with a weapon, either a firearm (or its impression such as replicas or barrels) or other weapons.

In terms of high-level attacks, the OCTF estimates that the number of armed robberies attributed to organised criminals dropped from 113 in 2002–2003 to 70 in 2003–2004 and 64 in 2004–2005.[49] It would mean that in 2002, organised groups were responsible for 7 to 8 per cent of all armed robberies. However, if we assume this refers to *firearm* robberies organised groups were responsible for 14 to 16 per cent of all robberies with a firearm for these periods. In terms of the figures cited above it would also mean that, for example, in 2002, 36 organised groups were responsible for 113 robberies. This would fit in with the idea that a small number of *organised* organised (sic) groups are responsible for a small number of robberies netting a substantial proportion of money taken.[50] As outlined in the book so far, all the main republican and loyalist paramilitary organisations have been responsible for substantial armed robberies, and may 'subcontract'[51] or 'sanction'[52] attacks. Paramilitaries appear to be responsible for the attacks which result in the largest financial 'take'. However, 'ordinary' organised criminals undertake the majority of high-level robberies.

Handguns and shotguns are used in the high-level armed robberies. For example in 2001 firearms were employed in 96 of the 120 cash-in-transit robberies and they remained the dominant weapon.[53] In the UK, 'some replica pistols are so realistic that it is difficult, even for firearms experts, to distinguish them from the real article … especially when one considers that they were seen, probably for a matter of seconds, in the highly charged context of an armed robbery'.[54] This is particularly the case in the Northern Ireland context, where a person brandishing a firearm is more likely to expect it to be believed to be real, considering the wider circulation of handguns and shotguns.

Nevertheless, armed robberies with firearms have declined after a peak around 2000–2003, as have attacks on cash-in-transit targets. Despite the

Table 4.1: Armed robberies in Northern Ireland 1988–2005

Year	Armed robberies recorded by police	Armed robberies recorded by police where firearm is used or the impression of a firearm is given	Take from armed robberies recorded by police where firearm is used or the impression of a firearm is given (£)
1988	805	742	1,389,000
1989	663	604	1,079,000
1990	579	492	1,729,000
1991	686	607	1,673,000
1992	866	739	1,666,000
1993	751	643	1,515,000
1994	657	555	1,709,000
1995	620	421	838,000
1996	655	405	2,840,000
1997	621	401	1,810,000
1997–1998	594	396	1,845,000
1998–1999	632	367	1,028,000
1999–2000	682	432	1,687,000
2000–2001	927	509	2,180,000
2001–2002	1191	636	7,405,000
2002–2003	1375	676	2,991,000
2003–2004	1042	485	3,034,000
2004–2005	812	343	29,925,000*
2005–2006	842	284	4,268,000

* Includes the Northern Bank robbery

Source: NIO, *A Commentary on Northern Ireland Crime Statistics 1997* (Belfast: TSO, 1997); Northern Ireland Statistics and Research Agency, *Northern Ireland Abstract of Statistics OnLine*, www.nisra.gov.uk/archive/uploads/publications/abstract_online/Table%206.2.xls; RUC/PSNI, *Annual Report of the Chief Constable*, various years.

media focus on high profile offences such as the Northern Bank robbery, the main increase in armed robbery since the peace process has been in low-level armed robberies committed by one or two individuals for small takes in terms of cash, and employing other weapons than firearms. Although the figures for this has also reduced, a marked increase took place from 2001, and constituted the major share of all armed robberies from 2002 to 2005 (see Table 4.1). Firearms may be used but a variety of 'kitchen sink' implements are used in the majority of cases. These include knives (kitchen and hunting), baseball bats, hammers, hatchets, iron bars and golf clubs. Certain aspects of this type of ODC armed robbery can be explained by reference to ethnographic research on offender motivation, situated in street or criminal subculture. Armed robbery enables offenders to enjoy alcohol, cigarettes and gain ready cash leading to increased consumption until the time when robbery is needed to replenish the coffers.[55]

A surge in armed robbery at both the high level in terms of audacious attacks and at the low level may have been facilitated by security normalisation measures such as the removal of roadblocks and vehicle check points, the reduction in army patrols and in technical surveillance from lookout towers. These made robbery less risky.

Volume crime

As police services know after two decades of New Public Management reform, volume crime is of great concern to the public, since they are most likely to be affected by it or know someone who has been. Since the peace process there has been a rise in burglary and vehicle crime. Some burglaries, particularly those against the elderly or those in rural areas have generated publicity and criticism of the police. This section concentrates on vehicle crime since it raises issues of Northern Ireland's similarity to the mainland. Vehicle crime rose markedly in Northern Ireland:

Table 4.2: Vehicle crime in Northern Ireland, 1997–2006

Year	Number of thefts/ unauthorised taking of motor vehicles	Theft from motor vehicles	Total
1997	8,633	5,416	14,049
1998–99	9,715	6,075	15,790
1999–00	10,196	6,327	16,523
2000–01	10,806	5,713	16,519
2001–02	11,635	6,584	18,219
2002–03	8,410	7,140	15,550
2003–04	5,369	7,506	12,875
2004–05	4,456	5,371	9,827
2005–06	3,721	4,404	8,125

Note: does not include attempts. From 1998–99 these were recorded as vehicle tampering/interference.

Source: RUC/PSNI, *Annual Report of the Chief Constable*, various years.

The rise in vehicle crime was as a result of youth-driven car theft but with more precautions taken and with new purchases having better security (involving unique electronically cut keys), the number of thefts has reduced.[56] However, a significant market for car theft remains. Firstly, there is still a large 'pool' of vehicles available which are not so protected. Secondly, as on the mainland there has been an increase in creeper burglaries by which offenders break into homes to steal car keys.[57] Linked to this, finally there is a top end market of 'steal to order' thefts of high performance models.[58] There is a move away from 'ringing' i.e. creating a false identity, towards dismantling for parts. In terms of thefts from cars the table shows a measure of crime displacement. As the crime prevention measures outlined above led to a reduction in theft of vehicles, offenders turned to stealing from cars (see Table 4.2), including individual parts which may be in demand such as airbags.[59] As the table shows, although this has also decreased numerically, it constitutes a higher percentage of all vehicle crime.

Fraud

Fraud has increased in volume since 1998 primarily due to two factors: some frauds have increased in number, but many were/are now being discovered or reported. As an example of the latter in the public sector, it is possible that the devolved Assembly's PAC led to more uncovering of activities and the passing of information to the PSNI. Indeed, the PAC identified a lack of control over accounting practices in the public sector.[60]

Public sector fraud

The high percentage of public expenditure in Northern Ireland's economic activity provides a number of opportunities for fraud. In terms of benefit fraud, £54 million was missing in 2003 either from administrative error or fraud,[61] while £30 million was specifically identified as being lost through benefit fraud in 2005, 'a small proportion of which would have been in the organised category'.[62] Indeed, the context is similar to the mainland and should be removed from scapegoating or panic. Increasingly complex claiming and reporting processes have created disincentives for declaring income accurately. Such fraud is correlated with areas of deprivation.[63] Other offences may be organised crimes committed by groups, or increasingly the case, by professionals, such as prescription fraud in the NHS. Again this may take a variety of forms, including doctors claiming for prescribing medicines which were never dispensed. Such individual cases can nevertheless amount to substantial sums.[64]

Private sector fraud

The private sector has seen the increased reporting/uncovering of frauds by professionals, such as solicitors. Criminal activities have involved internal frauds and money laundering for others[65] and the UK state has instituted a money laundering reporting framework to identify the placing of funds by organised criminals.

Insurance fraud appears a problem with certain areas such as mandatory public liability insurance providing opportunities. Due to the security situation the insurance market has been dominated by a small number of firms who charge high premiums. New providers may appear to offer a competitive service but this may be a cover for fraud. Part of the process of liability insurance has been the use of a chain of brokers linking the client to an insurance company. In this chain there is the opportunity for fraud in the gaining of quotations which are subsequently falsely quoted along the chain, allowing for each firm to take a 'cut'. Fraudulent claims have been processed through the use of false postcodes and fraudulent certificates (public liability insurance certificates must be on public view in the premises).[66] In one case the estimate in lost premiums was £3.5 million, with 1,000 victims. In addition, businesses who believe they are covered and are in fact not, are thus open to action. The uninsured risk arising from this case has been estimated at £1 billion.[67] An organisation in Scotland targeted Northern Ireland for public liability insurance for football, Masonic, Orange Order and other clubs. Recommendation of this supposedly reasonable business spread in the tight knit community in Northern Ireland. However, the fraud uncovered, in which the PSNI assisted the Central Scottish Fraud Unit, took 400 victims with an estimated £500,000 in lost premiums.[68] Such crimes, as the PSNI and other official sources are quick to point out are not victimless. Or, if we were to adopt the framework developed earlier, could cause significant harm.

From an almost zero level, 'Nigerian' or '419' or advance fee fraud, became a noticeable criminal activity in Northern Ireland in the 2000–2003 period.[69] The OCTF specifically identifies a lottery prize fraud and others[70] which are basically variants on the 419 fraud: they are schemes to obtain money 'up front', following which the offender disappears. As such they simply represent new methods to conduct deception. The internet is a situational aspect providing more potential victims, easier opportunities and little chance of apprehension. The internet particularly deskills and democratises fraud. It is a type of offence paramilitaries cannot monopolise. These are crimes identical to those on the mainland.

Conclusion

Much concern is displayed by official and other commentators about a wide range of criminal activity in Northern Ireland. Indeed the list of crimes covered in OCTF publications gets longer and longer every year with little differentiation as to their importance or the actual involvement of organised crime proper.

In terms of organised crime, ODCs may be former paramilitaries or new entrants. They may have close, tangential or no links to paramilitaries. Those links that do exist may be personal in the network society which is Northern Ireland. ODCs engage in crime areas not dominated by paramilitaries, such as armed robbery, in areas where there is a paramilitary presence and areas where some form of accommodation with such groups is required (such as drug distribution). However, this is not the case through all of the province, rather in certain areas known for paramilitary presence such as mid-Ulster, Armagh and Belfast. As with organised crimes related to paramilitaries, organised criminals are not developing new crimes or operating markedly differently to organised and other criminals on the mainland. Many of these crimes are identical to those committed on the mainland and stem from similar contexts: the opening of EU markets and relaxed duty free restrictions has led to personal and organised smuggling; the opening of world markets as countries accelerated the process of late industrialisation (China, India, southeast Asia) has seen great volumes of counterfeit goods produced which find ready markets in Western and Eastern Europe. Those who purchase such goods in Northern Ireland are merely one part of the culture of marketisation and consumption in late modern societies, and such illicit economies are ways of incorporating even relatively deprived consumers into market life.[71] The main feature is the disproportionate level of some crimes compared to the province's population size and socio-economic structure.

Many organised crimes (i.e. committed by individuals with more or less planning) show similarities with the context of such crimes on the mainland. In terms of public sector fraud this has risen on the mainland within organisations and against them (government departments, the NHS, local government). In terms of internal fraud, some would argue that this can be traced to the marketisation and absence of internal controls which has accompanied New Public Management reforms.[72] As on the mainland, some 'respectable professionals' in Northern Ireland are taking opportunities as budgets and other controls are devolved without effective supervision. In terms of external deception, benefit fraud for example, this is evident in urban and rural areas which have been left behind by the influx of public funds, and by structures which effectively mean that there is a disincentive for individuals to declare changes in income. Private sector fraud may also see organised crimes being committed by professionals for large sums.

One important area where Northern Ireland does differ from the UK mainland and the Republic of Ireland is in the area of drugs, due to a combination of specific cultural, political and temporal factors and it will be interesting to see whether by 2010 drug use has markedly increased on the model of England, Wales and Scotland, or whether Belfast might match Dublin in the expansion of drug use as a result of economic growth.[73] This appears doubtful, but it is likely that drug use will increase if some of the current social controls on it (some of them from paramilitary groups) dissolve.

In terms of volume crimes, car crime in effect replicated in a delayed fashion the pattern in the UK, where these offences rose sharply in the 1990s and then declined. In terms of other crimes such as assault, again they are similar to the UK. Offences of assault have risen although not as much as in England and Wales[74] and some of this can be traced to the development of the 'night time economy' again to less of an extent than the mainland, with clubbing and the presence of Male Volume Vertical Drinkers which creates a context for scuffles, slights and resulting violence.[75] The MVVD culture is relatively limited in Northern Ireland at present but one important variable in the near future may be the changes in licensing laws which may lead to an approach like that of cities in England and Wales and Dublin in the Republic in which high concentrations of drinking outlets appear in urban zones. In Northern Ireland of course some assaults are influenced by sectarianism or racism, but this is evident in the UK.

Now that crime has been examined, the next chapters concentrate on the state response to crime. However before pragmatic aspects such as law enforcement strategies and effectiveness can be discussed the next chapter focuses on the vital context for any policing of paramilitary and ordinary crime – the fundamental reform of the police which was a central component of the peace process.

Notes

1 *A Commentary on Northern Ireland Crime Statistics 2004* (Belfast: NIO, 2005), p. 7. See also J. Brewer, B. Lockhart and P. Rodgers, 'Crime in Ireland since the Second World War', *Journal of the Statistical and Social Inquiry Society of Ireland*, 27:3 (1996), 152.
2 Brewer, Lockhart and Rodgers, 'Crime in Ireland', 155.
3 Brewer, Lockhart and Rodgers, 'Crime in Ireland', 161–163.
4 B. French and P. Campbell, 'Crime victimisation in Northern Ireland: Findings

from the 2003/04 Northern Ireland Crime Survey', *Research and Statistical Bulletin*, 4 (2005), p. 8.

5   B. French, D. Donnelly and M. Willis, 'Experience of crime in Northern Ireland', *Research and Statistical Bulletin*, 5 (2001), p. 4; *A commentary on Northern Ireland crime statistics 2004*, fig. 2.1, p. 7; see also for comparison T. Dodd, S. Nicholas, D. Povey and A. Walker, 'Crime in England and Wales 2003/04', *Home Office Statistical Bulletin* 10/04 (2004).

6   French, Donnelly and Willis, 'Experience of crime in Northern Ireland', p. 4.

7   French and Campbell, 'Crime victimisation on Northern Ireland, p. 8.

8   *A commentary on Northern Ireland crime statistics 2004*, fig. 2.1, p. 7.

9   IMC, *Tenth Report of the Independent Monitoring Commission* (London: The Stationery Office, 2006), p. 25.

10 An assault committed by individuals unconnected to paramilitaries but motivated by sectarianism would still be politically motivated.

11 For a historical discussion see M. McIntosh, 'Changes in the organisation of thieving', in S. Cohen (ed.), *Images of Deviance* (London: Pelican, 1971), pp. 98–134.

12 D. Hobbs, 'Criminal collaboration: Youth gangs, subcultures, professional criminals and organised crime', in M. Maguire, R. Morgan and R. Reiner (eds), *The Oxford Handbook of Criminology* (Oxford: Oxford University Press, 1997), p. 818.

13 See D. Hobbs, *Doing the Business: Entrepreneurship, Detectives and the Working Class in the East End of London* (Oxford: Clarendon, 1988); D. Hughes, 'The Spivs', in M. Sissons and P. French (eds), *Age of Austerity 1945–51* (Oxford: Oxford University Press, 1986), pp. 69–89.

14 J. Pearson, *The Cult of Violence* (London: Orion, 2002).

15 For the Republic see I. O'Donnell, 'Violence and social change in the Republic of Ireland', *International Journal of the Sociology of Law*, 33 (2005), 101–117.

16 See Organised Crime Task Force, *Confronting the Threat. Strategy 2001–2* (Belfast: OCTF, 2001), p. 7; Organised Crime Task Force, *Threat Assessment. Serious and Organised Crime in Northern Ireland* (Belfast: OCTF, 2003), p. 2.

17 BBC, 'Organised Crime', *File on Four*, BBC Radio Four (15 March 2005).

18 Northern Ireland Affairs Committee, *The Financing of Terrorism in Northern Ireland* Vol. 1, HC 978-1 (London: The Stationery Office, 2001–02), para 66.

19 Author interview, Senior Detective, PSNI Serious and Organised Crime Squad, PSNI, 10 November 2005.

20 Northern Ireland Affairs Committee, *The Financing of Terrorism*, paras 22–24.

21 PSNI figures quoted in Northern Ireland Affairs Committee, *The Illegal Drugs Trade and Drug Culture in Northern Ireland*, Vol. 1 HC 1217-I (London: The Stationery Office, 2003), pp. 25–26.

22 I. S. Wood, *Crimes of Loyalty. A History of the UDA* (Edinburgh, Edinburgh University Press, 2006), p. 289.

23 Northern Ireland Affairs Committee, *The Illegal Drugs Trade*, para. 69; R. MacDonald and J. Marsh, 'Crossing the Rubicon: Youth transitions, poverty, drugs and social exclusion', *International Journal of Drug Policy*, 13 (2002), 27–38.

24 Organised Crime Task Force, *Confronting the Threat. Serious and Organised Crime*

in Northern Ireland (Belfast: OCTF, 2005), p. 50; K. McElrath, *Prevalence of Problem Heroin Use in Northern Ireland* (Belfast: Drug and Alcohol Information and Research Unit, 2002), p. 34.

25 University of Glasgow Centre for Drug Misuse Research, *Estimating the Prevalence of Problem Opiate and Problem Cocaine Use in Northern Ireland* (Belfast: Drug and Alcohol Information and Research Unit, 2006), p. 20.

26 Organised Crime Task Force, *Confronting the Threat. Serious and Organised Crime in Northern Ireland* (Belfast: OCTF, 2004), fig. 4, p. 24.

27 University of Glasgow Centre for Drug Misuse Research, *Estimating the Prevalence of Problem Opiate Use,* pp. 1–2; Organised Crime Task Force, *Annual Report and Threat Assessment* (Belfast: OCTF, 2006), p. 36.

28 From 2000–2003 the street price of heroin fell from £100–120 to £80–100 a gram. PSNI estimates quoted in House of Commons Debates, 22 January 2004, *Hansard,* Col. 543WH.

29 University of Glasgow Centre for Drug Misuse Research, *Estimating the Prevalence of Problem Opiate Use,* p. 5.

30 Organised Crime Task Force, *Confronting the Threat,* p. 24; Organised Crime Task Force, *Annual Report and Threat Assessment,* p. 36.

31 Northern Ireland Affairs Committee, *The Illegal Drugs Trade,* pp. 20–21.

32 NIO, 'Changing patterns of drug use in Northern Ireland – some recent survey findings', *Research Findings,* 1 (1997); S. McMullan and D. Ruddy, 'Experience of drug misuse: Findings from the 2003/04 Northern Ireland Crime Survey', *Northern Ireland Office Research and Statistical Bulletin,* 10 (2005).

33 PSNI estimates quoted in *Hansard,* 22 January 2004, Col. 543WH.

34 Northern Ireland Affairs Committee, *The Illegal Drugs Trade,* p. 6.

35 Northern Ireland Affairs Committee, *The Illegal Drugs Trade,* pp. 6–12; A. Barton, *Illicit Drugs: Use and Control* (London: Routledge, 2003).

36 Organised Crime Task Force, *Threat Assessment* (Belfast: OCTF, 2002), p. 6; Northern Ireland Affairs Committee, *The Illegal Drugs Trade,* pp. 9–10.

37 M. Simpson, 'The relationship between drug use and crime: A puzzle inside an enigma', *International Journal of Drug Policy,* 14 (2003), 307–19.

38 Organised Crime Task Force, *Confronting the Threat. Serious and Organised Crime in Northern Ireland* (Belfast: OCTF, 2005), p. 49.

39 K. Holloway and T. Bennett, 'The results of the first two years of the NEW-ADAM programme', *Home Office OnLine Report,* 19/04 (2004), www.homeoffice. gov.uk/rds/pdfs04/rdsolr1904.pdf.

40 D. Hobbs, P. Hadfield, S. Lister and S. Winlow, *Bouncers: Violence and Governance in the Night Time Economy* (Oxford, Oxford University Press, 2003); P. Chatterton, 'Governing nightlife: Profit, fun and (dis)order in the contemporary city', *Entertainment Law,* 1:2 (2002), 23–49.

41 *Chief Constable's Annual Report 2005–2006* (Belfast: PSNI, 2006), p. 11.

42 H. Parker, L. Williams and J. Aldridge, 'The normalisation of "sensible" recreational drugs use: Further evidence from the North West of England', *Sociology,* 36:4 (2002), 941–964.

43 McMullan and Ruddy, 'Experience of Drug Misuse', Table 4, p. 6; for a general comparison with England and Wales see N. Chivite-Matthews (et al), 'Drug Misuse Declared: Findings from the 2003/04 British Crime Survey',

Home Office Statistical Bulletin (May) 2005; see the comparison between England, Wales, Scotland and Northern Ireland in G. Eaton, 'Drug Use in the Population', in G. Eaton, M. Morleo, A. Lodwick *et al.* (eds), *UK Drug* Situation, 2005 edition (European Monitoring Centre for Drugs and Drug Addiction/Department of Health, 2005).

44   Although Europe is not uniform in respect of drug use. See G. Tremlett, 'Spain tops table of cocaine use', *Guardian* (7 September 2005); P. A. Sáiz, 'Use of cocaine by secondary school students in Northern Spain', *European Addiction Research*, 9:3 (2003), 138–143; UNODC, *World Drugs report* 2006 (Slovakia: UN, 2006).

45   Northern Ireland Affairs Committee, *The Illegal Drugs Trade*, para. 11.

46   For the former see 'Drug-related offences', Written Answers, 23 January 2006, *Hansard*, Col. 1870W and the latter see 'Drug-related offences', Written Answers, 24 July 2006, *Hansard*, Cols. 917–918W.

47   Organised Crime Task Force, *Threat Assessment* (Belfast: OCTF, 2002), p. 14.

48   Author interview, Detective Chief Superintendent, PSNI attached to the OCTF, Stormont House annexe, 25 July 2003.

49   Organised Crime Task Force, *Confronting the Threat*, p. 15.

50   OCTF analysis altered after 2002 away from identifying specific numbers of organised networks.

51   Northern Ireland Affairs Committee, *The Financing of Terrorism in Northern Ireland*, Vol. 1 HC 975-1 (London: The Stationery Office, 2001–02), para 62; author interview, Detective Chief Superintendent, PSNI attached to the OCTF, Stormont House annexe, 25 July 2003.

52   Author interview, Detective Chief Superintendent, PSNI attached to the OCTF, Stormont House annexe, 25 July 2003.

53   Organised Crime Task Force, *Threat Assessment* (2002), p. 14; Organised Crime Task Force, *Confronting the Threat*, p. 33.

54   I. O'Donnell and S. Morrison, 'Armed and dangerous? The use of firearms in robbery', *Howard Journal of Criminal Justice*, 36:3 (1997), 306.

55   N. Shover and D. Honaker, 'The socially bounded decision-making of persistent property offenders', *Howard Journal of Criminal Justice*, 31 (1982), 276–293; R. Matthews, *Armed Robbery* (Devon: Willan, 2002); M. Gill, 'The craft of robbers of cash-in-transit vans: Crime facilitators and the entrepreneurial approach', *International Journal of the Sociology of Law*, 29 (2001), 277–291.

56   Organised Crime Task Force, *Threat Assessment. Serious and Organised Crime in Northern Ireland* (Belfast: OCTF, 2003), p. 19.

57   Organised Crime Task Force, *Confronting the Threat*, p. 69.

58   Organised Crime Task Force, *Threat Assessment*, p. 12.

59   Organised Crime Task Force, *Confronting the Threat*, p. 69

60   Author interview, Detective Chief Inspector, PSNI, Belfast, 22 July 2003; see also Northern Ireland Assembly, 'Report on [1] Grants Paid to Irish Sport Horse Genetic Testing Unit Ltd. and [2] National Agriculture Support: Fraud', *Fourth Report of the Public Accounts Committee* (PAC, 2001); Northern Ireland Assembly, 'Report on Internal Fraud in the Local Enterprise Development Unit', *Eleventh Report of the Public Accounts Committee* (PAC, 2002).

61   *BBC Digital News Northern Ireland* (21 May 2004).

62 Organised Crime Task Force, *Annual Report and Threat Assessment* (2006), p. 44.

63 See the study of Belfast by E. Evason and R. Woods, 'Poverty, deregulation of the labour market and benefit fraud', *Social Policy and Administration*, 29:1 (1995), 40–54.

64 Author interview, Detective Chief Superintendent, PSNI, Belfast, 24 July 2003.

65 Author interview, Detective Chief Inspector, PSNI, Belfast, 22 July 2003.

66 Author interview, Detective Chief Inspector, PSNI, Belfast, 22 July 2003.

67 Author interview, Detective Chief Inspector, PSNI, Belfast, 22 July 2003; Organised Crime Task Force, *Confronting the Threat* (2004), p. 38.

68 Author interview, Detective Chief Inspector, PSNI, Belfast, 22 July 2003; see also Organised Crime Task Force, *Serious and Organised Crime in Northern Ireland. Threat Assessment and Strategy* (Belfast: OCTF, 2004), p. 38.

69 Author interview, Detective Chief Inspector, PSNI, Belfast, 22 July 2003.

70 Organised Crime Task Force, *Confronting the Threat*, p. 43; Organised Crime Task Force, *Annual Report and Threat Assessment 2006* (Belfast: OCTF, 2006), p. 33.

71 I. Taylor, *Crime in Context. A Critical Criminology of Market Societies* (London: Polity, 1999); M. Presdee, 'Volume Crime and everyday life', in C. Hale (*et al.*) (eds), *Criminology* (Oxford: Oxford University Press, 2005), pp. 185–201.

72 A. Doig, 'Mixed signals? Public sector change and the proper conduct of public business', *Public Administration*, 73 (1995), 191–212.

73 For a detailed analysis of the relationship between drug use and crime in the Republic see J. Connolly, *Drugs and Crime in Ireland. Overview 3* (Dublin: Health Research Board, 2003).

74 Offences against the person rose consistently from 26,104 in 2001/02 to 28,982 in 2003/04 and 30,953 in 2005/06. This category includes murder, attempted murder and explosives offences but these are a very low percentage of the total. In terms of individual assault categories the NIO argues, 'it is difficult to establish how much of the increase in recorded violent offences is genuine' because of recording changes. B. French and P. Campbell, 'Crime victimisation in Northern Ireland: findings from the 2003/04 Northern Ireland Crime Survey', *Research and Statistics Bulletin*, 4 (2005), p. 9. However, these changes have largely seen a switch between the category Assault Occasioning Actual Bodily Harm (AOABH), which has increased, while the category common assault has consequently decreased. Taking the bulk categories of common assault, AOABH and aggravated assault, they rose from 21,058 in 2002/03 to 23,165 in 2005/06. See Northern Ireland Office, *Recorded Crime in Northern Ireland* (various years).

75 Hobbs, Hadfield, Lister and Winlow, *Bouncers*; P. Hadfield, *Bar Wars* (Oxford: Oxford University Press, 2006).

5

From RUC to PSNI: Police reform and modernisation

They want to turn us into a county force.[a]

It suits a lot of people to airbrush us out of history.[b]

We were in turmoil two years ago.[c]

Proactively supporting Nationalist Ireland.[d]

Q: I'm basically saying that for all the fighting, what we still have is a British police force. It's a tongue in cheek question – you can pass on it.
Orde: Pass![e]

---

[a]   Comment regularly heard from police officers by the author in the 2003 period.
[b]   Author interview, Chief officer, Police Federation, Belfast, 25 February 2004.
[c]   Author interview, Chief officer, Superintendents' Association, Belfast, 26 February 2004.
[d]   Critics commenting on the PSNI following the Whiterock riots, 'Hearts and Minds', BBC TV (30 October 2005).
[e]   Interview, Hugh Orde, *The Blanket* (25 October 2004).

From RUC to PSNI

In his history of the IRA, Richard English argues that the organisation needs to be treated in context. Abstracting the role of one social force in the Northern Ireland conflict risks distorting 'the dynamics of political and historical interaction.'[1] However, this distortion is often evident with regard to studies of policing. Critiques of the RUC are legion, yet many of these analyses do not provide a full account of police practice since they do not situate the police in context.[2] There is often little analysis of the dynamism of the Northern Ireland conflict, involving patterns of attack and response, specialist 'versus' routine policing, the changing patterns of 'street' politics and national politics, regional political developments, and the differing political economies of conflict in South Armagh, mid-Ulster and Belfast. Instead the conflict, and the police are 'read' via the successive phases of British security policy.[3]

Despite this, three concrete interrelated problems surface again and again in accounts of the RUC: force identity, human rights and accountability. Force identity centred on the Britishness of the police and its overwhelmingly Protestant character.[4] The use of police powers and their effects on human rights were a constant course of criticism from the institution of Northern Ireland[5] but accelerated after 1968 with the actions of the 'B Specials' police reserve against civil rights demonstrators, the shooting of suspects by RUC specialist units in the 1980s and the collusion allegations concerning RUC Special Branch and loyalist paramilitaries and the activities of informants in republican paramilitary organisations.[6] Finally, criticisms of RUC accountability centred on its limited and centralised nature through the Police Authority for Northern Ireland (PANI). Although public accountability was problematic since PANI members were declared legitimate targets by the PIRA, there were regular accusations that the Chief Constable sidelined PANI, and there was an absence of local accountability.[7] With regard to communities, the RUC had patchy support in nationalist areas and faced implacable opposition in republican areas, based on their general perception as a colonial police, and on specific complaints such as their regular attempts at recruiting informants. But the RUC saw a reduction in its support in Protestant areas from the mid-1980s. This began after the Anglo–Irish Agreement was signed in 1985, which formalised Republic of Ireland involvement in Northern Irish affairs and led to demonstrations, and was recharged in the 1990s following the disturbances at Drumcree where the police clashed with Protestant protestors who opposed any restrictions on the traditional march by the Orange Order down the nationalist Garvaghy Road.[8]

This legacy meant substantial police reform would be central to any genuine peace process.[9] The Independent Commission on Policing in

Northern Ireland, chaired by Chris Patten, was established as part of the Belfast Agreement to examine the RUC. Its report, published in 1999, recommended a comprehensive programme of reform. The Patten recommendations can be crystallised into two aims: to create a 'police service not a police force',[10] and to take the politics out of policing.[11] Three main interrelated issues dominated the debate around the reform of the RUC, namely cultural reform, including recruitment and religious composition, key symbols, force name and badge; secondly, organisational reform, including police service size and the role of Special Branch and CID; and finally governance, including the mechanisms by which accountability was to be established, and linked to this the relationship between the police and the wider community.

Cultural reform

In November 2001 the Police Service of Northern Ireland (PSNI) replaced the RUC as the service's title, with the RUC remaining as part of the masthead. In line with Patten, both the badge and oath of allegiance were changed to emphasise human rights and the political neutrality of Northern Ireland. A programme of renovation and opening up of police stations began.[12] By 2005 'a programme of softening the appearance of existing stations' was under way at 40 of the then 135 police stations in the estate,[13] and the colour of police Land Rovers changed from grey to white.

Following Patten's recommendations, recruitment on a 50/50 non-Protestant/Protestant basis was implemented from 2001, with the process contracted out to a recruitment firm. The 50/50 target had not been met by 2006, although the policy has seen more Catholics join the PSNI. The percentage of Catholic officers increased from 8.28 per cent in November 2001 to 17.42 per cent in April 2005.[14] Recruitment was controversial. Desmond Rea, the chair of the Policing Board, argued that the disproportionate recruitment of Catholics was 'the price that has to be paid' to get Catholics up to 30 per cent of the force by 2010.[15] Here, cultural and organisational reform merged. However, there were clear issues with regard to basic organisational features of the police.

Organisational reform

In terms of the controversial uniformed Reserve forces which historically bulked up the police to large proportions, Patten recommended the phasing out of the Full Time Reserve (FTR), depending on the security situation, and reform of the Part Time Reserve (PTR) to attract more Catholic recruits. The FTR became a controversial issue. Nationalists and republicans called for its disbandment, although the FTR was effectively being quickly downsized, since 1,000 officers had already left by 2003 via early retirement. Some officers in the police viewed Orde's stand on the issue as a barometer of his intent to 'defend' the police in the midst of the intense reform process. Hugh Orde argued that the FTR was still required, particularly in the light of public order situations such as the loyalist intimidation at Holy Cross School, the Orange parades at Drumcree, the constant micro-disturbances caused by republican and loyalist groups across Belfast and the need to protect public buildings against attacks from dissident republicans. The highly political decision was taken to retain the FTR, and then begin a final phase-out from 2005 to 2007. The PTR continued in a reformed format, with moves to attract more Catholic recruits.

In the area of criminal intelligence and investigation the Patten Report concurred with those critics who identified Special Branch as being a force within a force and argued that it should be reduced in size, merged with the CID and thus brought under the aegis of a department of mainstream management of criminal investigation.[16] This partly occurred. The Crime Department of the PSNI was established, headed by one Assistant Chief Constable and covering serious and organised crime investigation and Special Branch. A number of Branch officers took early retirement. The PSNI discharged a number of its informants as part of repeated reductions. Existing and new informants were run under the new RIPA-proofed system, which was also affected by the National Intelligence Model (NIM), which aimed to improve information collection and exchange within the police. However, subsequently the Crompton Report called for the retention of Special Branch. Critics questioned the extent of change and actually pointed to the appearance of Special Branch personnel in important areas of criminal investigation. Patten had argued that with regard to national security the Chief Constable should report to the Secretary of State. However, from 2007 MI5 took over responsibility for counter terrorism from Special Branch. This solidified the control of national security matters from London and created further accountability issues which are dealt with in Chapter 8.

Governance and accountability

The Patten Report viewed the relationship between the police and the community as central to reform: 'We make proposals for a new structure of accountability which should ensure effective and democratically based oversight of policing and the creation of a close partnership between the police and every community'.[17] The Patten proposals envisaged a Policing Board, funded by the Northern Ireland Office (NIO) and with a substantial elected component, with a direct role in developing policing plans and highlighting human rights issues. Importantly, the Board would have the power to oblige the Chief Constable to produce a report on his duties or those of his officers if it felt this was necessary: 'the Policing Board should have the power to require the Chief Constable to report on any issue pertaining to the performance of his functions or those of the police service'.[18]

Then Secretary of State for Northern Ireland Peter Mandelson placed limits on this under the Police (Northern Ireland) Act 2000, by widening the areas in which the Chief Constable could question the Board's request for him to produce a report on a matter. To national security issues, pending court cases and personnel matters was added the more general criteria of crime investigation. As per Patten the issue would still then be referred to the Secretary of State who may or may not decide to overrule the Board. Interestingly Mandelson was probably the least biddable Secretary in terms of 'pushing things on' with regard to the peace process (ironic considering his closeness to Prime Minister Tony Blair), and his argument was that the Patten structure would not take politics out of policing so much as thrust them centre stage: 'I may have been cautious in placing safeguards on the powers of the Board, particularly in relation to the launching of inquiries. I wanted to avoid parties using the police as a battleground.'[19]

Critics argued the attempted changes to the Policing Board's authority constituted the British state playing its old game again. Clifford Shearing, one of the Patten commissioners argued that this and other measures had 'gutted' Patten.[20] Others argued that Mandelson should have 'reinforced [Patten] not meddled with it'.[21] Although the system received support from Patten himself,[22] to critics the practical legislative implementation of Patten had moved away from its original community based and driven policing structure, and the Police (Northern Ireland) Act 2000 was a traditional 'police' Act.[23] The Policing Board reform was heavily criticised by nationalists,[24] and was the pinnacle of a number of concerns expressed by republicans: 'Sinn Féin remained aggrieved over the changes to Patten in a number of key areas. These included the new oath (to be sworn only by new officers); the ban on former prisoners serving on District Policing Partnership Boards; the changes to DPPBs; the retention of plastic bullets; the retention of Special Branch (the "political police") and the Police Reserve; and the retention of the title RUC within the name of the "new" police force. Many of Sinn Féin's concerns were addressed in the 2001 Police Act.'[25] Indeed the renegotiation of policing saw 94 changes made to Mandelson's original Act,[26] including strengthening accountability to the Policing Board.[27] The SDLP joined the Policing Board in 2001. Sinn Féin did not, and the Party did not agree to support policing and justice arrangements and join the Policing Board until 2007, and this was conditional on the restoration of devolved government including policing.

A further Police (Northern Ireland) Act 2003 narrowed the scope for the Chief Constable to question a request by the Board for a report to national security issues, pending court cases and sensitive personnel matters. The issue would then be referred to the Secretary of State who would decide whether the request should be met by the Chief Constable. Depending on the decision of the Secretary of State, information might still be provided to a special purposes committee rather than the full Board. This power had not been exercised by 2007.

The new Policing Board had been established in 2001, drawn from elected local representatives (ten, chosen by parties) and independent members appointed by the Secretary of State. As per Patten, under the Police (Northern Ireland) Act 2000 the Board negotiates the annual policing budget with the NIO, allocates the budget to the Chief Constable, and monitors performance against this. The Policing Board develops a policing plan along with the Chief Constable, sets performance objectives and targets, and assesses police performance against these, and is under a general duty to secure the economy, efficiency and effectiveness of the service. This model of accountability is clearly drawn directly from New Public Management practices already operating in England and Wales, which aim to introduce business-style reforms to the public sector and brings its own debates in terms of its particular approach to ideas and practices of accountability.[28] However, the Policing Board is distinctive in that it also assesses specific issues central to Patten such as police ethics and community relations and its public meetings provide an additional heightened element of accountability. In practical terms the Policing Board required capacity- building in terms of expertise on policing issues, including organised crime and community policing, after initial concerns that members were not versed in applied policing issues.[29]

According to Patten, genuine local accountability required decentralised policing. Accordingly the PSNI was reorganised into District Command Units (DCUs) similar to Basic Command Units in England and Wales. These areas were under local commanders who had financial and organisational autonomy (to an extent) and clearer lines of communication to senior management. Twenty-nine DCUs were established in 2001 corresponding to Northern Ireland's local government districts. The second stage of the process was the institution in 2003 of District Policing Partnerships (DPPs), each one parallel to a DCU and composed of local community representatives. In regular private and public meetings the local commander reports to the DPP and receives views on what the local community feels should be the policing priorities.[30]

The 29 DCUs did see some diseconomies of scale in terms of the replication of management and administrative posts (crime manager, business manager, personnel, public relations), which did not bear the weight of the areas they were covering, and were too small to effectively implement and operate the National Intelligence Model.[31] (Within DCUs there were also concerns raised over a lack of genuinely devolved budgets which undermined ostensible devolution.)[32] In short, a general criticism was that Northern Ireland was 'over DCU'd'. Patten had acknowledged the disjuncture but argued that securing local accountability was at that time the most important process and that DCUs should match local District Councils.[33] However, in 2006/2007 a proposed local government reorganisation aimed to reduce local regions to nine. This would mean a corresponding reduction of DCUs to nine. The Police Oversight Commissioner argued that this would lead to a weakening of intelligence gathering, yet as mentioned, others argued that the number of DCUs had previously weakened the implementation of the NIM. However, if there is a revolving argument with regard to the most appropriate organisational form for economies of scale in police management and the intelligence cycle, another concern is whether a larger number of DCUs/DPPs facilitates genuine local accountability.

The establishment of District Policing Partnerships faced initial problems with regard to the intimidation of members and potential members by dissident republicans (see Chapter 8), and the criticisms which echoed those of the republican movement that DPPs were actually mechanisms by which dissent could be marginalised.[34] The roll out and running of DPPs has been costly. Some observers argue this is justified,[35] although others say it also runs against the idea that one role of policing accountability structures is to keep down costs.[36] DPPs have also been characterised by a lack of attendance but the importance in terms of long-term legitimacy appears to centre on having the structure in place. The lack of attendance can be viewed from a variety of perspectives, with some arguing that there would be a clear problem 'if people were climbing the walls to get in', and that lack of attendance was in line with that seen in other observed jurisdictions in the USA.[37] Perhaps the innovation of DPPs has been in line with the identified trend in the UK of heightened criticism of public officials combined with an apathy towards public participation.[38] This is reflected in the relatively poor public perception or lack of knowledge of DPPs.[39] In any case the presence of journalists at DPP meetings is a mechanism by which issues raised are given publicity[40] although this reflects the idea that journalists are the optimum method of securing accountability. Finally, the nature of DPPs predictably varies: some DPPs view their role as challenging; others as facilitative and supportive. This corresponds to those long-term debates about the governance of police and whether structures are 'captured' or independent.[41] Therefore, 'DPPs were both a promising local initiative and a reflection of continuing political conflict'.[42]

Perhaps the most significant development in terms of accountability has been the establishment of the Police Ombudsman for Northern Ireland

(PONI), which provides accountability via external investigation. Like much public sector reform in Northern Ireland the Police Ombudsman has assumed a heavy symbolic and practical role. The PONI, established by the Police (Northern Ireland) Act 1998 replaced the previous Independent Commission for Police Complaints[43] and has a number of powers beyond those of the previous system. These include the power to initiate investigations without complaint into matters of public interest (s55[6]), such as that into the Omagh bomb. The office also receives matters referred by the Chief Constable under law (s55), such as deaths in police custody, firearms discharge and the discharge of baton rounds. The office investigates matters as a result of complaint (s52), an example being the investigation into the sectarian murder of Sean Brown in 1997, and finally under s60 the Police (Northern Ireland) Act 2003, the Ombudsman can investigate a current policy or practice if s/he has reason to believe this is in the public interest (although matters relating to police covert investigation under the Regulation of Investigatory Powers Act 2000 are excluded). The PONI's powers include the capacity to conduct a retrospective examination of a case (again the use of police intelligence before the Omagh bomb), request forensic evidence and stage reconstructions. The office has approximately 40 investigators with powers of arrest, interview and search and seizure. The Ombudsman had a budget of £5.7 million in 2001/2, rising to over £7 million in 2004/5.[44]

The PONI took on a number of cases from the previous Independent Commission for Police Complaints and developed new investigations, the most notable and influential of which was that into the police handling of intelligence before the Omagh bomb. The report produced predictable political reactions. The Unionists declared the report partial and politically motivated. Sinn Féin argued the report justified its call for root and branch reform of the police;[45] the SDLP also swung behind the report. The Police Federation planned to challenge the report under Judicial Review. Downing Street, in its oscillation between unionist and nationalist interests on the policing issue, swung behind then Chief Constable Sir Ronnie Flanagan[46] particularly as his departure would have further destabilised the PSNI at that time. Mandelson, by then former Secretary of State, labelled the report 'politically charged' and 'a very poor piece of work', containing unwarranted conclusions.[47] However, the Omagh Report became highly influential in fuelling the reform and professionalisation of police investigation.

As Lustgarten argues: 'a prime indication of the maturing of state institutions is that provision for complaint and review becomes an integral part of the working of those institutions or their oversight bodies … In some case such organisations go further and fulfil the state's human rights obligations'.[48] Here the PONI has been productive in that it acts on multiple levels in raising accountability issues. For example, if there is debate over the scope for the Policing Board to require a report from the Chief Constable of the PSNI, the Ombudsman effectively functions as a generator of police reporting and reform, whether through self-initiated inquiries or complaints from the public. Further, the relationship between the PONI and parts of the PSNI remains unpredictable. The initial 'very strained relationship' between the police and PONI investigators particularly has lapsed.[49] Indeed, PONI reports often justify controversial police actions *ex post facto*. However, issues can easily produce strained relations such as the Ombudsman's 2007 report into Special Branch handling of informants in the loyalist paramilitary organisation the UVF, which was criticised in turn by the Northern Ireland Retired Police Officers Association.[50] The independence of the PONI allows it organisational space and it has clearly resisted 'capture'.

Nevertheless, in the highly charged universe of Northern Ireland the PONI has been charged with 'shooting from the hip'. After the Police Federation withdrew its application for a Judicial Review of the Omagh report, the PONI stated:

> The Ombudsman now acknowledges, with the benefit of hindsight, that certain PSNI members should have been given notice, or better notice, of the allegations against them and a better opportunity to respond, having regard to the requirements of natural justice. The Police Ombudsman believed, however, that there was considerable urgency in the production of the report.[51]

Indeed, the Police Ombudsman criticised the PSNI raid on Stormont in 2002 as part of the police investigation into alleged Sinn Féin spying, for its disproportionate nature,[52] but the same can be said for the PONI's high profile arrests of former RUC detectives and the press surrounding the publication of its report into the activities of police informants inside the UVF.

Overview

An evaluation of police reform depends on the methodology of change employed, but simply comparing the PSNI of 2005 with the RUC in 1995 clearly demonstrates the extent of reform.[53] Indeed the SDLP's policing spokesman argues that police reform has been 'the single greatest achievement of the Good Friday process'.[54] The point was later echoed with qualification by Sinn Féin MLA Gerry Kelly. Despite Sinn Féin's concerns over policing arrangements he argued that to say there is no difference between now and 1998 'is clearly not true' and commented that 'there has been a considerable mass of change … but we are going to get it right'.[55] Sinn Féin voted to support policing arrangements in 2007, on condition of the return of a devolved government which took place later in the same year.

However, there is a difference between organisational reform and engendering legitimacy.[56] Legitimacy can, for example, be based on techniques of policing. Police legitimacy in Northern Ireland has obviously been characterised by the techniques used ('hard' rather than 'soft' policing).[57] Police reform aims now to move to 'soft', consensual, community based policing. But although these different types of techniques are vital, police reform is more than moving from one technique to the other. Connected to this, the overall professionalisation and modernisation of the police also plays a role since it attempts to present the police as a responsive public sector service. Particularly in late modern societies, the police are viewed as organisations that should be as responsible and efficient as business units. There may be an ironic relationship between such reforms of the police and their legitimacy in that they may lead to a more cynical view of policing. More positive attitudes to the police in some areas of the UK since 2005 have stemmed not from the embedding of managerial reforms but as a result of the 7/7 terrorist attack in London, and this has of course helped to reduce police legitimacy amongst sections of the Muslim community. Indeed, this highlights the wider political context of police legitimacy.

While there have been constant complaints about police efficiency in Northern Ireland, particularly recently, this is of course not the central issue. The flexible business reform model has been 'sticky' in increasing police legitimacy amongst republicans and many nationalists because this is a model of reform which seeks to engender support through New Public Management procedures and 'consumer' responsiveness.[58] The reform outlined in this chapter is significant, but the changed policing structures seem to have fostered acceptance rather than active support on the part of many nationalists, and with regard to republicans the development of basic acceptance will be limited since the police remain a British police service. Over the long term the decentralisation of policing and other reforms may foster more of a de facto acceptance, and this will be one problem for Sinn Féin, if Northern Ireland's citizens become focused on the consumer side of policing and the essential debates about the PSNI being a 'colonial' police service fall away. As Patten argued, 'There are sharp disagreements among Northern Ireland people about the politics of policing, but there is less disagreement about policing itself.'[59]

Acceptance or otherwise of the police is also conditioned by the fact that the idea of 'policing' rather than 'police' influenced Patten,[60] meaning the development of the policing function across various quasi-public hybrids. This had in effect been in operation for some time (albeit in an antagonistic way) in the form of paramilitary 'policing' in republican and loyalist areas. The issue is whether this is formalised and brought within accepted systems of modern governance via restorative justice schemes or persists as part of a Balkanised system characterised by mere acceptance of the police for certain types of crime, while using local alternative schemes where they are viewed as more legitimate. Up until 2007 the community restorative justice schemes in republican areas did not cooperate with the police and negotiations were under way to ensure they were recognised by the NIO and cooperated with the PSNI at least formally.

Sinn Féin's participation in policing structures will heighten the issue over maintaining change in the police, which had already been highlighted by the SDLP. Even within the Policing Board the idea was evident that after six years of intense reform a period of consolidation might be required rather than the continuation of the reform process.[61] This would happen if the Policing Board should become 'captured' over the long term.[62] Capture in the short term was unlikely, since Gerry Adams argued that the Party's participation in policing structures would be to 'put manners' on the PSNI. Indeed the political nature of policing will continue as many republicans and some nationalists will seek to resist any long-term consolidation and legitimation of a specifically Northern Irish police.[63]

Important here is Sinn Féin's distinction between 'civic' and 'political' policing, which has been a tactic to enable accommodation with policing but which also reflects a political reality in terms of the republican critique of the police. The issue now and in future is what constitutes 'civic policing', i.e. the scope for cooperation in policing. Alternatively, even with regards to 'political' policing, Sinn Féin's acceptance of British government guarantees over the role of MI5 and its de facto co-operation with the PSNI over the last few years at the low level constitute remarkable change. Thus the idea of a Northern Irish police always being limited in its acceptance will persist with the practical consumerist demands for a responsive police force. But the overall change in policing is, to employ an over-used word in Northern Ireland, 'seismic'.

The role of crime management

The organisational, cultural and accountability streams of the reform process are integrated, but also display discrete identities. Further, the emphasis on each has changed as the reform process has evolved. Cultural change is ongoing but has been evident in the RUC's name change, the outside and inside of police stations, the new oath and cap badge, new recruitment and the policy of accelerated retirement. Organisational reform was also intense in the 2000–2002 period whereby the police slimmed down through early retirement and DCU decentralisation took place. Accountability reform was evident over the 2001–2003 period when a new Policing Board was instituted and DPPs established. However, an offshoot of all these reforms – but particularly organisational reform – has been managerial change, centrally in the area of crime management. This has become more important from the 2002 period with the establishment of Crime Department in the PSNI, a single department covering intelligence gathering and the investigation of serious crime.

The use of the term 'crime management' (the gathering, analysis and dissemination of intelligence on crime, the development of investigative strategies, the prevention of crime and the detection or disruption of offences) signals the extent to which the PSNI has become enmeshed in the universe of New Public Management, an ideological discourse and organisational practice which seeks to remould public sector organisations along business models with a consequent emphasis on financial management and control, efficiency and effectiveness. As applied to the police in England and Wales, this meant modernisation and continuing professionalisation of criminal investigation techniques, the dissemination of management training and ideology, the development of IT systems, the introduction of new systems for collecting and managing intelligence and the use of informants, and overall systems of performance measurement and reporting.[64] The Patten Reforms had almost nothing to say concerning crime management, since the Report concentrated on the overall structural themes of organisation, accountability and community policing. However, a more intense focus on crime management developed due to a number of factors.

Criticism of police practice

Firstly, reform arose as a result of the criticism of police practice in Northern Ireland by external bodies established to secure accountability on specific issues. In 2003 Sir John Stevens completed the third of his inquiries into events surrounding the murder of Patrick Finucane, a Belfast solicitor who was murdered by gunmen from the Ulster Freedom Fighters, the 'military' wing of the Ulster Defence Association. The Stevens Inquiry found that there had been collusion between police officers, army informant handlers and loyalist terrorists both in this murder and in another, and made a number of recommendations concerning the conduct of criminal investigation, intelligence gathering, sharing and quality control.[65]

Perhaps the most notable external inquiry in terms of initiating rapid change was that conducted by the Police Ombudsman for Northern Ireland into the (mis)use of intelligence before the 1998 Omagh bomb, in which the Real IRA exploded a device causing 29 deaths and 300 injuries. The report concluded that vital informant information would not have prevented the Omagh bomb, but that this intelligence was misused by the RUC, and this highlighted deeper problems with the use and access to information between Special Branch and the rest of the RUC.[66]

Although the Report was controversial to say the least, it became a crucial pointer in fuelling change in the PSNI. The recommendation that Her Majesty's Inspectorate of Constabulary (HMIC) should review terrorist-linked murder investigations led to the Policing Board requesting such an external review. The result was the 2003 HMIC *Report on Murder Investigation in Northern Ireland* (The Blakey Report), which argued: 'The emphasis placed by the PSNI on public order and the fight against terrorism has, not unnaturally had a detrimental effect on the status of the CID', and that murder investigation should be modelled along the lines of that in England and Wales, which itself underwent modernisation in the 1990s. Areas targeted for reform included the overall management of investigation, crime scene management, management of forensic science, and concentration on IT (e.g. utilising the Home Office Large Major Enquiry System (HOLMES 2) software).[67] The stress on the reinvestigation of murder cases was evident in the PSNI by 2003/4, with a large-scale programme under the Crime Department to review unsolved homicides via the Serious Crime Review Team in the short term, and in terms of pre-Belfast Agreement homicides, via the Historical Enquiries Team (HET). However, this was reinforced by a further PONI inquiry into the sectarian murder of Sean Brown, who was kidnapped, beaten and shot five times in the face in 1997, allegedly by Loyalist Volunteer Force paramilitaries. The PONI report focused on investigation management, the handling and sharing of intelligence, including between Special Branch and the Murder Investigation Team, and the handling of forensic and witness evidence. The criticisms were similar in some respects to those of the Omagh Report.[68] The case, along with a number of others was reopened, with a plea for information appearing on the BBC's 'Crimewatch' in 2005 and arrests taking place later in the year. Many of these external criticisms of the police overlapped, focusing as they did on problems with intelligence sharing and investigative tactics and illuminating problems in liaising with Special Branch. Again there was a link with developments in England and Wales with regard to employing new management and scientific techniques to undetected homicides.[69]

Police capacity

Secondly, reform was driven by a short-term 'crisis' in policing reflected in terms of the failure of the police to stem the rising tide of crime following the peace process, including the development of serious and organised crime in Northern Ireland. Crime patterns are dealt with in other chapters, but, briefly, volume and serious crime rose in Northern Ireland beyond that expected by the introduction of new recording methods.[70] As crime rose police detection rates plummeted. The police in Northern Ireland had historically achieved higher detection rates than forces on the mainland but from the late 1990s clear-up rates were poor. A number of serious offences such as murder, attempted murder, conspiracy to murder, extortion and financial crime such as deception offences saw a drop in the detection rate compared to three or four years previously.[71] As one officer put it simply at the time, 'we haven't had a proper grasp on crime'.[72]

Poor performance can be traced to a number of factors. Those responsible for implementing New Public Management reforms argued that the failure of the police to control crime replicated the similar failure of police services in the rest of the UK to respond to the doubling of crime from the late 1980s to the early 1990s: that is, the police required modernisation and professionalisation. These criticisms have been stated already with regard to external inquiries. In addition, according to some observers, as policy attention and resources were channelled into implementing the Patten reforms 'nuts and bolts' areas such as homicide investigation, serious/organised crime and financial crime investigation were not targeted for resources since they had (naturally) not been identified as priority areas in Patten.

The loss in experienced personnel played a role in reducing capacity. The proposal by Patten for a reduction in the number of officers engaged in specialist investigation was in effect rejected by the then Secretary of State for Northern Ireland, Peter Mandelson. Nevertheless, a large number of officers left the force through early retirement under the generous terms set up by Patten. Over 1,000 plainclothes and uniform officers had left the service by 2001 (rising to 2,138 by mid-2005) under the severance programme, a number of them senior officers with substantial operational experience,[73] with the crime department 'most affected' with the departure of 120 officers.[74] PSNI Chief Constable Hugh Orde argued 'We need more detectives. Patten did not forsee the amount of terrorism that would continue in "peacetime" policing and got rid of a disproportionate number … of the CID.'[75] One external inspection was 'very concerned about the short to medium term viability of the CID',[76] as concurrently terrorist investigations and public order problems swallowed up a significant amount of resources. A number of units involved in serious and organised crime investigation were hampered by a lack of staff or their replacement by inexperienced staff, and by a lack of resources.[77] The PSNI attempted to remedy this gap by recruiting experienced detectives from the mainland. However, this was a failure and the Patten severance packages had to be suspended in 2004 in order to retain experience in certain sectors since recruitment did not match exit. Apparently there was little or no 'knowledge management' policy towards individuals leaving the PSNI; individuals with experience in criminal investigation (and other areas) left without a replacement plan and few received exit interviews.[78] On the political level however, the NIO made capital out of this tsunami of retirements, since it represented the fundamental change required to entice Sinn Féin and the SDLP into accepting the new policing arrangements.

However, capacity was also clearly affected by the high rates of absenteeism and sickness in the PSNI, which rose during this period and stayed high, and was the subject of comment in successive external HMIC inspections. By 2000 it was noted that 'sickness amongst regular officers and full time reserve constables continues to rise at an alarming rate',[79] with average days lost via sickness at over 20 per year from 1999–2002 compared to just over 12 per year for England and Wales.[80] The PSNI and Policing Board addressed these and other concerns in a human resource strategy.[81] Although lower, sickness leave was still an issue in 2006, with the target set at 12 days per year.

New Public Management

Finally, in the absence of concrete recommendations from Patten, criminal investigation was influenced by mainland NPM/Whitehall thinking on policing, which led to the government developing police capacity in Northern Ireland, replicating the rest of the UK. New Public Management seeks to remould public sector organisations along quasi-business lines, stressing the use of management techniques, modernisation (particularly in IT) and financial control. Accountability is normally emphasised through the market mechanism. However, since this is limited in the public sector, even if quasi-markets are in operation, accountability is thus secured through the provision of a set of performance targets, the public dissemination of performance and internal and external inspection as a general principle and also to correct inefficiencies.[82] Like police services in England and Wales the PSNI was subject to a series of external inspections on general and specific themes which developed a framework for reform particular to the PSNI but based squarely along NPM lines. The HMIC conducted a 'Baseline Assessment' of the PSNI to establish a 'strategic overview' of operations, management, governance and community relations. This provides 'a baseline against which the Service's improvement will be monitored'.[83] This has also been buttressed by specific application of NPM via the recommendations of the external inspections already mentioned, such as the critical evaluation 'Murder Investigation in Northern Ireland' by the HMIC. Further, one of the strongest recommendations of the Patten Report had been that Special Branch and CID should be merged, to avoid Special Branch functioning as 'a force within a force'. The criticism of Special Branch in terms of human rights had been a constant in Northern Ireland, and reports such as that by the PONI into the Omagh bombing (mentioned above) had aimed the spotlight on Branch procedures. However, the HMIC conducted a report into Special Branch (The Crompton Report), which was firmly situated within Whitehall/ACPO/NPM thinking. Crompton stated: 'my review doesn't challenge the need for Special Branch, it is about improving efficiency and performance in the Police Service of Northern Ireland as a whole'.[84] Crompton argued that the Branch's concentration on the disruption of terrorist operations had mitigated against it developing standard criminal investigation skills and recommended that it should take cognisance of the implications of working towards a criminal prosecution, develop better intelligence evaluation, take regional input from Assistant Chief Constables on intelligence operations, develop more efficient intelligence sharing and adopt the National Intelligence Model.[85] The maintenance of Special Branch may have reflected the influence of the 'securocracy' but cannot be divorced from the post- 9/11 situation and also the failure of the PSNI to cope with rising (serious) crime.

Finally the National Intelligence Model (NIM) was implemented, following its rolling out in England and Wales. The National Intelligence Model seeks to 'promote effective Intelligence Led Policing (ILP) … and … standardise intelligence related structures, processes and practices across all forces'.[86] Simply, one model should provide a businesslike framework for the collation, analysis and dissemination of intelligence within and across police services. A number of previous criticisms of the police use of intelligence were evident concerning forces in England and Wales,[87] and the Police Ombudsman's Report into the Omagh bombing, the Blakey report into homicide investigation and the Crompton Report into Special Branch all had as a common theme a focus on the (mis)use of intelligence within the PSNI. The NIM was rolled out in mainland forces and also to DCU level in the PSNI by 2004. Some observers argued that the implementation in the PSNI was more effective, particularly spurred on by external criticism and its performance with regard to rising crime.

Thus a new framework of crime management resulted from the recommendations of these external inquiries and inspections, accentuated by rising crime problems and falling detection rates. Special Branch and CID were not merged but as per Patten they were both brought under the leadership of one ACC in a new department termed Crime Management. This was the framework within which the NIM was introduced. Finally, this reform was bolstered by an increase in police funding.

Public order problems such as the annual marching season, loyalist intimidation at Holy Cross School and the constant micro-disturbances

across Belfast, often encouraged by loyalist and republican groups constituted a drain on police manpower and resources. The PSNI had regularly applied for extra spending to cover overtime from the NIO Reserve.[88] Following the dying away of major public order disturbances
resourcing pressure decreased, and further, the NIO began to pump money
into the PSNI. The police budget, running at around £650 million per
annum from 2000–2003 stood at over £930 million in 2004–2005, falling
to £850 million in 2005–2006.[89] The police increased recruitment and
internal promotion into detective ranks. Over 200 detectives came 'on
line', although with a consequent gap before they achieved a level of
operational experience. Organisational reforms such as the NIM were
financed and NIO funding for the Historical Enquiries Team commenced.
The PSNI remained well resourced comparatively, and as one officer
pointed out, the distinction between Northern Ireland and the mainland
was evident in comparison with Nottinghamshire Constabulary, whose
Chief Constable publicly admitted his force was under strain in coping
with simultaneous major investigations. In 2004–2005 the PSNI was able
to simultaneously investigate the Northern Bank robbery, the McCartney
murder and other serious offences without sending police financing into
crisis.[90]

Situating police reform

Police reform has often been viewed as a process enveloped in the politics of the Northern Ireland peace process, a natural assumption considering the intense microscopic focus often adopted towards the Northern
Irish conflict. However, the process of police reform was inextricably
linked to a series of wider national, even global political and security
processes.

Even in terms of the specific Northern Irish context reform was often
more than it appeared to the naked eye. Particularly in the early stages,
some commentators appeared to view the process as being centred on
whether the Patten reforms had been implemented or not,[91] as though it
was not a template for reform but a writ from which no deviation was
permitted, while some police officers felt the process of police reform was
effectively part of a strategy whereby the RUC would be effectively turned
into 'an English county force',[92] and that this was part of a wider process
of appeasement of Republican/Nationalist politics.[93] Both analyses missed
the wider context. Rather then neutering the Northern Irish police, the
peace process and police reform actually provided the context for a
modernisation of the RUC, a modernisation clearly required following
the revelations of the Stevens Enquiries and the Police Ombudsman's

Report into the Omagh bombing investigation. Thus, while many reforms generated great debate as to their supposed ulterior political motive (e.g. human rights reforms were seen as appeasing the Nationalist/Republican community), they can in fact be situated firmly within the new governance of policing which had been applied to the police in the rest of the UK under the third Thatcher and Major administrations (1987–1997) and accelerated by the Blair Governments (1997–2007); that is, they were drawn from the New Public Management reforms which had been applied to the 43 forces of England and Wales from the 1990s.[94] The critical inquiries rooted in the Northern Irish experience often combined with NPM as in the reform of 'crime management', a process far beyond the Patten report for example. Thus the PSNI was becoming 'mainlandised', not as a minor English police service but as a major urban force.[95]

Indeed the development of crime as a political issue in moves to restore decommissioning tempered any large-scale 'downsizing' of the police. The role of the PSNI and from 2003 the Assets Recovery Agency in targeting loyalist paramilitaries was seen as important in drawing them into a process of reform and accommodation as well as building confidence in the nationalist community and in the Republic of Ireland. The Republic government concentrated political fire on PIRA crime and Sinn Féin's relationship to the republican movement, amply illustrated by the role of Justice Minister Michael McDowell, an implacable and vociferous critic of the Provisional IRA and Sinn Féin. The security situation added to this, not only involving the activities of republican dissidents and the feuds within loyalism, but also the change in context with regard to risk and security generally after 9/11.

A political charge to policing reform remained – and remains – evident. In terms of the reform process, while Secretary of State Peter Mandelson rejected some Patten-recommended reforms because, he argued, it would over-politicise the police,[96] Ronnie Flanagan, the Chief Constable who oversaw the transition from the RUC to the PSNI engaged in a highly charged public 'debate' with Police Ombudsman Nuala O'Loan over the Omagh Report. The subsequent Chief Constable Hugh Orde has been increasingly drawn into – and has voluntarily stepped into – what are in effect charged political debates where operational decisions and Orde's opinions key in directly with high-level developments in the peace process. Examples include statements concerning the alleged Sinn Féin spy ring in Stormont in 2003, the attribution of responsibility for the Northern Bank robbery in late 2004, his critical comments following the Loyalist/Orange-fuelled rioting in Belfast in 2005 and his comment in 2006 regarding Sinn Féin joining the Policing Board.

The British character of the PSNI, which emerged as a result of these reforms is thus more subtle. However, on a more fundamental level the mere existence of the PSNI rather than some all-Ireland transitional version of policing proposed by republicans represents a continuing problem of legitimacy. The police secure public order and thus the state, and a state which remains part of the UK despite the neutralisation of its symbolic Britishness. This will always place limits on police legitimacy although the future relationship between high politics and 'bread and butter' issues of civic policing will be an important variable, particularly if the SDLP and Sinn Féin become enmeshed in consumerist debates about policing effectiveness. If the link between policing and politics will not be broken as long as Northern Ireland exists, Chapter 6 turns from police reform to police tactics and performance with regard to serious and volume crime, and the political debates surrounding that.

Notes

1   R. English, *Armed Struggle. The History of the IRA* London: Pan, 2004), p. 376.
2   For standard critical accounts see G. Ellison and J. Smyth, *The Crowned Harp. Policing Northern Ireland* (London: Pluto, 2000); F. Ní Aoláin, *The Politics of Force. Conflict Management and State Violence in Northern Ireland* (Belfast: Blackstaff, 2000); J O'Brien, *Killing Finucane* (Dublin: Gill and Macmillan, 2005); Steve Bruce implicitly critiques much of the 'green' nature of security writing on the province. S. Bruce, *The Edge of the Union. The Ulster Loyalist Political Vision* (Oxford: Oxford University Press, 1994), Chapter 5 and S. Bruce, 'Loyalist assassinations and police collusion in Northern Ireland: An extended critique of Sean McPhilemy's *The Committee*', *Studies in Conflict and Terrorism*, 31:1 (2000), 61–80.
3   For sympathetic accounts of the RUC see J. Brewer and K. Magee, *Inside the RUC* (Oxford: Oxford University Press, 1991; J. Holland and S. Phoenix, *Phoenix. Policing the Shadows* (London: Hodder and Stoughton, 1996); C. Ryder, *The RUC. A Force Under Fire 1922–2000* (London: Arrow, 2000); C. Ryder, *The Fateful Split. Catholics and the Royal Ulster Constabulary* (London: Methuen, 2004). See J. Brown, *Into the Dark. 30 Years in the RUC* (Dublin: Gill and Macmillan, 2005) for a highly critical insider account of RUC Special Branch. For a thoughtful critical recent analysis of police legitimacy and the process of reform see A. Mulcahy, *Policing Northern Ireland* (Devon: Willan, 2006).
4   Ellison and Smyth, *The Crowned Harp*, pp. 21–23; 'It was in the area of security more than any other that Catholics were made to feel they did not belong.' M. Elliott, *The Catholics of Ulster* (London: Penguin, 2001), p. 379.
5   For the early period see K. Ewing and C. Gearty, *The Struggle for Civil Liberties. Political Freedom and the Rule of Law in Britain, 1914–1945* (Oxford: Oxford University Press, 2001) Chapter 7.
6   B. Dickson, 'Miscarriages of justice in Northern Ireland', in C. Walker and K. Starmer (eds), *Miscarriages of Justice* (London: Blackstone, 1999), pp. 287–303; Ryder, *The RUC*, Chapter 10; M. Urban, *Big Boy's Rules* (London, Faber,

1992), Chapters 16 and 17; M. Ingram and G. Harkin, *Stakeknife* (Dublin: O'Brien, 2004); PONI, *Statement by the Police Ombudsman for Northern Ireland on her Investigation into the Circumstances Surrounding the Death of Raymond McCord Junior and Related Matters* (Belfast: PONI, 2007). For a detailed response to the Ombudsman's Report see Northern Ireland Retired Police Officers Association, *A Rebuttal of the Statement by the Police Ombudsman for Northern Ireland on her investigation into the Circumstances Surrounding the Death of Raymond McCord Junior and Related Matters'* (Belfast: NIRPOA, 2007).

7   M. Connolly, J. Law, J. and I. Topping, 'Policing structures and public accountability in Northern Ireland', *Local Government Studies,* 22:4 (1996), 229–244; G. Hogan and C. Walker, *Political Violence and the Law in Ireland* (Manchester: Manchester University Press, 1989), pp. 35–36; Mulcahy, *Policing Northern Ireland,* pp. 36–45.

8   See Brewer and Magee, *Inside the RUC*; Ryder, *The RUC*; Mulcahy, *Policing Northern Ireland.*

9   C. Walker, 'The Patten Report and post-sovereignty policing in Northern Ireland', in R. Wilford (ed.), *Aspects of the Belfast Agreement* (Oxford University Press, Oxford, 2001) pp. 142–165.

10 *A New Beginning: Policing in Northern Ireland. The Independent Commission on Policing in Northern Ireland* (Belfast: The Stationery Office, 1999) para 1.17 (hereafter *The Patten Report*).

11 'Statement by Chris Patten on the future of Policing in Northern Ireland' (9 September 1999), para. 8. http://cain.ulst.ac.uk/issues/police/patten/cp9999.htm.

12 *The Patten Report*, Chapter 4, Chapter 8.

13 PSNI, *Annual Report of the Chief Constable 2004–2005* (Belfast: PSNI, 2005), p. 10.

14 PSNI, *Annual Report of the Chief Constable 2004–2005*, p. 8.

15 Quoted on *Hearts and Minds*, BBC Northern Ireland (30 October 2005).

16 *The Patten Report*, paras 12.11 and 12.12.

17 *The Patten Report*, para 1.15.

18 *The Patten Report*, para 6.22.

19 P. Mandelson, 'I am listening', *Guardian* (16 June 2000). See also D. Godson, *Himself Alone. David Trimble and the Ordeal of Unionism* (London: Harper Perennial, 2005) p. 620.

20 C. Shearing, 'Patten has been gutted', *Guardian* (14 November 2000).

21 Ryder, *The Fateful Split*, p. 309.

22 N. Watt, 'Patten attacks Sinn Féin over police', *Guardian* (29 November 2000).

23 Mulcahy, *Policing Northern Ireland,* p. 171.

24 Mulcahy, *Policing Northern Ireland,* p. 169.

25 G. Murray and J. Tonge, *Sinn Féin and the SDLP. From Alienation to Participation* (Dublin: O'Brien, 2005), p. 217.

26 Murray and Tonge, *Sinn Féin and the SDLP*, p. 207.

27 Mulcahy, *Policing Northern Ireland,* pp. 169–172.

28 I. Loader, 'Democracy, Justice and the Limits of Policing: Rethinking Police Accountability', *Social and Legal Studies,* 3:4 (1994), 521–544; P. Rogerson, 'Performance measurement and policing: Police service or law enforcement

agency?', *Public Money and Management*, Oct.–Dec. (1995), 25–29; J. Law, 'Accountability and annual reports: The case of policing', *Public Policy and Administration*, 16:1 (2001), 75–90; B. Loveday, 'The impact of performance culture on criminal justice agencies in England and Wales', *International Journal of the Sociology of Law*, 27 (1999), 351–377; B. Loveday,'Managing crime: Police use of data as an indicator of effectiveness', *International Journal of the Sociology of Law*, Vol. 28 (2000), 215–237.

29   Northern Ireland Affairs Committee, *The Functions of the Northern Ireland Policing Board: Responses by the Government and the Northern Ireland Policing Board to the Committee's Seventh Report of Session 2004–05*, HC 531 (London: The Stationery Office, 2005), pp. 7–8.

30   See for example, Coleraine District Policing Partnership, *Report of the Coleraine District Policing Partnership Public Meeting* (23 June 2003).

31   Author interviews, Chief officer, Superintendents Association, Garnerville, Belfast, 26 February 2004; Detective Chief Inspector, PSNI, 22 July 2003.

32   Author interview, Chief officer, Superintendents Association, Garnerville, Belfast, 26 February 2004.

33   *The Patten Report,* para 12.5.

34   Mulcahy, *Policing Northern Ireland*, p. 175.

35   Author interviews, Chief Officer, PSNI, Belfast, 26 January 2006; Alex Attwood, SDLP MLA and Policing Board member, Belfast, 6 October 2006; Ian Paisley Jr., DUP MLA and Policing Board member, Belfast, 5 October 2006.

36   Author interview, Danny Kennedy, UUP MLA and Policing Board member, Belfast, 4 October 2006.

37   'The public are only interested in policing when it affects the front door.' Author interview, Ian Paisley Jr., DUP, MLA and Policing Board member, Belfast, 5 October 2006.

38   *Power to the People. An Independent Inquiry into Britain's Democracy* (York: The Power Inquiry, 2006) identifies that there is vigorous comunity activism in a number of geographical and social areas but that this does not translate into support for formal political institutions.

39   Mulcahy, *Policing Northern Ireland*, pp. 175–176.

40   Author interview, Chief Officer, PSNI, Belfast, 26 January 2006.

41   T. Prenzler, 'Civilian oversight of police. A test of capture theory', *British Journal of Criminology*, 40 (2000), 659–674.

42   Mulcahy, *Policing Northern Ireland*, p. 176.

43   I. Topping, 'The police complaints system in Northern Ireland: a repeated transplant?', in M. Connolly and S. Loughlin (eds), *Public Policy in Northern Ireland; Adoption or Adaptation?* (PRI: Belfast, 1990).

44   PONI, *Annual Report and Statement of Accounts April 2004 to March 2005* (Ireland: The Stationery Office, 2005).

45   Sinn Féin, 'Durkan clutching at straws', *Sinn Féin Press Release* (29 August 2002); Sinn Féin, 'The king is dead. Long live the king. Chief Constables come and go but the central problem remains.', *Sinn Féin Press Release* (13 April 2002); 'Special Branch: Still untouchable', *Sinn Féin* (8 August 2002).

46   R. Cowan, 'PM backs Ulster police chief', *Guardian* (14 December 2001).

47 D. Sharrock, 'Mandelson attacks Omagh report', *Daily Telegraph* (15 December 2001). See also Mulcahy, *Policing Northern Ireland*, p. 177.

48 L. Lustgarten, 'Human Rights. Where do we go from here?' *Modern Law Review*, 69:5 (2006), 851.

49 Author interview, Chief Officer, Police Federation, Belfast, 25 February 2004.

50 PONI, *Statement by the Police Ombudsman for Northern Ireland on Her Investigation into the Circumstances Surrounding the Death of Raymond McCord Junior*; for a critique see Northern Ireland Retired Police Officers Association, *Rebuttal of the Statement by the Police Ombudsman for Northern Ireland on her Investigation into the Circumstances Surrounding the Death of Raymond McCord Junior*.

51 *Police Ombudsman Statement Following the Withdrawal of a Judicial Review by the Police Association for Northern Ireland to Quash her Report into Events Surrounding the Omagh Bombing* (Thursday 23 January 2003).

52 Mulcahy, *Policing Northern Ireland*, p. 180.

53 For a critical view which accepts the extent of reform see B. Dickson, 'Policing and human rights after the conflict', in M. Cox, A. Guelke and F. Stephen (eds), *A Farewell to Arms? Beyond the Good Friday Agreement* (Manchester: Manchester University Press, 2006), pp. 170–186.

54 Author interview, Alex Attwood, SDLP MLA and Policing Board member, Belfast, 6 October 2006.

55 Interviewed on 'Spotlight', BBC Northern Ireland (17 October 2006).

56 For a discussion of legitimacy see Mulcahy, *Policing Northern Ireland*, pp. 193–202.

57 Brewer, *Inside the RUC*.

58 For a discussion see I. Loader, 'Consumer culture and the commodification of policing and security', *Sociology*, 33 (1999), 373–392.

59 *Statement by Chris Patten on the future of Policing in Northern Ireland* (9 September 1999), para 8 http://cain.ulst.ac.uk/issues/police/patten/cp9999.htm. For a more detailed discussion of these issues see *Patten Report* (Chapters 1–3 particularly), which teased out the contours of policing specific to Northern Ireland and those in common with many other jurisdictions, particularly in relation to policing styles and community demands.

60 L. Johnston and C. Shearing, *Governing Security. Explorations in Policing and Justice* (London: Routledge, 2003); Mulcahy, *Policing Northern Ireland*, p. 195.

61 Author interview, Alex Attwood, SDLP, MLA and Policing Board member, Belfast, 6 October 2006.

62 Following devolution of policing and justice a new vista of problems opens up, and Patten flagged the warning that devolution should not lead to any weakening of the Policing Board. *The Patten Report*, para 6.15.

63 For an overview of these issues with regard to other jurisdictions see J. Brewer (ed.), *Restructuring South Africa* (London: Macmillan, 1994); M. Brogden and C. Shearing, *Policing for a New South Africa* (London: Routledge, 1997).

64 Audit Commission, *Helping with Enquiries. Tackling Crime Effectively* (London: HMSO, 1993); *Audit Commission, Cheques and Balances. A Management Handbook on Police Planning and Financial Delegation* (London: HMSO, 1994); Audit Commission, *Detecting Change. Progress in Tackling Crime* (London: HMSO, 1996); F. Leishman, B. Loveday and S. Savage (eds), *Core Issues in Policing*

   (Essex: Longman, 1996).
65   J. Stevens, *Stevens Enquiry 3. Overview and Recommendations* (2003), http://
     news.bbc.co.uk/1/shared/spl/hi/northern_ireland/03/stephens_inquiry/pdf/
     stephens_inquiry.pdf.
66   Police Ombudsman for Northern Ireland, *Statement by the Police Ombudsman
     for Northern Ireland on her Investigation of Matters Relating to the Omagh Bombing
     on August 15th 1998* (PONI, 2001); Police Ombudsman for Northern Ireland,
     First Annual Report November 2000–March 2002 (PONI, 2002), p. 37.
67   PSNI, *Report on Murder Investigation Procedures Presented to Policing Board*
     www.psni.police.uk/index/media_centre/press_releases/pg_press_
     releases_2003.
68   PONI, *The Investigation by Police of the Murder of Sean Brown on 12 May 1997*
     (PONI, 2004).
69   M. Innes, *Investigating Murder: Detective Work and the Police Response to Criminal
     Homicide* (Oxford: Clarendon, 2003); F. Brookman, *Understanding Homicide*
     (London: Sage, 2005).
70   Crime was also estimated to be rising on the previous recording system. For
     an estimate see B. French (*et al.*), 'Experience of crime in Northern Ireland',
     Research and Statistical Bulletin, 5 (2001), p. 4.
71   HMIC, *2002 Inspection: Police Service of Northern Ireland* (London: Home Of-
     fice, 2002), p. 23; D. Lyness, P. Campbell and C. Jamison (eds), *A Commen-
     tary on Northern Ireland Crime Statistics* (National Statistics, 2005), table 3.1, p.
     25.
72   Author interview, Chief Officer, Superintendents Association, Garnerville,
     Belfast, 26 February 2004.
73   HMIC, *2002 Inspection – Police Service of Northern Ireland*, p. 29.
74   HMIC, *2000/2001 Inspection: Royal Ulster Constabulary* (London: HMIC, 2001),
     p. 9.
75   Orde quoted in R. Cowan, 'I'll stay out of politics vows Ulster's new police
     chief', *Guardian* (2 September 2002).
76   HMIC, *2002 Inspection – Police Service of Northern Ireland* (Home Office, 2002),
     p. 26. The situation was exacerbated by the high levels of sickness in the
     PSNI noted in the same report, pp. 30–32.
77   Staffing information gained by the author in interviews with members of the
     Economic Crime Bureau and the Crime Department of the PSNI, February
     and July 2003.
78   Author interview, Chief officer of the Superintendents' Association,
     Garnerville, Belfast, 26 February 2004.
79   HMIC *2000/2001 Inspection – Royal Ulster Constabulary* (Home Office, 2001),
     p. 39.
80   HMIC, *2002 Inspection – Police Service of Northern Ireland*, fig. 10, p. 30.
81   Dickson, 'Policing and human rights after the conflict', p. 176.
82   C. Hood, 'A public management for all seasons?', *Public Administration*, 69:1
     (1991), 3–18; S. Jenkins, *Accountable to None. The Tory Nationalisation of Britain*
     (London: Penguin, 1996); C. Pollitt, J. Birchall & K. Putman, *Decentralising
     Public Service Management* (London:Macmillan, 1998).
83   HMIC, *Baseline Assessment of the Police Service of Northern Ireland* (London:

HMIC, 2004), para 1.3.

84 Northern Ireland Policing Board, *Policing Board Backs Recommendations on Special Branch* (2002) www.nipolicingboard.org.uk/text_only/to_pr_nov02.htm.

85 Northern Ireland Policing Board, *Policing Board backs recommendations.* Special Branch was renamed as Intelligence Branch though most observers still referred to it as Special Branch.

86 T. John and M. Maguire, 'The National Intelligence Model: Early implementation experience in three Police Force areas', *Cardiff School of Social Sciences Working Paper*, 50 (2004), p. 8.

87 John and Maguire, 'The National Intelligence Model', p. 8.

88 PSNI, *Annual Report of the Chief Constable 2002–3* (PSNI, 2003), p. 19.

89 PSNI, *Annual Report of the Chief Constable 2004–05*, p. 10; PSNI, *Chief Constable's Annual Report 2005–06* (PSNI, 2005), p. 9.

90 'Police force's murder "struggle"', BBC News (13 March 2005), http://news.bbc.co.uk/1/hi/uk/4344595.stm.

91 P. Hillyard and M. Tomlinson, 'Patterns of policing and policing Patten', *Journal of Law and Society,* 27:3 (2000), 394–415; C. Shearing, 'A "New Beginning" for Policing', *Journal of Law and Society,* 27:3 (2000), 386–393.

92 The police, in this period of demoralisation, also resent(ed) the importance placed upon paramilitaries which constituted a 'special culture'. As police officers pointed out on numerous occasions, criminal groups in Northern Ireland were/are given a status they would be denied in Glasgow, enhanced by a focus on titillation and information about the internal wranglings in groups such as the UDA.

93 D. Sharrock, 'Britain has no stomach for IRA fight', *Daily Telegraph* (5 December 2001).

94 See note 28.

95 The British government was already developing new strategies to combat serious/organised crime prior to police reform in Northern Ireland (including a new nationwide strategy for Customs and Excise, the development of asset recovery through what would become the Proceeds of Crime Act 2002, the Terrorism Act 2000 and ideas on data exchange and matching). Much of this was driven by research in the Performance and Innovation Unit of the Cabinet Office, and in the absence of concrete recommendations this applied to Northern Ireland.

96 P. Mandelson, 'I am listening'; Godson, *Himself* Alone, Chapter 29 and p. 479.

6

Policing serious and volume crime

Many people still have questions relating to unresolved deaths over a period of 30 years.[a]

If builders cooperated in [reporting extortion] cases we could have four a day.[b]

We are encouraged by Sir Hugh Orde's assertion that the battle against organised crime is 'winnable'. His putting it in these terms, however, shows that it has yet to be won.[c]

Problem solving is not something the police can do alone.[d]

[a]   Hugh Orde in Historical Enquiries Team, *Policing the Past. Introducing the work of the Historical Enquiries Team* (PSNI, n.d.)

[b]   Author interviews, Detective Chief Inspector and Detective Inspector, PSNI, Belfast, 24 February 2004.

[c]   Northern Ireland Affairs Committee, *The Financing of Terrorism in Northern Ireland*, Vol. 1 HC 978-1 (London: The Stationery Office, 2001–2002), para 86.

[d]   *Patten Report, A New Beginning: Policing in Northern Ireland. The Independent Commission on Policing in Northern Ireland* (Belfast: The Stationery Office, 1999), para 7.17

The new policing of crime in Northern Ireland

The criminal activity outlined in previous chapters obviously raises the issue of how law enforcement agencies, particularly the PSNI, are dealing with this. This chapter details the policing tactics and patterns involved in investigating serious and organised crime. A number of general themes are evident. Firstly, to repeat the point made in Chapter 5, the police have over the last decade become more thoroughly 'mainlandised' than at any time in their history. The Patten Report – anathema to Unionists – created a context wider than the report itself in which public sector changes that have been applied to the police in the rest of the UK have been rapidly applied to the PSNI. Some of these changes were already mooted under Ronnie Flanagan when Chief Constable of the RUC but without Patten and the Belfast Agreement it is unlikely that the change would have accelerated and broadened to the extent that it did. (This is evident in the investigation of homicide.) This process has been reinforced by the decision to retain Special Branch (against Patten's wishes), the impending role of the Serious and Organised Crime Agency in Northern Ireland (although as a partner within the OCTF) and the decision to transfer responsibility for national security to MI5 from Special Branch. While this overshadows the previous importance of Special Branch, both will work together and this represents a further mainland link.

Second are the deeply symbolic issues raised by certain areas of criminal investigation. Murder is one of these, and the controversy covers not only contemporary investigations but also those of murders officially deemed in the past (i.e. pre-Belfast Agreement) but now to be investigated by the Historical Enquiry Team. The issues surrounding this are deeply riven with alternative meaning and interpretation. Extortion is another crime whose investigation highlights a number of problems which seem to have deepened and expanded in the uneven soil of the peace process. To the public, media and other observers, the rise in extortion following 1998 seems to signal not only the problem of crime and the role of paramilitaries within it but seems to highlight the impotence of the criminal justice system in dealing with organised crime. Public perception and empirical reality are often at odds but these types of crime and their investigation do reveal evident problems in the control of organised crime, both paramilitary and non-paramilitary.

Finally, and following on from the previous point, is the simple but pressing issue of the effectiveness of policing. Has policing 'reduced', 'undermined', 'disrupted' or 'stabilised' organised crime in Northern Ireland, and what do these terms actually mean? It is interesting here not only to attempt to evaluate the policing of organised crime but also to assess the terminology used. Long-term actions such as the 'war on drugs', and now the seemingly endless 'war against terror(ism)' imply that organised crime resembles an army (perhaps a guerrilla army more than a regular one) and that its battalions can be defeated, if not in open 'warfare' then through an effective 'counter insurgency' approach. Other analyses would argue that the problem can be, at best, managed to a certain level.[1] This chapter, for reasons of space, cannot deal with every form of investigation and thus deals with specimen areas which illustrate the current landscape of criminal investigation: homicide, extortion and armed robbery and ends with a general discussion of the role of policing in Northern Ireland.

Homicide investigation

Murders in Northern Ireland have encapsulated a number of important issues: their political 'reading' and whether they might destabilise the peace process; their significance as symbols of the persisting power of paramilitary groups; their significance as products of disputes within and between paramilitary groups; their significance as actions permitted by the collusion of police officers, and their significance as barometers of street-level sectarianism and the (im)possibility of community integration. Thus in Northern Ireland there is a political economy of murder and it has many facets. In the fraught period after 1998 the crime of murder can be separated into three approximate categories. The first concerns those connected to paramilitaries (those committed by paramilitaries on what they regard as legitimate targets: informers, members of groups involved in conflict with other groups, or witnesses in upcoming criminal cases). Although Northern Ireland seems far removed from the visceral period of the 1970s, paramilitary murders in the contemporary period have included attacks of some intensity. Former PIRA member Eamon Collins was stabbed in the head and face a number of times, rendering him almost unrecognisable. The murders in 2000 of David McIlwaine and Andrew Robb, killed by the UVF as part of its feud with the LVF were similar frenzied cases involving multiple stabbings. UDA man George Legge's 2001 torture-murder lasted a number of hours and was later (2006) described by the coroner as resembling the ferocity of the Shankhill Butchers.

The second type of murder, what might be termed with a grimace, 'normal' attacks are those committed for the same reasons as in any other jurisdiction. Some attacks, particularly those influenced by alcohol and sectarianism, are often brutal. The nature of some attacks also might see them linked to paramilitaries. The disappearance of 25-year-old Lisa Dorrian after a party in 2005 was for a period laid at the door of the LVF.

Finally, hovering over Northern Ireland are the 2,000 victims of the period of conflict whose killers have never been identified. These dead are termed in modern professional language 'historic undetected homicides'. In Northern Ireland it is 'deaths attributed to the security situation'. The term homicide or death caused by another is employed because although most of these cases are murder, the generic term is used until information as to motivation and context confirms this. The following section deals with each of these in turn.

Paramilitary and 'normal' homicides

Despite the substantial number of murders which occurred during the period of conflict, the RUC had a relatively high (if fluctuating) clear-up rate. This rate nevertheless left a number of problems. Firstly, some murders were misattributed. Michael Stone is only the latest in a long line of paramilitaries to claim he confessed to murders he did not commit.[2] Secondly, it is clear that wider imperatives of national security had affected 'traditional' policing and clear-up rates. The problem of some unsolved murders was connected to the intervention of Special Branch, which led to murderers being sheltered from normal criminal investigation since they were informants. This was a process alleged with regard to Ken Barrett, the UFF operative eventually convicted of murdering Pat Finucane as a result of the Stevens Enquiries, with regard to the UVF on Mount Vernon,[3] and with regard to high-level British military intelligence informers inside the Provisional IRA, who were not prevented by their handlers from organising the murders of other PIRA men suspected of being informants or members of the security forces. These actions (or rather, omissions) were justified as being necessary to protect their identities.[4]

Thirdly, beyond the intense focus on these high profile murders and the role of Special Branch, there had been problems with murder investigation. The Blakey Report on murder investigation, in the understated language of such official documents, argued that the structure of murder investigation required reform: 'The emphasis placed by the PSNI on public order and the fight against terrorism has, not unnaturally, had a detrimental effect on the status of the CID.'[5] There was under investment in homicide investigation. Indeed although the HOLMES system was employed, the PSNI lacked a specific HOLMES room as late as the period of the Patten inspections. At another stage, eight murder investigations were being run from one HOLMES room. There was a lack of communication not just between intelligence and investigation but between investigation teams. The responsibility for major crime investigation overall (of which murder was a central example) was split between five Assistant Chief Constables.[6] These technical issues were part of a wider problem, in that overall, in New Public Management jargon, no one 'owned' homicide investigation.[7]

The Blakey Report, as the quote above signifies, acknowledged the historical context of murder investigation. However, the report concentrated on the contemporary situation and the 'nuts and bolts' of murder investigation. Its recommendations lay in the areas of the management of investigation, storage and management of evidence and forensic science and review. A process of reform was developed which consolidated Major Incident Teams (MIT). These units deal with serious crimes including homicide and terrorism. There are ten MITs with 20 staff in each, with dedicated HOLMES rooms, based in Belfast, mid-Ulster and the west. In theory they operate via the integration of intelligence and investigation. The tool for this is the National Intelligence Model mentioned in Chapter 5, which seeks to gain intelligence from a variety of sources (rather than sidelining it if it comes from sources regarded as less important such as the uniform branch) and integrate it with investigation. The teams employ more surveillance on murder investigations, widening the previous focus on its use for investigating terrorist offences. Homicide investigation teams of younger and more experienced detectives are mixed.[8] A Serious Crime Review Team reviews investigations after four weeks, and also examines past cases which took place after the 1998 period.[9] Although the Northern Ireland context has provided its own specific focus, it is clear that homicide investigation in the Metropolitan Police emerges as a template for reform, itself the product of external criticism and review in the wake of the Stephen Lawrence investigation.[10]

Undetected homicides

In England and Wales between 1988 and 1997 the detection rate for homicide was 93.5 per cent. Even then, this still left 751 homicides where no suspect had been charged or a suspect charged had been acquitted.[11] From 1970 to 1999 1,682 homicides remained unresolved.[12] In Northern Ireland the detection rate was lower, amidst a catalogue of murders which in the 1970s ran to around 200 a year, and in the early 1990s ran to 70 and above. Thus, over the course of the Troubles the aggregate number of undetected killings mounted up. This virtual monument of the dead demanded some sort of political response. However, and with respect to the strange perception of crime in Northern Ireland at times during the peace process these victims seemed destined for continuing neglect.[13] There were of course exceptions: those like Pat Finucane whose deaths have become political shibboleths overshadowing the path of peace negotiations. However the idea that 'something should be done' to investigate all these deaths developed during the peace process, fuelled by political representatives and families from both sides.[14] Thus, in 2005 the Historical Enquiry Team (HET) was established.

The HET is funded from the NIO until 2012, with a current budget of

£30 million per year. The Team is headed by retired Metropolitan Police Commander, David Cox. The HET aims to review 400 cases per year from 2006–2008 and 600 cases per year from 2009–2012. Not all cases will have the same attention, and in 'many, frankly, we will not have any evidential opportunities to pursue'.[15] Many cases will be in effect confirming responsibility.[16] Nevertheless, the task is formidable. Although estimates of unsolved terrorist murders hover around the 2,000 mark, the HET is tasked with reviewing all killings connected with the security situation from 1968–1998 and the full total here is a mammoth 3,268. It is no surprise that an Assistant Chief Constable (Alistair Finlay of Strathclyde) with specific responsibility for the HET was appointed because of the pressure of work.[17] The HET's case management is split between externally seconded officers (for example from the Garda and the Metropolitan Police) who deal with cases where, as the official account diplomatically puts it: 'independence is essential and where sections of the community or individuals are not yet comfortable working with the Police Service of Northern Ireland'.[18] The other cases are managed by the PSNI. (The PONI is effectively functioning as an adjunct to the HET, since it has examined on the basis of complaint a number of undetected homicides, including those of Eoin Morley, murdered in 1990; Sean Brown, murdered in 1997; the murder of Raymond McCord also in 1997 being a killing of great controversy because of the alleged role of UVF informants in the attack).

The HET is deeply political. Some expect it to function as a quasi-Truth Commission, and if this is the case it will certainly not replicate South Africa's model since that had 'Reconciliation' affixed to it. The HET has already been accused of being a tool to lay to rest murders by the security forces, since the involvement of state agencies in murders only adds accelerant to the combusting issue of state legitimacy in Northern Ireland. Critics of the republican movement hope it will uncover the last of the 'disappeared', those murdered by the IRA and INLA and buried in unmarked graves, and highlight the role played in murders by individuals who may be current members of Sinn Féin. Hugh Orde has repeatedly stated that the families of the bereaved remain the most important constituency for the HET, an attempt to anchor the HET's legitimacy away from the choppy waters of politics. However, this is difficult in a situation in which every politically motivated murder has been invested with layers of meaning over the decades. Perhaps the only satisfactory solution would be an international team of investigators on the model of the Independent Monitoring Commission. Alternatively and more cynically, historical murders may finally be laid to rest when in the years to come those parties involved in devolution in effect defuse the issue because it destabilises power sharing. Indeed, following the publication of the Police Ombudsman's inquiry into the murder of Raymond McCord by the Ulster Volunteer Force members who were police informants, Sinn Féin stated that the inquiry proved that the party's longstanding allegations about collusion between the British state and loyalist paramilitaries were accurate. At the same time Gerry Adams argued this meant it was more important to sign up to policing and work for reform from within. It is unlikely this would have been the reaction in previous decades.[19] Further, after the establishment of a power sharing government between the DUP and Sinn Fein, a mini crisis arose in October 2007 with the murder of Paul Quinn, allegedly by members of the PIRA as part of a punishment attack. The DUP used careful language arguing that if it could be shown that the PIRA was 'corporately involved' with the murder this would lead to the end of power sharing. Such delicate terminology and distinctions were not employed by the DUP in the period before power sharing.[20]

Extortion

Extortion is another symbolic crime. It is emblematic of the worst side of paramilitarism, the image of the group preying on its own community for money which may not even go to the organisation but is sidelined into private wealth. Extortion has been the subject of much debate following 1998 because it is also illustrative of the inability of the forces of law and order to control criminality and the role of paramilitaries in crime.

The primary problem in investigating extortion is simple: the crime is not reported. An in-depth study of the construction industry alone showed that 96.42 per cent of respondents who had been the subject of such demands had never reported them to the police.[21] The main reason cited for not reporting an extortion demand is simply that it is easier to pay. This begs the question of why it is easier, and thus subsidiary reasons are fear of damage to property, disruption to the business concerned (and in the case of building sites the incurring of penalty clauses due to the non completion of houses), down to fear of physical intimidation, which was certainly a factor but less than expected compared to damage to livelihood.[22] Even when an initial report to the police is made there is a large attrition rate, that is, only a small proportion of initial complaints eventually lead to prosecution/conviction.[23] The intimidation of potential witnesses has a long pedigree in Northern Ireland, but is rife in extortion cases. According to detectives the practice was 'endemic' throughout the 1990s, and the situation has not changed.[24] While extortion has increased since 1998, 65 per cent of extortion cases in 2003 could not be pursued due to the complainant requesting no police action, a figure which rose to 85 per cent by 2005.[25]

Thus alternative police tactics had to be developed. The framework for investigating extortion was developed in the early 1990s by the C1(3) of the RUC, the unit tasked with dealing with racketeering.[26] Information about these activities came from intelligence, victim reports and the identification of the problem by business associations. Problems in securing witness cooperation in the long term (i.e. to trial) led to undercover officers being placed in businesses following a report of extortion, who would then deal with the negotiations. Surveillance was also employed, including room, phone devices and body fits. The strategy, as one officer stated, was for the undercover officer to 'create the scenario' and dictate the pace of negotiations rather than the extortionist. This included the amounts to be paid, the timing of phone calls, the location of meetings and handovers of funds. Reaching the necessary evidential point (the delivery of threats, exchange of money) required management since in the initial stages requests for protection money would not be stated as such.[27] This process by which police dictate the development of the case remains the framework. Extortionists alter tactics, for example returning to face to face negotiations to avoid surveillance.[28] The police may in return employ stalling methods to provoke a clear threat in a recordable manner, or use evidenced money, such as a £5,000 payment to develop the negotiations and provide a convincing incentive for the extortionist(s) to continue. The varying dynamics in such investigations mean that although cases last on average 3–4 months, some are over within a week.[28]

Structural problems in investigating extortion

Police resources never match demand. And police organisations always demand more resources. However, within this general truism an increase in resources, or their targeting, can have an impact. Particularly during the recent reorganisation which created the PSNI, criminal investigation faced a squeeze in resources in terms of budgets and due to staff departure. The extortion unit was working with an overtime rather than a specific cash budget. The situation improved following the initial Patten-inspired staff exits and reforms, and the Organised Crime Task Force promoted inter-agency cooperation. However, the use of undercover officers and surveillance was not matched by a sufficient stock of evidenced money i.e. funds to be used as payments in extortion cases, and no funds were specifically earmarked for use in extortion cases.[30]

Following a trough, there was an increase in enforcement. In 2001 no one was sentenced to custody for extortion; nine individuals were in 2002.[31] Of those arrested under the Terrorism Act 2000, charges of blackmail rose to 17 in 2005 compared with 19 during the 2001–2004 period and charges of fund-raising under s15 stood at 7 in 2005 alone compared with 21 from 2001–2004. In 2005, 26 individuals were arrested and 24 prosecuted in the same year,[32] including figures from the UDA and UVF. Figures from the UVF were convicted in 2006 following police undercover operations. Having said this, although an increase in capacity would have an effect in allowing major paramilitary extorters to be tackled it could not meet 'demand'. The problem of underreporting is often cited as a block to the investigation of extortion but 'if builders cooperated in [reporting] cases we could have four a day.'[33] and then police could not cope with the caseload. The key would be targeting the prolific networks in paramilitary organisations.

Criminal investigations which are based on the testimony of witnesses remain subject to a clear constraint. If witnesses do cooperate there are a number of problems concerning their treatment, some of them similar to those on the mainland. Individuals at risk and thus placed in the Witness Protection Programme (WPP) lose their livelihood, homes, routines and regular income. In other cases it is not feasible for witnesses to relocate, for example those with small, locally based businesses such as taxi firms. The opportunity cost of cooperating with the police is thus significant. One witness threatened to expose police officers and operations unless he was awarded 'appropriate' compensation for the costs of his participation in the WPP. Whatever the realities – it is unlikely the complainant would possess such information – this complaint reflects the general cause for concern at the treatment of witnesses, particularly in cases involving organised crime.[34] The publicity given to such cases means there is a well-known disincentive to come forward.

The PSNI admit that extortion will not be tackled through police activity, a statement with which few would disagree, since policing alone rarely removes a criminal problem. Structural change is needed in both the public and private sector. In terms of public sector contracts, additional external control and surveillance has been applied. In practice, over the period of conflict the public sector has been effectively complicit in the development of the paramilitaries' operations. Funds have been disbursed with shaky mechanisms of accountability and surveillance. Indeed contracts were allegedly nodded through which had parts of their budgets set aside to cover extortion payments. On the advice of consultant Professor Ronald Goldstock, the NIO has introduced a pilot Independent Private Sector Inspector General (IPSIG) system for public contracts.[35] IPSIGs are in effect independent inspection organisations, usually private accounting firms, which 'have the expertise to evaluate the industry's racketeering susceptibility and … to help in the design of more effective laws and regulations',[36] but they also engage in enforcement in that they verify information provided by contractors, with sanctions including disqualification, civil or even criminal penalties for false reporting, such as concealing extortion payments in accounts.[37] This is apparently suited to public sector contracts and charities, based on the experience of New York state and other jurisdictions.

Similarly, the development of regimes of surveillance and reporting systems for the private sector has been suggested as important in the effort to limit extortion.[38] The surveillance does not refer to police surveillance, but rather the organisational function of gathering and reporting information and duties of reporting. This might be facilitated by instituting financial governance on the model of the mainland, 'trapping' businesses into a model of reporting and disclosure which might squeeze out major extortion demands if businesses are able to inform the extorters that all financial transactions of a certain type or over a certain limit have to be reported.

There are problems with this. This disclosure would, therefore, not cover small businesses or individuals who do not operate in a regulated sector with large transactions. Secondly, extortion payments can still be disguised, and the incentive is still with businessmen not to report, if they fear paramilitaries more than the authorities. This might be resolved by a Proceeds of Crime Act (POCA)-style reverse burden of proof whereby non-reporting would be a criminal offence. Whether this would be workable is problematic to say the least. In addition it subjects business to a potential legal penalty in addition to facing the extortion demand.

In effect, this would be a quasi-privatisation of the problem. This would be similar to the anti-money-laundering policies which have developed in the OECD since the 1990s. In the UK under the Proceeds of Crime Act 2002 financial institutions and individual professionals are under a duty to report suspicious transactions to relevant agencies (now the Serious and Organised Crime Agency). This is one part of a wider system of governance aimed to prevent financial crime by increased reporting, overseen by the Financial Services Authority. In other words the FSA-type model compels the private financial sector to 'police' itself and its clients. This is also problematic. However, these systemic suggestions illustrate the idea that regulation and surveillance for preventative purposes, known as 'new policing' is an important variable rather than traditional policing.[39] The idea of governing down crime, increasingly seen in the late modern state, will be addressed in Chapter 7, but the next section also addresses the balance between conventional policing and prevention in tackling serious crime.

Armed robbery

The detection of armed robbery by specialist police squads can have an impact on offending, particularly with regard to high-level armed robberies requiring organisation and planning and often committed by networks of individuals.[40] In Northern Ireland the police have focused on prolific groups, both ODC and those units in the UDA, UVF, PIRA and INLA which specialise in this, with some success (in cases using informant intelligence). However, this has involved disruption rather than prosecution. Clearance rates for armed robbery have historically been low, limiting its effect as a deterrent. Detection rates were at a low point around 2000.

Table 6.1: Clearance rates for armed robbery in Northern Ireland, 1995–2006

Year	%
1995	17.0
1996	19.0
1997	22.0
1998–1999	19.3
1999–2000	19.4
2000–2001	12.4
2001–2002	13.4
2002–2003	14.5
2003–2004	15.0
2004–2005	19.3
2005–2006	18.6

Source: NIO, *A Commentary on Northern Ireland Crime Statistics 1997* (Belfast: TSO, 1997), p. 18; PSNI, *Annual Report of the Chief Constable,* various years.

OCTF figures state that from the latter half of 2002 to the middle of 2004, 183 armed robberies were committed by organised groups. This figure includes paramilitary and non-paramilitary groups. However, if we examine paramilitaries alone, from 2002–2004 inclusive 20 paramilitaries were charged, and some of these were groups of individuals involved in one robbery. Therefore, a small number of paramilitaries are being charged with armed robbery, while official (OCTF) and external (IMC) reports argue that *all* major paramilitary groups are continuously involved in armed robbery.

Although the police have targeted prolific high-level armed robbers, serious armed robbery appears to have been reduced by situational crime prevention measures rather than police detection, although the police have played a role in this. This can be illustrated via an examination of the 'classic' armed robbery technique, cash-in-transit robbery. Under the aegis of the OCTF, a number of areas were examined in response to the

Table 6.2: Individual paramilitaries charged with armed robbery, 1999–2005

Year	Number
1999	28
2000	16
2001	3
2002	6
2003	5
2004	9
2005	3

Source: PSNI, *Number of persons charged with Terrorist and Serious Public Order Offences 1990/91–2005/06* (2005), www.psni.police.uk/persons_charged_fy-19.doc; National Statistics, 'Statistics relating to the security situation 1st April 2005–31st March 2006' *Statistical Report*, 6 (2006).

marked rise in cash-in-transit robbery. These included the transfer of banknotes to cash machines or ATMs (ATM robberies were a significant component of cash-in-transit robberies), the improvement of the quality of cash boxes and other security mechanisms such as moving beyond automatic dye marking of cash in the event of cash-box penetration (such marking can be neutralised), to better cash degradation systems and/or tracking systems such as smart water (marked with DNA). Since a large proportion of cash-in-transit robberies occur in specific locations the police provided situational crime prevention advice via the PSNI Architectural Liaison Officer, which led to the removal of bollards and the lowering of pavements to allow vans better access to more secure, less public locations while transferring money.[41]

In terms of preventative policing, the PSNI and security companies dealing with cash-in-transit robbery cooperated operationally along the lines of initiatives in the rest of the UK such as Operation Hawk and Hawk-Eye.[42] Operation Hawk, launched in 2000 and again in 2002, involved Greater Manchester Police (GMP) and the British Security Industry Association. During vulnerable periods such as Christmas, GMP, Merseyside, Lancashire, Cheshire and North Wales forces cooperated to monitor cross-boundary deliveries by overt and covert methods. Hawk-Eye involved Greater Manchester Police mounting overt CCTV surveillance on cash-in-transit delivery routes and destinations as a preventative measure and to record suspicious activity.[43] In Coleraine District Command Unit, for example, the PSNI has engaged in 'anti robbery patrolling of outlying areas which have previously been targeted; the shadowing of cash-in-transit deliveries by Technical Support Group personnel

and snap Vehicle Check Points on arterial routes ... to deter armed robbery teams from moving into the area'.[44]

These measures have reduced cash-in-transit robbery, although there
are fluctuations. Official sources, for example, the OCTF lauded a decline in cash-in-transit robberies as they fell to 46 in 2004 but in 2005
they rose again to 62. Further, in the first quarter of 2005, 20 cash-in-
transit robberies yielded over £1.5 million, a major proportion of all the
cash stolen by this method in the UK: the Northern Ireland figures for
just the first half of 2005 amounted to 10 per cent of the entire take for the
UK in 2005.[45] The OCTF states that Northern Ireland now ranks fifth in
the UK in terms of cash-in-transit robberies.[46] But in terms of population
size Northern Ireland remains disproportionate.

Table 6.3: Number of cash-in-transit robberies in Northern Ireland, 1998–2005

Year	Cash-in-transit robberies
1998[a]	12
1999[a]	15
2000[a]	33
2001[a]	120
2002[a]	113
2003[a]	68
2004	46
2005	62

[a] figures for Post Office and Securicor only

Source: OCTF, *Threat Assessment,* 2003, p. 21; OCTF, *Confronting the Threat,*
2005, fig. 2, p. 57.

The same is true of major robberies as a whole. Although the figures have
reduced, those in 2004 included the Northern Bank robbery. Thus there
is a split between the quantitative picture (the number of armed robberies
and serious armed robberies is declining) and a qualitative picture (the
number of serious armed robberies with a substantial take in money remains disproportionate). The decline might be also partly explained by
the fact that sufficient money has been taken to secure the retirement
funds of paramilitaries.

PSNI effectiveness in context

The police role in reducing crime is a complex one,[47] but there is evidence to show that although generally crime is 'sticky' the police can have an effect in certain areas, such as public order offences, serious offences and certain types of volume crime, either through poor performance or effective performance. Police performance was lacklustre in the 2000–2002 period, an important time frame within which paramilitary and organised crime groups expanded operations. Police detection rates fell markedly from 30 per cent in 1999/2000 to 20 per cent in 2000–2001, then rose again to 27 per cent by 2003–2004 and 30 per cent by 2005–2006.

Table 6.4: RUC/PSNI crime clearance rates (%), selected years

Year	1990	1992	1996	1997 -98	1998 -99	2001 -02	2002 -03	2003 -04	2004 -05	2005 -06
overall clear-up rates	38	34	34	31	27	20.1	23	27.4	28.2	30.6
murder[a]	28	51	63	61.7	43.6	59.2	66.7	80.8	79.4	192
drug trafficking[b]	x	92	97	93	92	78.6	69.8	77.5	83.5	86
armed robbery	20	17	19	22	17.6	13.4	14.5	15	19.3	18.6
offences against the state	84	80	81	78	73.9	33.6	33.4	41.6	45.9	50.3
arson	22	22	12	14	8.8	5.5	5.4	9.4	8.8	7.7
explosives	37	12	29	24	18.2	3.2	3.9	11.9	28.6	25
fraud/forgery	74	61	64	56	44.3	23.3	28.4	32.4	36	34.3

[a] 2005–2006 figure includes the Omagh bombing prosecution.
[b] figure for 1990 not available; figures for 1992, 1996 and 1997 cover total drugs offences.

Source: abstracted from NIO, *A Commentary on Northern Ireland Crime Statistics 1997* (Belfast: TSO, 1997), p. 18; National Statistics, *Recorded Crime in Northern Ireland 2002/03* (2003).

However as might be expected the effectiveness or otherwise of policing is not just down to simple rises in clear-up rates. Firstly, numerically by 2006 the police were clearing nearly twice as many crimes as in 1997. However, if statistical changes affected crime rates they also affected clear-up rates: since a proportion of the rise in crime was statistical, a proportion of the clear-up was also. The main effect here was in volume crime, but as an example of these problems with accuracy with regard to serious crime, the Omagh case raised controversy as the prosecution of one man, Sean Hoey is classed as a clear-up of the 29 murders caused by the explosion. Secondly, what counts as a clear-up can include witnesses withdrawing their complaint, informal resolution, and many other actions short of prosecution. The PSNI is altering its crime clearance counting to stress sanctioned clearances (i.e. the number of crimes which result in some kind of formal penalty) rather than all clearances (i.e. including those where the victim/witness withdraws the complaint).[48] However, despite all these caveats a trend to increased police effectiveness is evident.

Table 6.5: Numbers of crimes cleared in Northern Ireland, 2000–2006

Year	Number
2000–01	35,522
2001–02	28,142
2002–03	32,806
2003–04	35,093
2004–05	33,344
2005–06	37,664

Source: PSNI, *Annual Report of the Chief Constable*, various years.

Finally, overall detection rates are only crude approximations of the real picture of crime: they need to be separated geographically and qualitatively (for example, serious offences might be concentrated in certain urban zones), and another crucial variable is whether the main offenders or groups of offenders are being targeted, a point discussed below in terms of police effectiveness.

Thus, if overall clear-up rates may have a problematic relationship to crime control, the levels of recorded crime provide one alternative. There are still difficulties in that recorded crime does not catch the 'dark figure' of unreported crime. However, it does have a relationship in signifying trends and levels of overall crime, and certain offences can be accurately mapped, including those volume crimes such as car crime and burglary which are reported for insurance purposes and those serious crime such as murder/manslaughter and terrorist offences, which are generally accurately recorded.[48] In these terms, crime levels did reduce quite markedly after 2001 (see Table 4.2) although they were rising again by 2006. If we examine the core geographical area for crime, Belfast, responsible for around one-third of all recorded crime, a decline is evident, as illustrated in Table 6.6.

Table 6.6: Offences recorded, Belfast 2000–2006

	2001 –02	2002 –03	2003 –04	2004 –05	2005 –06
North Belfast	12,605	12,137	9,698	8,637	8,435
South Belfast	18,191	18,389	15,267	14,500	13,080
East Belfast	7,164	8,429	6,531	5,455	5,372
West Belfast	6,511	6,346	5,431	5,337	6,625
Totals	44,471	45,301	36,927	33,929	33,512

Source: abstracted from National Statistics, *Recorded Crime in Northern Ireland*, various years and National Statistics, *Recorded crime and clearances 1st April 2005–31st March 2006.*

What might explain the reduction in offences recorded? Targeted policing, involving concerted investigations and resources (here we are in the field of politics once more) can attain results, for example, serious charges being laid against the members of one group, or sustained charging of those investigated for serious offences. Examples might include the targeting of the North Belfast UDA leadership, the LVF in mid-Ulster and elsewhere. The number of persons charged with terrorist and serious public order offences rose from 273 in 2000–2001 to 359 in 2003–2004, with 164 identified loyalists charged in 2002, and 166 in 2003 (at the height of the loyalist feuding discussed in Chapter 3), dropping to 59 in 2004 and rising to 145 in 2005–2006,[50] which fits with the argument in chapter four of a 'screw tightening' towards loyalist paramilitaries to facilitate political transformation (and a variable largely ignored by loyalist groups themselves for predictable reasons). This raises the question of why it cannot be conducted all the time. In terms of serious offences the answer is limited resources. The evidential examination of one organised criminal group can take 12–18 months, involving (expensive) surveillance, forensic accounting and the cultivation of informants/witnesses. At one stage the PSNI organised crime unit was running 40 investigations concurrently.[51]

Short of a formal strategy to charge offenders, there are also disruptive operations, which may reduce crime but not show statistically. The targeted disruption of crime has been a controversial area, particularly regarding the role of Special Branch in Northern Ireland. There is a delicate balance between disruption which prevents individual offences (arrests, searches, seizures), disruption which undermines and incapacitates (through surveillance, repeated arrests, asset seizure) and disruption which is constricted and allows the individual or groups to persist in their activities, because it is part of an effective long-term management strategy. It is the latter for which Special Branch was criticised, since its sheltering of informants did not lead to any coherent end result.[52] The PSNI have engaged in such disruption of loyalists during the feud and of republicans in the south of Northern Ireland. The balance can be problematic: critics have argued that the influence of Special Branch in normal criminal investigation following their being brought into the mainstream Crime Department is leading to the use of disruption tactics, although such activities have also led to the charging of individuals for drugs and other serious offences.

In terms of volume crime, targeted policing is a prospect involving less expenditure in resources than the investigation of serious crimes/groups. DCUs have targeted prolific offenders, since for example, if burglars realise one DCU is an 'easier touch' they move there. Better fingerprint and forensic analysis has enabled the targeting of prolific offenders.[53] External reports mentioned previously had mentioned the need to improve forensic capability and procedures, although the fact that individual DCUs are reporting to the Policing Board and District Policing Partnerships constitutes a pressure with regard to their performance in controlling volume crime. As on the mainland, the police have undertaken 'hotspot' policing, for example the West Belfast Auto Crime team tackled joyriding. In Greater Belfast the removal of unlicensed vehicles apparently had a knock-on effect in reducing the number of burglaries and 'drive offs' from petrol stations.[54]

One manifestation of general enforcement can be seen in arrest figures (as well as search, seizures and other disruption). Arrests under PACE rose from 2002, and in 2006 were at their highest level in six years. Again, the figures show a slump in the 2001–2002 period, as demonstrated in Table 6.7.

Table 6.7: Arrests under PACE, 1998–2006

Year	Overall	Notifiable offences
1998–99	26,297	19,636
1999–2000	28,082	20,082
2000–01	25,330	18,890
2001–02	24,147	17,641
2002–03	25,613	18,557
2003–04	27,221	20,616
2004–05	27,748	20,556
2005–06	31,961	23,535

Source: PSNI, *Annual Report of the Chief Constable,* various years.

Thus it would be problematic to argue that the fall in crime in recent years has no connection to law enforcement activity, just as the slump in enforcement against both serious and volume crime which can be seen across the board in around 1999–2001 had an effect in facilitating the expansion of crime. However, the 'stickiness' of policing means other structural variables play a major role in crime reduction. For example, with regard to serious crime, the varying level of activity of paramilitary groups is a core variable, to which the police may be reactive. The UDA–LVF and UVF–LVF feuds were responsible for a large percentage of murders between 2000 and 2005.[55] In terms of volume crime, crime prevention has played a large role here, particularly with regard to the sharp reductions in burglary and car crime. The police play a role in providing advice here but one main variable is simply people who have been victimised sharing prevention information through family and personal networks. Other variables which affect crime involve the spread and depth of social controls.

Crime and social control

As mentioned, paramilitary controls have played a role in managing the drug trade down either through their opposition to it or 'licensing', and it appears that the republican movement has also played a cooperative role with the PSNI in crime prevention in West Belfast.[56] Restorative justice schemes in republican and loyalist areas play a role in crime prevention, with many schemes endorsed by paramilitary groups.

Other social controls in Northern Ireland have acted to dissuade large numbers of people from taking drugs, although this may change, as the example of Dublin demonstrates.[57] In other areas of social control there is little difference between Northern Ireland and the rest of the UK. For example, in terms of counterfeiting, official exhortations that it is not a victimless crime have not succeeded in preventing the purchase of such goods, and seizures will not control the production and sale of counterfeit goods because the technology has decentralised and deskilled. Other tactics might be required, such as improving counter-technology and civil lawsuits by manufacturers. With regard to the relationship between policing and social controls, the police have closed 60 brothels in South Belfast since September 2005, but prostitution is expanding, characterised by an 'entrepreneurial culture' at the top end of the market and catering to increased local demand.[58]

Conclusion

It is clear that if the police are stabilising crime, they (and law enforcement generally) operate within a political economy of crime composed of

structural factors such as economic change, the operation of crime prevention by the public and private sector, the depth of social controls, and
agent-centred variables such as the extent to which certain potential targets are seen as politically off limits, the power and scope of organised
crime groups, the spread of personal crime prevention and so forth. With
these caveats in mind this chapter has examined some specific areas of
criminal investigation. In terms of those areas, homicide investigation –
the subject of some critique in Northern Ireland across the spectrum – is
modelling the mainland, particularly the Metropolitan Police. Both current and previous homicide cases remain highly charged. Homicide investigation is in effect split across the PSNI, HET and even the PONI.
The HET is heavily burdened in terms of workload and politics. As on
the mainland, the HET's clear-up rates might be assisted by DNA and
other technology, depending on the survival and quality of forensic ex-
hibits. However, unlike the mainland the role of state informants in past
murders will raise the question of whether in many cases the state had
effectively quasi-nationalised murder. This is the case not only with regard to those informants in loyalist organisations, about which much ink
has been spilled, but also with regard to republican informants. The question of the political impact of such revelations rests on the development
of devolution over the longer term and the possibility that the main actors involved will themselves decide to 'move on' and manage the political controversy down. This appeared to be the case following the
Ombudsman's Report into the murder of Raymond McCord Jr by loyalist paramilitaries who were also Special Branch informants. The British
government and even Sinn Féin to an extent argued that policing had
moved on since these occurrences (although the report dealt with crimes
committed by UVF paramilitaries from the early 1990s to 2003).[59]

With regard to organised crime, the perceptions and panics about a
'mafia society' and a 'crime wave' in Northern Ireland following 1998
have been overplayed. As mentioned in previous chapters, law enforcement capacity has increased since 2000. The police are part of a system
which has the ability to police down organised crime, stabilising it to an
'acceptable' level. However, neither should the role of organised crime
be marginalised out of existence. In many areas Northern Ireland has an
organised crime problem out of proportion to its socio-economic profile
and population size. Nor, in terms of the paramilitary component, should
the focus on political normalisation obscure the problem that paramilitaries
will not dissolve overnight. The use of organised violence remains an
enduring and flexible form of social power.

With regard to volume crime, the poor police performance around the
1999–2001 period has been followed by targeted policing and the spread
of crime prevention. Crime did rise in Northern Ireland following 1998

but stabilised within a short period. Northern Ireland has not seen the sharp rise in crime that took place on the mainland followed by gradual stabilisation over a long period. However, as Northern Ireland develops economically and certain social patterns are evident (for example those centred on the night-time economy mentioned in Chapter 4), crime will rise.

These patterns have implications for strategy. Police investigation has to be the 'cutting edge' of law enforcement practice. However, the more the police and other agencies call for reporting, the more the police will be overwhelmed, unless the reporting leads to the charging of serious individuals responsible for a number of offences. If extortion and robbery require the targeted policing of the most prolific offenders, it is clear that as on the mainland other strategies are seen to be required to tackle organised crime: these are discussed in the next chapter. The OCTF's constant talk of the 'disruption' of criminal groups could not hide the fact in its own publications that these groups were reforming. Part of the problem is the exceedingly wide definition of organised crime employed in the UK, but it is also the case that criminal activity is network based, whether within paramilitary organisations, within the ODC 'community' or between paramilitaries and ODCs, and these networks can form relatively easily. Thus if the police have the role of targeting major groups, other strategies have been sought to tackle organised crime: prevention and regulation strategies and incapacitation strategies.

Many of the offences discussed above imply the need for 'multi-agency working', the mantra of the New Public Management state. This implies the regulatory state rather than the punitive state. That is, rather than relying on the national security or police-led law enforcement model of crime control, the state, via a range of public and quasi-public bodies, develops a system of reporting and surveillance, expands prevention and a wide range of methods of enforcement and penalty ranging from criminal to regulatory and administrative. This has not been applied in Northern Ireland to the extent that it has in the rest of the UK. Although a major amount of the economy is constituted by, or reliant on, or connected to, state spending, the regulatory state we associate with late modernity has not been instituted in the province. We should remember it is never fully instituted in any jurisdiction – mainland Britain has the Financial Services Authority (FSA) and a plethora of other regulatory agencies but a significant black economy, for example. However, there are many areas of Northern Ireland which are physically and organisationally under- or even unregulated. According to the state, charities, taxis, construction and the private security business are all in line to be subjected to regulation. These types of policy concerns are represented in the Organised Crime Task Force, whose main tasks are to promote cooperation within the public sector and between the public and private sector to combat crime. Thus the OCTF in a sense constitutes law enforcement functioning as a template for late modern governance.

Another major development in crime control has been incapacitation strategies, which have expanded on the UK mainland, particularly since 1997. These are strategies aimed at effectively immobilising offenders through restrictions on their liberty or behaviour. They can be applied without the need for a criminal conviction. For example an Anti Social Behaviour Order may be applied to an individual on evidence of a pattern of anti-social behaviour. Or they may be enabled as an alternative to custody, for example Drug Testing and Treatment Orders and Home Detention Curfews. Or they may be general controls which follow a specific conviction such as Sex Offender Protection Orders.[60] However the main device, and one presented as the 'magic bullet' for tackling organised crime, has been asset recovery. If paramilitaries cannot be convicted, or not convicted of serious offences, then the state incapacitates them through confiscation or taxation on the basis that their assets have been gained unlawfully. Thus the criminal law recedes as asset recovery – often on the basis of civil law – takes its place. This raises clear issues of effectiveness and civil liberties.

It is to these examples of late modern law enforcement, the Organised Crime Task Force and the Assets Recovery Agency, that the next chapter turns.

Notes

1   M. Levi and M. Maguire, 'Reducing and preventing organised crime: An evidence based critique', *Crime, Law and Social Change*, 41 (2004), 379–469.
2   M. Stone, *None Shall Divide Us* (London: John Blake, 2004).
3   J. Brown, *Into the Dark: 30 Years in the RUC* (Dublin: Gill and MacMillan, 2005), particularly Chapter 10 onwards.
4   M. Ingram and G. Harkin, *Stakeknife* (Dublin: O'Brien, 2004); J. Brown, *Into the Dark*; PONI, *Statement by the Police Ombudsman for Northern Ireland on her Investigation into the Circumstances Surrounding the Death of Raymond McCord Junior and Related Matters* (Belfast: PONI, 2007); for a critique see Northern Ireland Retired Police Officers Association, *Rebuttal of the Statement by the Police Ombudsman for Northern Ireland on her Investigation into the Circumstances Surrounding the Death of Raymond McCord Junior and Related Matters* (Belfast: NIRPOA, 2007).
5   *A Report on Murder Investigation in Northern Ireland* cited in PSNI, 'Report on Murder Investigation Procedures Presented to Policing Board', *Press Release* (13 June 2003).
6   The information above is drawn from an author interview with Chief Officer,

PSNI, Belfast, 26 January 2006.

7 PSNI, Report on Murder Investigation Procedures Presented to Policing Board, Press Release (13th June 2003), http://www.psni.police.uk/index/media_centre/press_releases/pg_press_releases_2003.

8 The information above is drawn from author interviews with Chief Officer, PSNI, Belfast, 24 February 2004 and 26 January 2006.

9 For example, the investigation of the murder of Brian McDonald in 2002 was the subject of a complaint to the PONI. The complaint was not upheld but a team started to review the investigation in 2006. Pre-1998 homicides are dealt with by the Historical Enquiries Team, mentioned in the next section.

10 M. Innes, *Investigating Murder: Detective work and the Police Response to Criminal Homicide* (Oxford: Clarendon, 2003); F. Brookman, *Understanding Homicide* (London: Sage, 2005).

11 D. Gaynor, *Getting away with Murder. The reinvestigation of Historic Undetected Homicide* (Centrex/Home Office, 2002), p. 1.

12 Abstracted by the author from Gaynor, *Getting Away with Murder,* Appendix 4, p. 41.

13 For a discussion of the 'framing' of victims around the time of the Belfast Agreement see M. Smyth, 'Lost lives: victims and the construction of "victimhood" in Northern Ireland', in M. Cox, A. Guelke and F. Stephen (eds), *A Farewell to Arms? Beyond the Good Friday Agreement* (Manchester: Manchester University Press, 2006), pp. 170–186.

14 One striking contemporary example of this being the campaign by Raymond McCord Sr over his son's death, allegedly at the hands of the UVF.

15 Chief Constable Hugh Orde, oral evidence to the Northern Ireland Affairs Committee, *BBC Parliament* (9 November 2005).

16 In August 2006 the HET informed the family of Henry Cunningham that the UVF was responsible for the teenager's murder in 1973, to which Henry's brother responded that the family had been fully aware of this.

17 *UTV News* (4 July 2006) http://u.tv/newsroom/indepth.

18 Historical Enquiries Team, *Policing the Past. Introducing the Work of the Historical Enquiries Team* (PSNI, n.d.).

19 'Adams urges SF support for the police', *BBC News Northern Ireland* (28 January 2007), http://news.bbc.co.uk/1/hi/northern_ireland/6306179.stm.

20 'Murdered man in IRA linked fights' *BBC News* (22 October 2007) http://news.bbc.co.uk/1/hi/northern_ireland/7056388.stm.

21 E. Adair, 'To pay or not to pay. The extent of paramilitary extortion within the construction industry', MSc dissertation, University of Leicester, 2005, p. 75.

22 Adair, 'To pay or not to pay', pp. 76–77.

23 '… the very name or even the impression that it is a paramilitary group can silence anyone that might otherwise have chosen to take a stance against them … we lose a lot of cases in terms of people not reporting them in the first place … We lose a lot of cases between reporting and appearance in court because the victim makes a choice of not choosing to go ahead with the prosecution or claiming that there has been no further contact from the

extortioner.' PSNI ACC White, quoted in Northern Ireland Affairs Committee, *The Financing of Terrorism in Northern Ireland*, Vol. 1, HC 978-1 (London: The Stationery Office, 2002), para. 50.

24   J. Moran, 'Paramilitaries, "ordinary decent criminals" and the development of organised crime in Northern Ireland following the Belfast Agreement', *International Journal of the Sociology of Law*, 32 (2004), 267.

25   See Organised Crime Task Force, *Threat Assessment. Serious and Organised Crime in Northern Ireland* (Belfast: OCTF, 2003), p. 15; Organised Crime Task Force, *Annual Report and Threat Assessment 2006* (Belfast: OCTF, 2006), p. 41.

26   K. Maguire, 'Policing the black economy: the role of C13 of the RUC in Northern Ireland', *Police Journal*, LXVI:2 (1993), 127–135; Author interview, Detective Constable, PSNI (formerly in CI3 and involved in investigating extortion in the 1990s), Belfast, 23 July 2003.

27   Author interview, Detective Constable, PSNI (formerly in CI3 and involved in investigating extortion in the 1990s), Belfast, 23 July 2003.

28   Author interviews, Detective Chief Inspector [a] and Detective Inspector [b], PSNI, Belfast, 24 February 2004.

29   Author interviews, Detective Chief Inspector [a] and Detective Inspector [b], PSNI, Belfast, 24 July 2003.

30   Author interviews, Detective Chief Inspector [a] and Detective Inspector [b], PSNI, Belfast, 24 July 2003.

31   House of Commons, Written Answers, 19 April 2006 *Hansard*, Col. 728W.

32   D. Lyness, 'Northern Ireland Statistics on the operation of the Terrorism Act 2000: Annual statistics 2005', *Research and Statistical Bulletin*, 4 (2006), 2–3; Organised Crime Task Force, *Annual Report and Threat Assessment 2006* (Belfast: OCTF, 2006), p. 41; 'Extortion helpline is launched', *BBC News*, 15 May 2006, http://news.bbc.co.uk/1/hi/northern_ireland/4771751.stm.

33   Author interviews, Detective Chief Inspector [a] and Detective Inspector [b], PSNI, Belfast, 24 July 2003

34   Moran, 'Paramilitaries, "ordinary decent criminals" and the development of organised crime in Northern Ireland', 267.

35   Organised Crime Task Force, *Annual Report and Threat Assessment 2006*, 2006), p. 19.

36   R. Goldstock, *Organised Crime in Northern Ireland. A report for the Secretary of State and Government Response*, (n.p., n.d.), p. 24.

37   Goldstock, *Organised Crime in Northern Ireland*, p. 24.

38   Author interview, member of the NIO dealing with financial matters, Stormont House annexe, 25 July 2003.

39   M. Levi, 'Evaluating the "new policing": attacking the money trail of organised crime', *Australian and New Zealand Journal of Criminology*, 30:1 (1997), 1–25.

40   R. Matthews, *Armed Robbery* (Devon: Willan, 2002); R. Matthews, 'Armed robbery: Two police responses', *Police Research Group Crime Detection and Prevention Series Paper*, 78 (1996); M. Gill, 'The craft of robbers of cash-in-transit vans: Crime facilitators and the entrepreneurial approach', *International Journal of the Sociology of Law*, 29 (2001), 277–291.

41   Author interviews, Northern Ireland Office official member of OCTF, Stormont House annexe, 25 February 2003; Detective Chief Superintendent,

PSNI and member of OCTF, Stormont House annexe, 25 July 2003.

42   Author interviews, Detective Chief Superintendent, PSNI and member of
     OCTF, Stormont House annexe, 25 July 2003; Northern Ireland Office offi-
     cial member of OCTF, Stormont House annexe, 25 February 2003.

43   British Security Industry Authority, *BSIA and Greater Manchester Police join
     together in Operation Hawk-Eye* (2002), www.bsia.co.uk/cgi-bin/WebObjects/
     BSIA.woa/wo/39.0.12.3.28.3; British Security Industry Authority, *BSIA teams
     up with North West police forces* (2003), www.bsia.co.uk/cgi-bin/WebObjects/
     BSIA.woa/wo/30.0.12.3.9.3.

44   Coleraine District Policing Partnership, *Report of the Coleraine District Policing
     Partnership Public Meeting* (23 June 2003), p. 22.

45   '£40,000 stolen in cash van raid', *BBC News Northern Ireland* (3 May 2005),
     http://news.bbc.co.uk/1/hi/northern_ireland/4510429.stm. A total of £15
     million was taken in 836 attacks. 'Rise in security van cash attacks', *BBC
     News* (18 April 2006) http://news.bbc.co.uk/1/hi/uk/4917344.stm.

46   Organised Crime Task Force, *Annual Report and Threat Assessment 2006*, p. 40.

47   See R. Mawby, *Policing the City* (England: Saxon House, 1979); Home Office,
     'Crime and Police Effectiveness', *Home Office Research Study*, 79, (London:
     HMSO, 1984); J. Brewer, A. Guelke, I Hume *et al.* (eds), *Police, Public Order
     and the State* (London: Macmillan, 1996); T. Coupe and M. Griffiths, 'Catch-
     ing offenders in the act', *International Journal of the Sociology of Law*, 28:2 (2000),
     163–176; B. Bowling, 'The rise and fall of New York murder: Zero tolerance
     or crack's decline?', *British Journal of Criminology*, 39:4 (1999), 531–554; N.
     Tilley and J. Burrows, 'An Overview of Attrition Patterns', *Home Office Online
     Report* 45/05 (2005); for the USA see: J. Skolnick, *Justice without Trial. Law
     Enforcement in a Democratic Society* (New York: John Wiley, 1967); J. Donohoe,
     'Did *Miranda* diminish police effectiveness? *Stanford Law Review*, 50, April
     (1998), 1147–1180; N. Dennis, G. Erdos and D. Robinson, *The Failure of
     Britain's Police. London and New York Compared* (Civitas, 2003).

48   Comment by Hugh Orde at the Policing Board meeting, Belfast, 5 October
     2006.

49   M. Maguire 'Crime statistics: The "data" explosion and it implications', in
     M. Maguire, M. Morgan and R. Reiner (eds), *The Oxford Handbook of Crimi-
     nology*, Oxford: Oxford University Press, 2002), pp. 322–376.

50   See National Statistics, *Statistics Relating to the Security Situation in Northern
     Ireland*, various years.

51   Author interviews, Detective Chief Inspector [a] and Detective Inspector [b],
     PSNI, Belfast, 24 July 2003; Detective Chief Inspector [a], PSNI, Belfast, 10
     November, 2005.

52   For a related critique with regard to the mainland, see C. Dunnighan and C.
     Norris, 'The detective, the snout, and the Audit Commission: The real costs
     in using informants', *Howard Journal of Criminal Justice*, 38:1 (1999), 67–86. A
     prime is example is the connections between police and the informants in-
     side the UVF outlined in PONI, *Statement by the Police Ombudsman for North-
     ern Ireland on her Investigation into the Circumstances Surrounding the Death of
     Raymond McCord Junior and related matters* (Belfast: PONI, 2007).

53   Author interview, Chief Officer, PSNI, Belfast, 26 January 2006.

54   House of Commons Written Answers, 27 April 2004, *Hansard* Col. 926W.
55   See the *British Irish Rights Watch* site at www.birw.org.
56   A. McIntyre, 'Catching the monkey', *The Blanket* (4 April 2006).
57   J. Connolly, *Drugs and Crime in Ireland. Overview 3* (Dublin: Health Research Board, 2006).
58   For a recent overview see the three-part series, 'Sex Crime Northern Ireland' broadcast on *UTV* in October 2006.
59   'Reaction to Ombudsman's Report', *BBC News Northern Ireland* (22 January 2007), http://news.bbc.co.uk/1/hi/northern_ireland/6286657.stm.
60   R. Matthews and J. Young (eds), *The New Politics of Crime and Punishment* (Devon: Willan, 2003).

7

Political policing?
The Organised Crime Task Force and
the Assets Recovery Agency

David Liddington (Con): Can the Minister give us an unqualified assurance that no political limits are being imposed on investigations by the Assets Recovery Agency?
Ian Pearson (Security Minister): Yes.[a]

Mr. Gray was a notorious figure in the UDA and in organised crime in Belfast. Many people will be surprised to see the low value of the money recovered in this case, but the reason is simple. While Mr. Gray led a flamboyant lifestyle, our investigations showed that, at the end, this was really all that was left.[b]

While directly attributable quantifiable effects are hard to demonstrate it is clear that financial investigation and asset recovery will show that crime will not pay.[c]

[a]   Oral Answers, House of Commons, (8 March 2005), *Hansard,* Cols. 10–11.
[b]   Alan McQuillan, head of the Assets Recovery Agency in Northern Ireland, quoted in S. Gordon, 'Exposed: Jim's Gray days', *Sunday Life* (21 January 2007).
[c]   Performance and Innovation Unit, *Recovering the Proceeds of Crime* (London: Cabinet Office, 2000), p. 16.

Introduction

The previous chapter argued that organised criminality could not be managed to an 'acceptable level' by the PSNI alone. The role of public and private sector governance in preventing and reducing crime has expanded in many late modern societies characterised by notions of risk and anxiety. Such societies, far from being overseen by the retreating or shrunken state, are actually governed by embedded and widening mechanisms of regulation and discipline. This state control is not as overt as in the 1970s but is in some senses more sophisticated and pervasive. Although state power has been evident in the province, a movement towards modernisation has been evident, one relevant to the structure of law enforcement. It is evident in two organisations discussed in this chapter, the Assets Recovery Agency (ARA) and the Organised Crime Task Force (OCTF). The operations of these agencies raise questions about the most appropriate organisational models for coordinating law enforcement responses, state power, the notion of political policing and last but not least the issue of effectiveness.

The new regulatory state

One aspect of the late modern state is the way in which its drive for modernisation has contradictory results. The 1980s and 1990s saw states in Western Europe and North America subject their public sectors to business-style reforms. These reforms aimed to produce decentralised, flexible, financially 'responsible' units across the public sector. If appropriate, functions were privatised to a greater or lesser extent. But both the implementation of the reforms themselves and their end result required more pervasive central control. In the UK even conservatives identified the ironic increase in central state control which had been a direct result of the Thatcher government's reform of the public sector.[1] Thus targets are set for the giant functions of education, health and social services. The organisations involved are surveilled and inspected. With regard to the semi-privatised sectors of the economy such as the utilities and transport, surveillance, reporting and regulation is undertaken. Regardless of the success or failure of such systems, this is the 'new regulatory state'.[2]

In terms of criminal justice, central control has been creeping across the plain for some time as these NPM reforms have been applied to the criminal justice system.

The judiciary are hedged by the extension of mandatory sentencing, and an elaborate inspection regime covers the major sectors of the criminal justice system, such as prisons and probation, framed by compulsory planning and an abacus of performance measurement.

In addition, a progressive centralisation of policing has taken place. The 1990s was a decade in which panic ceased to roll in successive waves across policy and media networks, and began to churn incessantly around vortices of drugs, money laundering and organised crime.[3] The panic was nevertheless connected, albeit often loosely, to empirical phenomena, and much attention was paid to developing the most appropriate organisation for combating organised crime. In the UK it is possible to detect a long-term move towards a more centralised law enforcement structure, although progress has been slow. It was not until the 1990s that the UK gained a National Crime Squad (or NCS, formed from the Regional Crime Squads) and a National Criminal Intelligence Service (NCIS). The third Labour government, elected in 2005 and obsessed with public sector organisation and reorganisation, drove the process forward by establishing the Serious and Organised Crime Agency (SOCA) in 2006, an organisation which replaced the NCS and NCIS and took on the investigation arm of Customs and Excise. Touted as 'the British FBI', SOCA initially had 4,200 staff and was tasked with tackling high-level organised crime, drug trafficking and fraud.[4] This development was accompanied by moves to merge the UK's 43 police services down to a dozen super forces, although the latter move met with some resistance. In 2003 the Assets Recovery Agency (ARA) was created. This process raised two issues: the first is that this progressive if uneven process of centralisation raised the spectre of direct political influence of policing priorities, since SOCA and the ARA report to British government ministers. Indeed in 2007 SOCA absorbed the ARA. Critics would argue policing has always functioned according to political priorities but the debate over the level of operational control, which has traditionally rested with the police, is a genuine one.[5] The issue of political influences on policing, and accountability is clearly implied by such changes and this is intensified in the Northern Ireland context, discussed below.

A further important issue, and one often overlooked, is simply whether this reorganisation works. Modern bureaucratic societies are characterised by the search for 'perfect' organisation, particularly one overarching organisation that will solve all previous 'problems' of coordination. Past experience shows that successive organisations are rarely dismantled and thus the governmental landscape becomes littered with bodies that in their time were hailed as the solution to various problems. This is particularly evident with regard to criminal justice (particularly in the USA, for example), and although SOCA has swallowed up a number of agencies in the UK the issue remains as to whether any new agency improves coordination.

Governing through crime and governmentality

In terms of criminal justice the movement can be taken further, via the idea of 'governing through crime'. As states undergo legitimacy crises, often based on public anxiety about crime and disorder, state power is extended.[6] One process via which increases in state power occur is that in which the state takes measures to combat 'exceptional' crime, but the list of exceptional crimes requiring such attention grows ever longer (in the UK in addition to terrorism it now encompasses, drugs, money laundering, violent and sexual offending and anti-social behaviour).[7] Thus have New Labour governments created over 1,000 new criminal and regulatory offences since 1997,[8] continuing a trend established under previous Conservative governments, particularly in the 1987–1997 period. The government has also established the Assets Recovery Agency, a body with powers to recover assets via the criminal or civil law. As a complement to the system of financial governance it seeks to deprive individuals of assets if it can demonstrate they have gained them through unlawful conduct. As befits the late modern state, if it cannot achieve this following an individual's criminal conviction, it will do so via civil law or a tax demand. Thus the state taxes the profits of crime and extends its regulatory reach. The ARA's power has been subject to a number of unsuccessful challenges under the Human Rights Act. The police's powers of seizure and recovery have also been expanded.

This can be reinforced by the movement to view more areas of social life as being relevant to crime,[9] a process which leads to the increasing surveillance of the private sector and social life. The UK financial sector is governed by the Financial Services Authority, which sets guidelines, monitors financial governance and institutes penalties for breaching rules. With regard to the coverage in this chapter, in the financial sector almost any form of financial provision is covered by anti-money- laundering and other strictures. In terms of the family and education, in late 2006 the government was suggesting (not for the first time) that children should be identified as 'at risk' of future criminality. Once in this category 'interventions' would ensure the individual was turned towards the path of social responsibility. This buttresses developing systems of surveillance on children who are seen as being at risk of either abuse or themselves becoming criminals.[10] There are systems of licensing and inspection for private security, an industry that has expanded markedly over the last decade. Increasingly the private sector is retaining data for is own fraud prevention purposes and for possible future access by law enforcement. Although this should not be overestimated, it represents 'governmentality', the extent to which an ever wider set of policy issues are evaluated in terms of their possible effects on generating or helping to reduce crime and the idea that a network of public and private agencies should take a role in this.[11]

Governing through crime in Northern Ireland

In Northern Ireland these processes are evident. The extension of state power by the 1970s as a result of the conflict has been noted. The peace process has not seen any real reduction, rather, modernisation. A comprehensive review of criminal justice was undertaken which predictably concluded that the system required modernisation in terms of human rights and efficiency: reform, an expansion of regulation and monitoring was proposed. Thus inspectorates of criminal justice have blossomed in the province, and as mentioned, New Public Management has been applied to the PSNI and is being targeted at prisons and probation.

However, the focus of this chapter is two organisations which are part of the new regulation of Northern Ireland from a criminal justice standpoint: the Organised Crime Task Force and the Assets Recovery Agency. Both represent the idea of governing through crime, and the ARA represents an important expression of state power. The OCTF's main role is to promote coordination within law enforcement. However, although the OCTF is not directly concerned with promoting regulation, via its deliberations on areas seen to be affected by organised crime (private security, intellectual property, taxis, direct and indirect tax, charities and so forth) it has also encouraged public and private cooperation on reform and regulation. The involvement of relevant departments of the Northern Ireland Office in the OCTF from 2005 in examining regulation is evidence of this. The Belfast office of the Assets Recovery Agency takes a direct enforcement role via substantial legal powers, and its actions raise questions of effectiveness (a different issue from state power) and issues of political policing. These new law enforcement bodies represent late modern governance and the extension of state power. Space precludes a full examination of the wider implications of the existence of these bodies: the focus here will be on role and effectiveness.

The Organised Crime Task Force

Northern Ireland was affected by the development of the ARA and had its own reorganisation in the form of the Organised Crime Task Force (OCTF), established by then Secretary of State Peter Mandelson in 2001. The OCTF predated 9/11 and was in part a response to the acceleration of crime as an issue following the peace process. As mentioned in previous chapters, the symbolic nature of crime was particularly powerful in Northern Ireland because of the paramilitary issue, particularly the idea that paramilitaries from both sides were benefiting from crime in the new political climate. Mandelson made a number of public comments about the need to tackle organised crime, and clearly linked the legitimacy of the peace to tackling what he termed the 'rump of paramilitarism': 'Our focus rightly has been on defeating terrorism, we must now reach further and grip the organised crime that terrorism has formed.'[12] However, the development raised issues of central (political) control as well as effectiveness.

The OCTF is not a police organisation with its own powers. As argued previously, this was a period in which the PSNI was at a low ebb and its performance was below par, but the establishment of another law enforcement agency was out of the question considering the turf wars this would have promoted, in addition to the constitutional issues. The OCTF aimed to solve the problems of strategy and coordination with regard to law enforcement, not replace it. At the time of its establishment it was composed of an overall committee chaired by the Northern Ireland Security Minister, subgroups which were organised on functional lines (Strategy, Legal, Analysis, Coordination, Publicity) and expert groups which concentrated on crime areas (Intellectual Property, Armed Robbery, Extortion, Fuel Oils, Drugs and so forth). The OCTF's main roles lay in developing strategy, information sharing and promoting coordination.[13]

However, a political element was evident: although the OCTF did not seek executive authority, the ministerial component still raised issues of control. The OCTF was an organisation that could be used to provide subtle pressure on law enforcement, particularly the police in terms of the issue of crime. Although attendance was voluntary the 'costs' of not attending were clear. If agencies did attend then collective priorities would be set and organisations were required to report back. Thus a subtle game was in operation; although the operational independence of the police remained sacrosanct, political priorities could influence policing priorities – the fact that a British government minister chaired the OCTF provided constitutional 'muscle' particularly since ministers would have to answer questions in parliament regarding the response to organised crime and this directly involved the police. Thus in one sense the OCTF was reflecting crime as a political issue, something that the Policing Board as the formal mechanism of accountability for the PSNI reinforced on a more direct level.

This set-up might have been expected to produce friction between the OCTF and the PSNI. In practice, tension did not develop between the OCTF and the PSNI. Early on, police officers were concerned that the OCTF was a political organisation and not happy with the level of 'spin' involved, but over time approval increased. One point might have been the fact that as events unfolded, the OCTF was no threat to the PSNI and the initial hype around the organisation died down, reducing ideas that the OCTF 'grabbed headlines'. As well as the PSNI, the OCTF worked with other agencies. Revenue and Customs (previously Excise) had its own national strategy and the OCTF attempted to tweak it to Northern Ireland conditions. For example with regard to drugs, cannabis is the main drug problem in Northern Ireland (see Chapter 4), but it is not seen as the main threat on the mainland (where the focus is on crack cocaine and amphetamines). In some areas the strategies gelled: in terms of oils fraud Northern Ireland was out of proportion to the rest of the UK and thus a priority target in the Revenue's national strategy.

In addition to cross-organisation communication, the OCTF also facilitated cooperation within the prosecution system, in areas such as charge laying. Police officers (as in all jurisdictions) see prosecutors as displaying a tendency to negotiate following initial charge laying, or as viewing some offences (in Northern Ireland, counterfeiting for example) as less serious. Such criticisms were also evident from the private sector in regard to offences relevant to it (counterfeiting again, bank robbery). The OCTF has assisted an integrated approach via more communication and cooperation between the PSNI and the DPP in terms of PSNI laying and sustaining charges and DPP/PPP prosecution policy.[14]

In terms of prevention, subgroups adopted the models of situational crime prevention which had already been influential within the UK Home Office, whereby offences are seen as a 'script' and broken down into individual components which make the crime possible: 'One must examine what the offenders or sets of offenders require to be able to do in order to accomplish different sorts of crime and volumes of crime efficiently.'[15] In terms of cash-in-transit robbery this involved overt patrolling by the PSNI, altering access in the public spaces where most attacks took place, changing designs on security boxes, the use of professional witnesses and so forth (see Chapter 6). In terms of financial crime this involved a focus on changing regulation and licensing. NIO departments joined the OCTF in 2005 and by 2006 were examining licensing regimes in various areas,[16] replicating the mainland.[17]

The subgroups also deal with technique. The OCTF could be an efficient manner of securing cooperation which was going to be requested in any case; or developing personal links; or strategy, or in effect pooling training. However, the effectiveness of OCTF subgroups is dependent upon the individuals in attendance; they require relevant authority and expertise[18] and in some a 'cascade effect' (the process by which in terms of increasing or decreasing seniority attendees come to match rank) led to some groups losing gravitas. Some expert groups were proactive; others less so, and the Northern Bank robbery was the catalyst for a general review of the OCTF.[19]

One of the main issues with regard to the OCTF is that of analysis. There has not been a shortage of intelligence on crime in Northern Ireland; the key has been putting it into a useable framework.[20] Special Branch intelligence and criminal investigation intelligence are two different products, and this had been particularly the case in Northern Ireland. The OCTF acted as one framework for driving a more integrated analysis of organised crime groups and criminality, although the main factor became the establishment of the Crime Department in the PSNI in 2003 and the implementation of the National Intelligence Model in the PSNI. The analysis in OCTF reports has oscillated. In some respects the earlier reports were tighter, based on crime groups; later this was changed to crime areas. The argument was that a focus on groups was not effective since they dissolved and reformed flexibly[21] but one problem with identifying crime areas as threats is that the list grows longer each year, and requires some sort of weighting. The focus switched back to groups again, as the strategy group 'is moving away from targeting commodity types such as oils fraud or armed robbery to identifying and targeting the main criminal gangs who move between commodity types'.[22] In fact a focus on either groups or crime areas has methodological difficulties, even when tying them together through network analysis.[23] The qualitative analysis of the OCTF does not (in open source terms) identify the major areas or groups in terms of impact, although there were also issues of rigour in the closed product. Following reorganisation the OCTF has now slimmed its structure to focus on fewer main areas: revenue, drugs, armed robbery and criminal finance. Although two of these are wide categories, there is a core list of groups involved in these activities who will be targeted.

Finally, cooperation with the Republic, historically a sensitive issue, has been subject to OCTF ministrations. The wider post-Belfast Agreement political context has assisted cooperation and the stabilisation of relations between the Gardai and PSNI, as did individual disasters such as the bomb exploded by the Real IRA at Omagh in 1998, and under the OCTF cooperation has become more formalised,[24] via attempts to develop formal policy networks linking tax and police officials. Following cross-border seminars, ten investigative operations were launched.[25] However the main variable here remains relations 'on the ground', particularly in border areas; these were the historical basis of cooperation since formal channels could seize up following disapproval of either government's actions by the other.

Since its inception, the OCTF's four main objectives have been:

1. To confront the activities of organised crime networks in Northern Ireland, concentrating on serious illegal activities and the major criminal networks, 2. To

develop cooperation between law enforcement and other operational agencies in the planning and conducting of operations, 3. To develop intelligence gathering capabilities against organised crime networks and improve understanding of the activities of those networks, 4. To develop cross-community support and work, where appropriate with the private and public sector.[26]

The first objective is undertaken in practice by the PSNI and Revenue and Customs. The OCTF's effectiveness is most evident in terms of the second objective: its role in improving communications and long-term strategic thinking. This is important, since, while policing is the cutting edge of law enforcement by nature it 'lacks the crucial dimension of a focus on longer term outcomes and on the structures and conditions which facilitate organised criminal enterprises'.[27] Police analysis was improving due to the NIM, but the OCTF facilitated its development before this, and stressed the strategic aspect. In addition, networks in subgroups and expert groups have reduced the 'transaction costs' involved in expanding communications within traditional law enforcement (PSNI, DPP) and between law enforcement and the private sector. The development should not be overstated: the police and Customs had a long tradition of joint working in the areas of drugs and oils fraud. Finally, the frameworks of the OCTF have facilitated crime prevention in areas such as oils fraud, armed robbery (and have functioned as an arena for private sector complaints about law enforcement (in)activity). As befits a virtual organisation the OCTF and its groups are only as effective as its 'software' (in this case the Minister and the members). Ministerial commitment has varied, and as mentioned, the organisation also lost momentum as expert groups varied in energy and quality.

Comparison with the mainland is illuminating. The OCTF stands as a stark contrast to the Serious and Organised Crime Agency, which represents the alternative route to solving problems of coordination, that is, to establish a new agency. SOCA incorporates the National Crime Squad, The National Criminal Intelligence Service, the National Investigation Service of what was then Customs and Excise, part of the Home Office Immigration and Nationality Directorate and part of the Inland Revenue. This mainland behemoth was seeking an expanded budget and personnel after being in operation less than a year. SOCA had large start-up costs even before operations were conducted, and for the financial year 2006–2007 its funding was estimated at £457 million.[28] Further, SOCA was already being criticised by some of its own officers for a lack of coordination and proactivity.[29] The resources needed to fill the maw of this organisation will in all likelihood continue to grow, particularly as it swallowed up the ARA in 2007. The OCTF is a type of flattened organisation which claims limited resources in terms of set-up or dissolution and operation. The OCTF on average costs around £330,000 per year.[30] The costs are not exactly comparable, since the cost of the work prioritised by the OCTF which is then undertaken by the relevant organisations has to be factored in.[31] However, the total is still substantially less, as would have been the case for an equivalent of the OCTF established on the mainland.

Financial investigation and the Assets Recovery Agency: the magic bullet for organised crime?

The financial operations of organised crime and paramilitary groups have long been seen as a vulnerable point for criminal investigation, but this idea has grown in influence since the early 1980s. A national and transnational policy focus on the financial aspect of criminal offences became evident with regard to drug trafficking in the 1970s and money laundering from the 1980s. The United States drove forward the development of an international regime from the 1970s, and this accelerated in the following decade with the 'war on drugs' declared by then US President Ronald Reagan. The international regime comprises, partly, United Nations, OECD and EU soft and hard law and the regulatory surveillance of the Financial Action Task Force (FATF), and is concerned with identifying suspicious transactions and verifying customer identity (as a preventative tool but also to provide information for investigation) and standardising the criminalisation of money laundering across jurisdictions. If these two processes were part of a system of prevention and for providing intelligence for possible investigation, asset recovery completed the financial circle to an extent. That is, it involves mechanisms to seize (permanently if possible) the assets of those formally designated as having the proceeds of criminal activity or even a 'criminal lifestyle'. Asset recovery is less generalised internationally but the US has had a role in policy transfer, influencing countries such as the UK, Australia and Canada to institute such powers. Following 9/11 a media and policy panic over terrorist financing led to further measures being adopted in many countries.[32] Nevertheless, developments in individual jurisdictions not unnaturally played a key role. In the 1990s in the Republic of Ireland the murder of Garda Jerry McCabe by a Provisional IRA unit during a robbery and the murder of investigative journalist Veronica Guerin by drug traffickers are said to have played a major role in the development of Irish financial legislation tackling organised crime/paramilitary structures and the establishment of the Criminal Assets Bureau (CAB). In the UK, following convictions arising from the police's Operation Julie, a court ruling that the Crown had no right to the assets of a convicted trafficker led to a post mortem in the form of the Hodgson Report, and 'one of the specific points it raised concerned the seizure of assets of drug dealers'.[33] The Drug Trafficking Offences Act (1986) was one result, and problems with this led to the Drug Trafficking Act (1994) and the Proceeds of Crime Act (1995), a not exhaustive list which reflected concerns over the non-use of these powers.

Investigation and recovery in Northern Ireland

In Northern Ireland the conflict had seen the wider and more effective use of financial investigation. A wide range of paramilitary fundraising activity was evident by the 1980s and the republican movement was already gaining a substantial part of its revenues from video piracy in the early 1990s.[34] The RUC had established an anti-racketeering squad in 1982 which included a Tax Exemption Unit and a Counterfeit Products Unit to tackle black markets, extortion and related activities. The scope of normal criminal investigation powers were later extended by the Northern Ireland (Emergency Provisions) Act 1987 which granted special finance powers to police investigators, including a licensing system to prevent, for example, the provision of private security services by paramilitaries to building firms.[35] The idea that a wider financial and regulatory scope could buttress policing was formalised by the establishment of the Terrorist Finance Unit (TFU) in the NIO in the late 1990s. Initially the TFU was to drive forward the practice of financial investigation and 'examine whether or not the security forces required extra powers to investigate racketeers and secure prosecutions against them. The recommendations of this study were put into effect in the Prevention of Terrorism (Temporary Provisions) Act 1989',[36] including powers for the forfeiture of assets following conviction. In bureaucratic terms the NIO recognised police primacy but also the lack of specific financial expertise in the RUC. Thus the TFU seconded personnel from Customs, Inland Revenue and accountancy and the legislative change already mentioned enabled them to be appointed Authorised Investigators with the power to issue production orders, which required the presentation of financial documents without 'proof of a specific offence'.[37] The TFU had a number of interrelated functions. Firstly, in terms of disruption, visits and the use of production orders had the effect of undermining 'easy money' practices such as cash payments and lax accounting regimes, particularly in the entertainments sector. Open source material such as publicly advertised entertainment events could lead to an examination of accounts which might reveal weak or absent accounting for payments from bar takings, music nights and so forth.[38] Indeed, 'The RUC's Anti-Racketeering Squad forced the closure of 54 republican drinking clubs by 1992 merely by inspecting the audited accounts.'[39] Secondly, as a result of open source and Special Branch intelligence gathering, the TFU assembled packages which either guided a criminal investigation or could be used to change regulatory policy. For example, the Registration of Clubs (Northern Ireland) Order 1996 was one of a number of licensing measures which aimed to squeeze out particular financial practices which were used by paramilitaries to gain funds. Overall the aim was to restrict financing from a cash based system to a more regulated and theoretically more accountable system. Paramilitaries' 'access to funds had been diminished' by TFU activity, but not all areas had been successfully restricted,[40] and the enthusiasm and policy fervour for financial investigation died down in the mid-1990s. The TFU was merged into the RUC.[41]

One issue had been the balance between disruption and prosecution, but cynics might argue that financial investigation was out of sync with the need to draw republicans particularly into the peace process following 1994. This is not the first time that law enforcement priorities have coincided with wider political priorities or strategy (see Chapters 2 and 3). Overall the financial approach suffered not only from a lack of political support but also from a lack of state legal power behind it: investigation and disruption only went so far, according to the critics. This was not entirely the case since the 1989 Prevention of Terrorism (Temporary Provisions) Act provided powers of forfeiture on conviction but these had not been used. However, even as the TFU was being sidelined, a number of wider developments on the mainland returned financial investigation to the foreground, and fuelled the later development of state power in the areas of asset seizure and recovery, which has been evident in Northern Ireland.

The new structure of financial governance and investigation

One factor influencing the UK was the Criminal Assets Bureau (CAB) in the Republic of Ireland, which began to receive attention as an effective example of tackling drugs related organised crime and republican paramilitary organisations. There, the Proceeds of Crime Act (POCA) 1996 and the Criminal Assets Bureau Act 1996 created a structure by which a specific organisation had powers of financial investigation. Further, there were a range of financial measures that could be taken against those deemed to have gained their funds through criminal activity. Once the CAB has prima facie evidence of unexplained wealth the burden of proof shifts to the defendant to explain it has not been gained from unlawful activity. Under the POCA an order can be obtained initially to prevent disposal of the assets, following which an order may be given to freeze them. If a confiscation order is subsequently issued by the High Court, after a period (or sooner if the parties agree) the assets can be sold and the funds are transferred to the Ministry of Finance. Alternatively a tax demand can be served if the property can be shown to have been gained without tax payments.[42] In 2004 the Irish state netted 6.75 million euros from confiscation and 16 million in unpaid tax.[43] The fact that these are civil procedures to a lower burden of proof clearly raises questions of state power and accountability but following the high profile murders of McCabe and Guerin and concerns about organised crime, the political context was ripe for the introduction of special powers. Omagh would later see a repeat of this process with regard to anti-terrorism legislation.

The experience of the Republic connected with the ongoing New Public Management of criminal justice in the UK. In 2000 the Cabinet Office Performance and Innovation Unit (PIU) produced a report arguing asset recovery had not been utilised effectively in the past and was not cost effective. A new strategy, according to the Home Office would be: '[l]ed by intelligence ... gathered in the course of financial investigations and through suspicious transaction' reporting.[44] The PIU report predictably gained added impetus following 9/11, and resulted in specialist legislation, the Proceeds of Crime Act (POCA) 2002 which created a specific organisation, the Assets Recovery Agency (ARA).

The POCA is important for a number of reasons. First, it aims to increase the surveillance carried out by the financial sector to prevent the disguising of criminal funds and increase the supply of intelligence on suspicious transactions. The 'regulated financial sector' covered by POCA began as traditional financial institutions but has spread to estate agents, dealers in high value goods and casinos. 'Sections 330, 331 and 332 impose a duty to report suspicion [of money laundering] upon anyone in the regulated sector' and nominated officers outside the regulated sector; and sections 333 and 342 create criminal offences for tipping off those subject to a money laundering investigation or prejudicing an investigation. In addition Money Laundering Regulations impose duties for surveillance and Know Your Customer procedures.[45]

Secondly, POCA introduces legislative powers to remove assets from the control of those deemed to have gained them unlawfully. Prior to POCA, legislation on the mainland and Northern Ireland had progressively expanded asset seizure and recovery. Laws had permitted the prosecutor to recover the means used to commit an offence (forfeiture). Later, they covered the confiscation of the assets of those convicted of certain offences, such as drug traffickers whose assets were classed as the proceeds of crime. This spread to other relevant offences, and the test was altered to the civil standard of proof. POCA now enables the recovery of the proceeds of criminal activity following any conviction, if the authorities can demonstrate that a benefit has been derived from a specific criminal activity relevant to the conviction *or* from general criminal conduct.[46]

However, there are two other methods which can be employed, without the requirement of a conviction. Through an application to the High Court the state can employ the civil law, i.e. on the balance of probabilities to initially restrain (for example through injunction) assets it claims have been gained through criminal conduct. Following this, an investigation of the provenance of the individual's assets is conducted, and the state may then apply for a confiscation order to permanently deprive the individual of his/her assets. Finally, the normal tax powers may be used to tax criminally acquired assets. It is these methods which the ARA concentrates on in Northern Ireland.

The state has assumed the power to strip an individual of his/her assets on a civil standard of proof on the basis of a general assertion regarding criminal conduct and via a process in which the burden of proof is partially reversed, with the individual having to show his/her assets were gained lawfully. An appeal under the Human Rights Act argued that these procedures effectively constituted a criminal penalty and should be on the basis of a criminal standard of proof. Interestingly, one of the reasons stated by the Northern Ireland Court of Appeal in its dismissal of the challenge was: 'If recovery proceedings could only be taken on proof beyond reasonable doubt that the person from whom recovery was sought had benefited from the crime, the efficacy of the system would be substantially compromised.' Thus it appears that the need to deprive criminals of assets by what appears to be effectively a penalty is in the end judged on grounds of efficiency.[47]

However the main focus of the rest of this chapter, following on from the previous chapter on policing, is simply whether the strategy works. The justification for the strategy is that, firstly, the current surveillance and reporting systems make it more difficult for criminals to hide their assets and, secondly, the asset recovery procedures deprive them of past profits, destroying their criminal lifestyle and sending out a signal *pour encourager les autres*. This chapter will concentrate on the latter, since in public statements and comments to the author a number of individuals argued that the ARA should be given two years to show its worth and that it in effect would be the 'magic bullet' which would hobble paramilitary/organised crime.[48]

Financial reporting

With regard to the duty to report suspicious transactions, this is part of a new governance regime aimed at managing down crime. In another sense it represents the culmination of a process commenced in the 1980s by the TFU, in which better financial surveillance would in theory squeeze out financial transactions by paramilitaries in particular. However, this new regime mandates reporting by the private sector itself, with the burden on it for failures. As mentioned, the procedures centre on surveillance of customers (Know Your Customer procedures involving requesting identity documents and confirmation of the source of funds to be deposited/transferred) and Suspicious Activity Reports (SARS) which should be filed by those in the regulated sector with regard to actions which they suspect involve the laundering of criminal proceeds. As is often the case with such systems, the publicity given to initial cases sends out a signal. In 2003 the Northern Bank was fined £1.25 million by the Financial Services Authority (FSA) for not making proper checks on its customers and not taking prompt action to remedy this.[49] Northern Ireland contributed 6,000 out of the 200,000 SARS filed in 2005, and the state clearly wishes reporting to increase. The OCTF called for more reporting from the private sector.[50]

However, the issue is not necessarily number but quality. The PSNI had already seen an increase in SARS, although as on the mainland there was the problem of defensive reporting in order to guarantee that prosecution will not result, particularly as designated individual persons, Money Laundering Reporting Officers are legally liable for not reporting suspicious transactions. With regard to banks, an initial defensiveness has given way to an increased number of quality reports which provide the police with worthwhile intelligence on which to conduct investigations.[51] However a large increase in such reports would not automatically lead to more investigations. As on the mainland, SARS themselves only give rise to a small number of investigations in relation to the proportions received, and a large level of reporting simply overshoots the capacity of the system to handle them. Even in the Republic, classed as a success, a major task is the sifting of the mass of information which is constantly reported to the Bureau.[52]

If SARS are serving a function it may be through developing governance generally with regard to middle and lower ranking offenders (e.g. professional and other individuals seeking to convert frauds and so forth) rather than leading to criminal investigations against high profile Level 3 targets (serious criminals who operate across borders)

Asset recovery

The Belfast office of the ARA is the most active in the UK. The Belfast office deals mainly with civil cases, criminal confiscation being handled by the PSNI. As a result of the ARA's actions (freezing orders, interim receiving orders, settlement, tax) in the 2005/2006 period, the total amount of money in the UK under some form of criminal or civil restraint stood at £85.7 million. The total money involved in civil disruption stood at £47.4 million, £15.9 million of which came from Northern Ireland.[53] Moving to assets actually recovered after criminal or civil action has finished, Northern Ireland is still far ahead of England and Wales.

Table 7.1: Assets recovered in England and Wales and Northern Ireland, 2004–2006

Year	Total assets recovered £m	England and Wales £m	Northern Ireland £m	England and Wales assets recovered per 1000 of population £	Northern Ireland assets recovered per 1000 of population £
2004–05	4.3	3.9	0.4	74.1	265.03
2005–06	4.1	3.3	0.8	63.1	450.54

Source: Written answers, House of Lords, 4 July 2006, *Hansard*, Col. WA30

Thus, with around 15 per cent of the organisation's total budget,[54] the ARA's Northern Ireland office has been responsible for around 20 per cent of all assets under restraint in the UK, approximately 30 per cent of all assets under civil restraint, and for between 9–20 per cent of all assets recovered in the UK.

Two questions arise from this hyperactivity: has the seizing of assets significantly curtailed paramilitary activity? Secondly, have the actions which have taken place been affected by 'political policing', particularly since the ARA is a non-departmental government body reporting to a Government Minister, the Home Secretary?

This latter critique was trumpeted by the DUP. Following a parliamentary question from Nigel Dodds, then Security Minister Ian Pearson replied: 'The Assets Recovery Agency is not a prosecuting authority and does not hold information on individual affiliation. However of cases perceived to be from the loyalist community, there are currently assets to the value of £350,000 under interim receiving orders, and £1.25 million has been agreed for recovery. Of cases perceived to be from the republican community, assets to the value of £173,332 have been frozen and £225,000 has been agreed for recovery.'[55] Thus for every £1 under restraint by the ARA which is associated with republican paramilitaries, £4 associated with loyalist paramilitaries has been under restraint.

Any accusation of partiality must be qualified. The ARA is not a prosecuting agency; it receives referrals from the PSNI or Revenue and Customs and its caseload is large scale or complex cases. The ARA can only deal with those cases which are referred to it, and we do not have detail on those cases which are not proceeded with (a significant number) each year. Further, again according to Ian Pearson, some cases take a long time,[56] and this might be connected to the issue of how well the assets are hidden. Indeed, according to the Northern Ireland Affairs Committee, 'The disparity in referrals may reflect the greater sophistication of republican organisations.'[57] It seems loyalists were the more available targets (although this then tends to undermine the theory that the ARA is a magic bullet).

Judgements of partiality can only be made if one ascertains which paramilitary 'community' has the largest assets,[58] and overall republican groups do have a greater financial capacity than loyalist groups. Capacity is not the same as use, but it is at least a reasonable guide as to how much money is flowing around an organisation. According to the PSNI, republican organisations as a whole had an estimated fundraising capacity of between £10.5 and £13.5 million per annum. Loyalist groups had an estimated fundraising capacity of between £4 million and £4.5 million per annum.[59] Further, the PIRA takes the largest amount of money as a single organisation (although according to Secretary of State for Northern Ireland Peter Hain the PIRA has transformed from taking and spending millions per year in 2002 to a desistance from organised criminality). Finally, these figures are also representative of the historical accumulation of assets. Thus, remembering that the ARA has wide and intrusive powers to seize assets gained by general criminal conduct, there would be scope for wide-ranging restraint of republican movement assets in the first instance. The case of Thomas 'Slab' Murphy mentioned in Chapter 2 would be an example of this. Security Minister Pearson argued that he would expect cases to even out in the long run. This is a misreading of the purpose of the ARA since the point of the organisation is surely to tackle those groups with the most illegal assets, not to engage in 'birth certificate counting', to use one police officer's phrase i.e. evening-out between Catholic republican and Protestant loyalist paramilitaries.[60]

In order to refute claims that it is partial the ARA relies on a YouGov poll which states that 71 per cent of people do not believe it is treating the communities differently (although interestingly the number of people who believe loyalists are being focused on increased from 9 per cent in 2005 to 11 per cent in 2006).[61] Following the debate in parliament and elsewhere, in 2005 the ARA did focus on smuggling in South Armagh, although the individuals concerned have not been labelled as republicans (criminals subject to asset restraint are often publicly identified as loyalists by the ARA). In 2005–2006 over £5 million of assets belonging to alleged fuel smugglers in South Armagh was frozen and placed under investigation. However, those labelled as having links with Loyalist paramilitaries continued to be targeted, with £9 million of their assets being subject to investigation in 2005–2006.[62]

On the available public data (and one would think the relevant agencies would place accurate and representative information in the public domain) there appears to be evidence of partiality in the operations of asset recovery. What might lie behind this? A prosaic reason for the ARA targeting loyalists rests on the pressure under New Public Management to meet targets. The ARA's business plan sets a series of performance indicators of which the most important are, of course, amounts of assets seized and subsequently recovered. Apparently Loyalist assets were more clearly visible over the investigative parapet. This led to the ARA not only targeting living loyalists but deceased ones. When Stephen Warnock of the LVF was shot dead in his car, £40,000 was found in the vehicle. This was recovered by the ARA, while £200,000 from the estate of UDA figure Jim Gray was frozen, as was £1.2 million from the estate of Red Hand Commando leader Jim Johnston. As one observer puts it: 'it is difficult for dead people to give any explanation of the origins of their assets and their relatives may be ignorant of the minutiae of their origins'.[63]

However, another question is extant: has the ARA been used as a tool for manoeuvring paramilitary groups towards the negotiating table and undermining those who have not 'signed up' to the peace process, or are lacklustre in their commitment? It appears that the organisation, or those bodies which refer cases to it, did not target those throbbing targets of republican or loyalist paramilitarism whose departure would destabilise the ongoing institutionalisation and demilitarisation of paramilitary groups and in practical terms, affect the prospects for devolution in 2006/2007. The ARA has targeted a number of individuals connected to the LVF and smugglers in South Armagh. Thomas 'Slab' Murphy has been targeted: the man alleged to be one of the PIRA's most prodigious fundraisers has been the subject of substantial investigation and his financial assets have been frozen. But this is in fact acceptable to the republican movement leadership since his opposition to the peace process became stronger over time and he presented a threat to the PIRA if he switched allegiance and gave his financial backing to republican dissidents. This can be compared to remarks made in the Policing Board meeting of 5 October 2006, when Hugh Orde stated that the assets of the republican movement were effectively clean, a remarkable assertion considering the self-stated remit of the ARA is that it can touch the assets in space and time that other organisations cannot. One observer argues that this was a clear political message to Sinn Féin.[64] Whatever the case, as of 2007 the information regarding the merger of the ARA with SOCA seems unclear at best as to the number of staff, although the resourcing is apparently to remain constant. In one answer it appeared that the staff of the Belfast office would be sharply reduced if, as stated, SOCA will have 'a designated officer responsible for Northern Ireland'.[65]

ARA: the magic bullet?

This new governance may be marginally increasing the costs of doing business for paramilitaries and organised criminals. But in overall *quantitative* terms the ARA has not dented organised crime in Northern Ireland in the four years of its operation. This is evident from the government's own estimates of organised crime in Northern Ireland. Official estimates should be treated with caution because of their clear political provenance. They can be used to downplay or overplay a particular crime problem in order to generate policy consensus. The government estimates the criminal economy in Northern Ireland as standing at £700 million p.a.[66] This is an astronomical figure and is somewhat a hostage to fortune if it is not being reduced by reporting or ARA activity, but again the official figures are not made any more sensible by the fact that the definition of money laundering, like organised crime, is very wide.

If we adopt a more restricted approach, according to the Organised Crime Task Force, in 2005/2006 'intellectual property theft is estimated at £200 million', extortion generates £10 million per annum, seizures of drugs alone amounted to over £7 million and the 35 million cigarettes seized amounted to £7 million in lost revenue.[67] We can conservatively treble the drugs figure to £21 million (indeed Northern Ireland's biggest single drug seizure of £18 million worth of cannabis took place in late 2006) and treble cigarettes to £21 million also. Although drug dealers have been targeted, the price of drugs continues to fall. Specific surveys of Belfast show price declines in cannabis, heroin, amphetamines, LSD and crack.[68] Approximately £245 million revenue is lost each year by cross-border shopping (which is legal) and oil frauds. This is an overall figure but if we simply take fraud as 10 per cent (quite low) this is £24.5 million.[69] The dumping of illegal waste, which creates substantial environmental harm and in which organised criminals are active brought in £25 million.[70] We might halve this to £12 million. Further, despite the publicised case of armed robber Cecil Walsh, cash-in-transit robberies increased again from 2005 to 2006 (from 46 to 62). Cash-in-transit armed robberies had netted approaching £1.5 million in the first half of 2005 (see Chapter 6). Fuel smuggling has been relatively stabilised at a high level but this is attributable to Revenue and Customs activity since major asset freezes by the ARA came largely in 2006. All this approximates at £300 million. Unless this money is being stashed under beds across the province it is being laundered, or perhaps more to the point, it represents the idea that much of this money is spent at a low level, as the ARA discovered after its investigation into loyalist paramilitary Jim Gray (see Alan McQuillan's quote at the start of this chapter). This calls into question the argument that the ARA acts as a deterrent.

The ARA argues that the process of going through appeals to set precedents has taken up much time and this will decline now that major challenges have been dismissed. That is debatable. Debates over the exact interpretation of the Theft Acts (1968/1978) are still ongoing and indeed seem to have confused the issue of theft beyond normal human understanding. There are likely to be more challenges in future to asset recovery via judicial review and under the European Convention on Human Rights.[71] If there remains a legal constraint on rapid ARA operations this will limit its function as a *general* deterrent to criminal activity. Studies of the death penalty in the USA have shown that for it to be effective as a deterrent the punishment must be connected in time and space. The system of appeals introduced after 1976 led to the connection between a sentence and its being carried out stretching enormously and dissolving its deterrent effect.[72] This is particularly the case since offenders display 'bounded rationality' that is, individuals do not make long-term cost benefit calculations, and the calculations they do make often involve a small number of variables.[73]

The deterrence effect is further limited by the ARA targeting the dead. In addition, the issuing of press releases and news items may have a time limited effect, for the reasons mentioned. Where the deterrent may operate is in geographical terms; if individuals literally see a house sold, luxury cars impounded, bundles of cash being removed from premises and so forth. Northern Ireland is a small jurisdiction. Its inhabitants do not like to leave (one of the reasons why exiling is such a punishment) and word of mouth spreads quickly. The deterrent effect has to be set against the idea that taking out one large criminal *via* asset recovery may encourage others to take his/her place, or may encourage the individual to work harder to regain the nest egg. Here there would be the debate about whether paramilitaries particularly had lost their status by being stripped of assets, or whether they could still trade on this.[74]

Finally the ARA will have to take account of counter measures. Although Northern Ireland does have a hold on many individuals, if some paramilitaries are becoming more internationally oriented, the ARA may face the same problem as the Republic. It seems that some criminals there have moved to other jurisdictions, taking their assets with them, to avoid the attentions of the CAB. This immediately creates problems, because, despite much talk of globalisation and the development of bilateral agreements, 'the processes for identification, restraint and recovery of such assets is a complex matter'.[75] Although this is not an insurmountable obstacle.[76]

Where the ARA has been effective is not in terms of general deterrence but in specific targeting, i.e. in qualitative terms. If the PSNI and Revenue and Customs target paramilitaries concertedly they can inflict organisational damage. The ARA's targeting of the LVF, coupled with the PSNI-targeted policing of the LVF (from which referrals to the ARA originate) and the LVF's hammering at the hands of the UVF led to the LVF standing down in 2005. The targeting of other prominent loyalists such as the UDA's Jim Gray, as well as of the UDA's North Belfast leadership, sent out a signal to the UDA and other paramilitaries (at least high profile ones) that their careers might be in jeopardy and created some instability in conjunction with other factors outlined in Chapter 3. Asset seizure assisted in the dissolution of a mainstream organised criminal network involved in illegal waste disposal in Fermanagh.[77]

The role of the PSNI

The capacity of the ARA to process cases has been mentioned as a constraint. But it is unlikely that the agency's caseload will expand short of a massive increase in expenditure, and the situation became more uncertain following the organisation's merger with SOCA in 2007. As mentioned, there were criticisms of the under-use of confiscation measures by UK police but despite this £2 million was placed under restraint by the RUC in 1997.[78] The PSNI passes large/complex cases to the ARA for civil action, but the other criminal asset restraints made by the PSNI (cash seizures and confiscation orders) remain substantial.[79] Capacity could be furthered bolstered by recent policy moves to 'decentralise' asset seizure. There has been a reduction of the amount which can be seized by officers from £5,000 to £1,000. The PSNI had been increasing financial training coverage amongst all uniform and plainclothes officers in the use of seizure powers under PACE and POCA, including a marked expansion in 2006.[80] The spread of this tactic would create the platform for a plausible system of disruption of lower level criminals, particularly since the PSNI conducts approximately 25,000 arrests each year. However in the final analysis the PSNI's capacity is finite.

Conclusion

In this and the previous chapter the argument has been adduced that organised crime can be at best managed down to a certain level because policing is limited by the laws of time and resources and its effectiveness is 'sticky'. The developments outlined here have increased the costs of doing business for organised criminals. The issue is whether they have increased the costs so substantially that organised criminality will decline. The ARA exemplifies the idea that specialist organisations are not magic bullets. They are powerful ammunition but prone to misfiring. This does not mean that their power is a trivial issue; rather that their power is not targeted or effective according to their own aims.[81] Advocates of the ARA might argue that it needs more time to prove itself but long-term comparisons provide cold comfort: 'the experience of the United States is some way from providing the unqualified success claimed for it by the advocates of such a system'.[82] Indeed, in Los Angeles, often the site of cutting-edge (and controversial) policing techniques, despite asset seizure and forfeiture laws which allow the seizure or demolition of properties used for drugs sales, extensive conspiracy and public order laws and SWAT teams, 'the LAPD have been unable to keep track of all the bodies on the street, much less deal with common burglaries, car thefts and gang organised protection rackets'.[83] The ARA is potentially powerful in terms of its symbolic retributivist role but the keys to policing down organised crime (disregarding the structural context for a moment) may not lie in specialist organisations but are traditional, based on the targeted policing of networks of individuals, crime prevention and low cost ways of improving information collection and exchange.

As mentioned, Northern Ireland is a small jurisdiction, and in this context the question is evident as to whether policing has been targeted at bringing certain paramilitary groups in from the cold via 'screw-tightening' and targeting others who were/are clearly outside the framework of the peace process. There are high-level targets aplenty amongst major republican and loyalist groups but their departure would destabilise the ongoing institutionalisation and demilitarisation of paramilitary groups, not merely in terms of creating antagonism between these groups and the state. By also simply depriving certain individuals of their nest eggs it would create the incentive for individuals and groups to carry on activities to recoup their losses. There is debate (see Chapter 2) as to the extent to which crime has been a pension fund for the republican movement before it goes into stasis (or terminates, depending on one's point of view). The same applies to loyalists. In the end, the question is whether the ARA is either consciously or unconsciously affected by the overall political strategy. Such issues remained in the air while the ARA was accountable to the Home Secretary, and are not changed with the merger of the ARA into SOCA, which also reports to the Home Secretary. Indeed with the Northern Ireland section apparently now with a reduced staff this calls into question any further long-term proactive approach to asset recovery from paramilitaries or their political wings.

The structural conditions for organised and paramilitary crime might change, but the movement of historical time and social change in the 1990s saw a flourishing of organised crime and organised crime groups. The paramilitary structures within which they operate may be dissolving, but the political context is not the only frame of analysis since some of these groups have social power, and are satisfying social and economic demands. The issue is the extent to which they can be 'managed down' or dismantled.

Notes

1   S. Jenkins, *Accountable to None. The Tory Nationalisation of Britain* (London: Penguin, 1996); S. Jenkins, *Thatcher and Sons. A Revolution in Three Acts* (London: Allen Lane and Penguin, 2006).

2   M. Moran, 'The rise of the regulatory state in Britain', *Parliamentary Affairs,* 54 (2001), 19–34; M. Moran, *The British Regulatory State. High Modernism and Hyper-Innovation* (Oxford: Oxford University Press, 2003).

3   For a general account see F. Furedi, *Culture of Fear: Risk Taking and the Morality of Low Expectations* (London: Continuum, 2002); A. Edwards and P. Gill, 'The politics of "transnational organised crime": discourse, reflexivity and the narration of "threat"', *British Journal of Politics and International Relations,* 4:2 (2002), 245–270; P. van Duyne, 'The phantom threat of organised crime', *Crime, Law and Social Change,* 24 (1996), 341–377; P. van Duyne, 'Pavlov's dog and beyond', *Howard Journal of Criminal Justice,* 37:4 (1998), 359–374; M. Levi, 'Evaluating the "new policing": Attacking the money trail of organised crime', *Australian and New Zealand Journal of Criminology,* 30:1 (1997), 1–25.

4   A. Doig, 'Joining up a response to terrorism? And agency shall speak unto agency', *Crime, Law and Social Change,* 44: 4/5 (2005), 433–435.

5   R. Reiner, *The Politics of the Police* (Oxford: Oxford University Press, 3rd edn, 2000).

6   J. Simon, 'Governing through crime', in L. Friedman and G. Fisher (eds), *The Crime Conundrum* (Boulder, CO: Westview, 1997).

7   S. Cohen, *Visions of Social Control* (Cambridge: Polity, 1985); D. Garland, *The Culture of Control. Crime and Order in Contemporary Society* (Oxford: Oxford University Press, 2001).

8   'More than 1000 new crimes under Labour', *Daily Mail* (8 February 2005).

9   Cohen, *Visions of Social Control.*

10 S. Penna, 'The Children Act 2004: Child protection and social surveillance', *Journal of Social Welfare and Family Law,* (27:2) 2005, 143–157.

11 Garland, *The Culture of Control.*

12 Secretary of State's Announcement, 25 September 2000, quoted in Organised Crime Task Force, *Confronting the Threat. Strategy 2001–02* (Belfast: OCTF, 2001).

13 Author interview, member of the NIO, also an OCTF member, Stormont House annexe, 25 February 2003.

14 Author interview, Detective Chief Superintendent, PSNI and member of OCTF, Stormont House annexe, 25 July 2003.

15 M. Levi and M. Maguire, 'Reducing and preventing organised crime: An evidence based critique', *Crime, Law and Social Change,* 41 (2004), 432; P. Ekblom and N. Tilley, 'Going equipped: Criminology, situational crime prevention and the resourceful offender', *British Journal of Criminology,* 40 (2000), 376–398.

16 Author interviews, two officials in the Northern Ireland Office, Stormont House annexe, 10 November 2005.

17 The OCTF also moved into the development of 'consumer psychology' with public advertising framing counterfeiting as not a victimless crime, and raising

    ideas about reporting organised crime.

18   Author interview, Detective Inspector, PSNI, Belfast, 11 November 2005.

19   Author interviews, two officials in the Northern Ireland Office, Stormont House annexe, 10 November 2005.

20   Author interviews, NIO official involved in financial matters, Stormont House annexe, 25 July 2003 and Detective Chief Superintendent, PSNI and member of OCTF, Stormont House annexe, 25 July 2003.

21   Organised Crime Task Force, *Confronting the Threat. Serious and Organised Crime in Northern Ireland* (Belfast: OCTF, 2005), p. 28.

22   Organised Crime Task Force, *Annual Report and Threat Assessment 2006* (Belfast: OCTF, 2006), p. 51.

23   N. Coles, 'It's not what you know – it's who you know that counts', *British Journal of Criminology*, 41 (2001), 580–594.

24   Northern Ireland Affairs Committee, *Organised Crime in Northern Ireland*, Vol. I HC 886-II (London: The Stationery Office, 2006), para 72.

25   Author interviews, two officials in the Northern Ireland Office, Stormont House, 10 November 2005.

26   See Organised Crime Task Force, various years.

27   Levi and Maguire, 'Reducing and preventing organised crime', 410.

28   *Serious and Organised Crime Agency Annual Plan 2006/07*, www.soca.gov.uk/downloads/annualPlan.pdf.

29   *Channel 4 TV News* (23 January 2007).

30   OCTF costs were £178,677 in 2000–2001; £460,451 in 2001–2002; £302,161 in 2002–2003; £363,822 in 2003–2004; 136,326 in 2004–2005 (to December 2004) Written Answers, House of Commons, 13 January 2005, *Hansard*, Col. 658W.

31   Thus the costs of the officials in the PSNI, Revenue and Customs and the private sector working on tasks set by the OCTF would have to be incorporated into a comprehensive estimate. However, this would still be relatively smaller since a new policing organisation has not been created with substantial start-up costs, and if the tasks have been more efficiently organised there may be a saving.

32   P. Alldridge, *Money Laundering Law* (Oxford/Portland: Hart, 2003); R. Noble and C. Golumbic, 'A new anti-crime framework for the world: Merging the objective and subjective models for fighting money laundering', *New York University International Journal of Law and Politics*, 1/2:30 (1997/98), 79–144; J. Reynolds, 'The new US anti-money laundering offensive: Will it prove successful?', *Cross Cultural Management*, 9:3 (2002), 3–31.

33   K. Maguire, 'Policing the black economy: The role of C13 of the RUC in Northern Ireland', *Police Journal*, LXVI: 2 (1993), 134.

34   P. Norman, 'The Terrorist Finance Unit and the Joint Action Group on Organised Crime: New organisational models and investigative strategies to counter "organised crime" in the UK', *Howard Journal of Criminal Justice*, 37:4 (1998), 378, quoting RUC estimates.

35   Norman, 'The Terrorist Finance Unit', 378.

36   Maguire, 'Policing the black economy', 134.

37   Norman, 'The Terrorist Finance Unit', 379.

38   Author interview, NIO official involved in financial matters, Stormont House annexe, 25 July 2003.

39   Norman, 'The Terrorist Finance Unit', 380.

40   Author interview, NIO official involved in financial matters, Stormont House annexe, 25 July 2003.

41   Norman, 'The Terrorist Finance Unit', 380–381

42   P. Alldridge, 'Money laundering law', p. 225.

43   D. Morrison, 'What measures can be taken to increase confiscation of criminal assets in Scotland?' MA Dissertation, Business School, University of Teesside, 2006, p. 4-40-1.

44   Cabinet Office, *Recovering the Proceeds of Crime* (Performance and Innovation Unit, 2000).

45   P. Sproat, 'The social impact of counter terrorist finance policies in the UK', *Crime, Law and Social Change,* 44:4/5 (2005), 442 .

46   See ARA, *Annual Report 2005–06* (London: ARA, 2006).

47   The court argues it is not a penalty to the individual, it is recovering assets gained by unlawful conduct. Cecil Walsh and the Director of the Assets Recovery Agency (2005) NICA 6, para 33; for a defence see A. Kennedy, 'Civil recovery proceedings under the Proceeds of Crime Act 2002', *Journal of Money Laundering Control,* 9:3 (2006), 245–264.

48   See, for example, Cabinet Office, *Recovering the Proceeds of Crime* (Performance and Innovation Unit, 2000); ARA, *Annual Report 2005–06.*

49   BBC *Newsline* (7 August 2003).

50   BBC *Newsline* (7 September 2006). Money laundering charges brought against estate agent Philip Johnston (he was charged for not reporting) saw his business effectively ruined. The charges were later dropped. 'Spotlight', *BBC Northern Ireland* (5 September 2006).

51   Author interviews, Detective Chief Superintendent, PSNI, Belfast, 24 July 2003; Detective Inspector, PSNI, 11 November 2005.

52   Morrison, 'Measures to increase confiscation', pp. 4–42.

53   ARA, *Annual Report 2005–06,* p. 11.

54   The Northern Ireland office had declining share in relative terms from 2004 to 2005 although a sharp rise in 2006 to 20 per cent of the overall budget.

55   Oral Answers, House of Commons, 9 March 2005, *Hansard,* Col. 11.

56   Oral Answers, House of Commons, 9 March 2005, *Hansard,* Col. 10.

57   Northern Ireland Affairs Committee, *Organised Crime in Northern Ireland,* Vol. I HC 886-II (London: The Stationery Office, 2006), para 163.

58   P. Sproat, 'The new policing of terrorist finance in Northern Ireland', paper delivered to the British Society of Criminology Annual Conference, University of Leeds, July 2005.

59   PSNI figures quoted in Northern Ireland Affairs Committee, *The Financing of Terrorism in Northern Ireland,* Vol. 1, HC 978-1 (London: The Stationery Office, 2001–02), para 33.

60   'I should like, and would expect in time, more balance between the amount of assets seized from the republican and loyalist sides', Oral Answers, House of Commons, 9 March 2005, *Hansard,* Col. 11.

61   ARA, *Annual Report 2005–06,* p. 33.

62 Abstracted by the author from ARA publicity 2003–2006.
63 Sproat, 'The new policing of terrorist finance in Northern Ireland'.
64 Author interview, Alex Attwood, MLA and Policing Board member, Belfast, 6 October 2006.
65 Written Ministerial Statements, House of Commons, 11 January 2007, *Hansard*, Col. 21WS; see also Written Answers, House of Commons 28 February 2007, *Hansard*, 1415W.
66 BBC *Newsline* (7 September 2006).
67 Organised Crime Task Force, *Annual Report and Threat Assessment 2006*, 27.
68 'Street Drug Prices', *Druglink*, Jan/Feb (2004), 24; 'Street Drug Prices', *Druglink*, Sep/Oct (2005), 32.
69 Organised Crime Task Force, *Annual Report and Threat Assessment 2006*, p. 31.
70 Northern Ireland Affairs Committee, *Organised Crime in Northern Ireland*, Vol. I, HC 886-II, paras 47–48.
71 Kennedy, 'Civil recovery proceedings under the Proceeds of Crime Act 2002', 262.
72 I. Erlich, 'The deterrent effects of capital punishment', *American Economic Review*, 65 (1975), 397–417; I. Erlich, 'Capital punishment and deterrence', *Journal of Political Economy*, 85 (1977), 741–788; K. Smith, 'Explaining variation in State level homicide rates: Does crime policy pay?', *Journal of Politics*, 59:2 (1997), 350–367.
73 N. Shover and D. Honaker, 'The socially bounded decision-making of persistent property offenders', *Howard Journal of Criminal Justice*, 31 (1982), 276–293.
74 See J. Braithwaite, 'Following the money trail to what destination?', *Alabama Law Review*, 44:3 (1993), 657–668; M. Levi, 'Evaluating the "new policing": attacking the money trail of organised crime', *Australian and New Zealand Journal of Criminology*, 30:1 (1997), 14.
75 Morrison, 'Measures to increase confiscation', pp. 5–34.
76 Kennedy, 'Civil recovery proceedings under the Proceeds of Crime Act 2002', 250–51.
77 Author interview, Detective Chief Inspector [a], PSNI, Belfast, 10 November 2005.
78 RUC, *Annual Report of the Chief Constable 1997–1998* (RUC: Belfast, 1998), p. 39.
79 Amounting to £1.4 million in 2003–2004; £600,000 in 2004–2005 and £1.7 million in 2005–2006. Written Answers, House of Commons, 6 June 2006, *Hansard*, Col. 563W.
80 C. Goddard, *POCA 2002: Implementation and Financial Awareness Training Within the PSNI* (PSNI, 2005).
81 M. Cuellar, 'The mismatch between state power and state capacity in transnational law enforcement', *Stanford Public Law and Legal Theory Research Paper*, 70 (2003).
82 Alldridge, *Money Laundering Law*, p. 223; Levi, 'Evaluating the "new policing"', 22.
83 M. Davis, *Ecology of Fear. Los Angeles and the Imagination of Disaster* (London: Picador, 2000), p. 378.

8
Counter-terrorist policing

The [security normalisation] programme requires the vacation and demolition of the remaining towers in South Armagh, and the return of the sites to green field status as rapidly as possible thereafter.[a]

Republican ultras operate in perhaps the most unfavourable climate ever for the physical force tradition.[b]

They have no support in places like Ardoyne and have no coherent strategy. They are nothing but a collection of thugs and hoods.[c]

Last week's Real IRA bomb attacks … targeted vital British military installations including Carpetrite, TK Maxx, JJB Sports and MFI.[d]

[a] IMC, *Eleventh Report of the Independent Monitoring Commission* (London: The Stationery Office, 2006), p.18.
[b] J. Tonge, '"They haven't gone away you know." Irish republican "dissidents" and armed struggle', *Terrorism and Political Violence*, 16:3 (2004), 673.
[c] PIRA source speaking on the CIRA, quoted in S. Breen, 'Dissidents in drive for new recruits', *Sunday Life* (17 July 2005).
[d] 'Letter from Ulster', *Private Eye* (18–31 May 2006), p. 7.

Counter-terrorist law and security

The policing of terrorism in Northern Ireland following the Belfast Agreement presents three notable features. First is the (often controversial) assessment of the threat posed by groups both on and off ceasefire; second is the comparison between the mainland and the Republic of Ireland in counter terror policy, and third is the notion of the continuing 'Britishness' of security policy centred on the role of MI5.

Northern Ireland has often been characterised as being influenced by the contagion model: anti-terror laws were implemented in the province and then spread across the mainland.[1] The relationship was more complex than this[2] but the body of anti-terror controls appeared to be about to decline after 1998 as Northern Ireland lost its place at the centre of British security policy. Internment without trial had finally been officially ended by the Northern Ireland (Emergency Provisions) Act 1998 although it had not been used since the 1970s.[3] Following the Omagh bomb in 1998 it was the Republic's government that changed the law and engaged in a proactive investigation into many aspects of dissident republicanism: 'senior figures in the Irish state knew that the centre of gravity of Real IRA activity was south of the border and that it was imperative for the confidence of Unionists – and indeed the loyalist paramilitaries who might have been contemplating retaliation – to be restored quickly'.[4] In contrast, 'New Labour was sceptical about the efficiency of draconian measures.'[5]

Following this brief period of liberalisation came the development of more comprehensive anti-terror legislation, and ironically as it lost its connection with Northern Ireland it arguably became more stringent. Before the 9/11 attack in the USA the British government had passed the Terrorism Act 2000 which replaced the Prevention of Terrorism Act and the Emergency Powers Act. It expanded the definition of terrorism (s1) and extended its coverage across the UK permanently. Pre-charge detention was initially set at seven days, as it had been in Northern Ireland. Section 3 of the Act allows the executive to specify organisations as terrorist (known as proscription). A number of offences flow from this, including membership and organisational support (ss11–13). Other offences include providing financial and organisational support to terrorists, and failure to report terrorist activity (ss14–19). Therefore, charges are easier to lay if an organisation is proscribed. Part 7 has powers specific to Northern Ireland and is limited to five years, being renewed every year. These powers cover the retention of non-jury trial (Diplock courts), onus of proof (s77), powers of entry and arrest and seizure by police officers and Army, stop and question, land control and road closure (ss81–92) and organisations specified as terrorist (s107–108).

Following 9/11, internment returned in the form of the Anti-Terrorism Crime and Security Act 2001. Originally this applied only to foreign citizens classed by the Home Secretary as being terrorist. Following legal challenges the House of Lords decided that this was discriminatory and disproportionate since it only applied to foreign citizens. The Prevention of Terrorism Act 2005 was passed which provides for indefinite house arrest (via Control Orders) and is applicable to all citizens across the UK.[6] The Terrorism Act 2006 extended pre-charge detention to 28 days, short of the 90 days requested by the government and supported by a clearly political intervention by the higher echelons of the Metropolitan Police.[7] The Serious Organised Crime and Police Act 2005 introduced restrictions on protest in Westminster and at areas designated as important to national security. Thus the 9/11 attacks led to the deepening of anti-terror powers across the UK, but their enforcement was focused on the mainland.

While the war on terror has raged abroad the Government continued with security normalisation in Northern Ireland. Military presence was reduced, as were roadblocks and helicopter flights. Watchtowers were dismantled, including the archetypal towers in South Armagh and on the Divis flats. In December 1999 the British Army used 19 sites for observation and communications; this was down to 2 by July 2006.[8] Other military bases and installations reduced from 32 in December 1999 to 22 by July 2006,[9] and troop deployments (defined as those in Northern Ireland and available for deployment to the province), which stood at 16,344 in 1999[10] almost halved to 8,300 in July 2006.[11] Following this brief description of changes in the UK's security architecture, the sections below detail the perceived threats to national security and the operation of legislation and counter-terror policing.

The republican movement

The main controversy was whether the actions of the PIRA breached the ceasefire and would cause the PIRA to be specified. Some of the murders alleged to have been committed by republicans have been detailed in Chapter 2 but the ceasefire has been held to be adhered to 'in the round'. Two other issues were the conviction of individuals for the smuggling of arms from Florida, USA, for the republican movement and the arrest of the 'Colombia Three', republicans alleged to have trained members of the Revolutionary Armed Forces of Colombia (FARC) in mortar techniques. The three were initially found not guilty (but guilty of travelling on false passports) but following a prosecution appeal against their acquittal they were found guilty of the original charge. The three fled Colombia. The Northern Bank raid was so substantial as to raise the question of whether it was in fact a 'military operation' and breached the ceasefire. This led to tension between the British government and the PIRA and sanctions on Sinn Féin. Finally, the practice of spying continued to provoke criticism. There was concern over the PIRA's practice of 'targeting', the collection of intelligence (names, addresses, routines) on public officials including politicians, police, prison officers and the judiciary. The arrests of Sinn Féin workers at the Northern Ireland Assembly in 2002 were aimed at investigating a republican spy ring. Lists of addresses were found after searches. According to NIO minister Paul Goggins, '2,195 individuals were informed of their details having been compromised. This included 77 PSNI/Garda officers, 1,583 prison officers, 13 army personnel and 37 politicians.'[12] Following a break-in at the PSNI complex at Castlereagh earlier in the same year, lists of Special Branch informants and sensitive addresses were stolen. Police searches following these developments led to arrests and the seizure of the stolen documents.[13] However in the hall of mirrors that is Northern Ireland some of this highlighted continuing controversies over the security activities of the British state. For example, the spy ring arrests in the end forced one of those arrested, Denis Donaldson, to admit he had been a British agent for decades. (There were also allegations that the Castlereagh break-in had actually been facilitated by disgruntled Special Branch or MI5 officers). In any case surveillance did continue. There had been talk of moving PIRA Volunteers into a Political Intelligence Unit as the organisation demilitarised[14] and apparently intelligence gathering was still in full swing in 2006 for political purposes, with regard to the threat from dissidents and even in monitoring the activities of criminals.[15] However, in the delicate judgement of the IMC this did not constitute proactive (tasking) intelligence-gathering outside the aims of the PIRA's July 2005 statement.[16] The final sequence of IMC reports concerning the republican movement stated that the PIRA was dismantling its military capability in engineering and logistics, capabilities which intelligence-gathering underpinned for decades.[17]

Dissidents

The prospect of a split in Sinn Féin and the republican movement which might produce a powerful dissident military and political challenge was seen as very real in the lead-up to the peace process. Indeed moves towards peace did produce a split in the form of the Real IRA. However, dissident republicans have been constrained by a number of factors: the political advance of Sinn Féin; the inability of the dissidents to develop credible alternative organisations to mainstream republicanism; and their constricted room for manoeuvre in the North and in the Republic due to police and security agencies' activities (the organisations are penetrated by informants).[18]

There had been a split in Sinn Féin in 1986 after the party voted to end abstentionism and take up any seats it won in the Irish Parliament. A group defected and formed Republican Sinn Féin (RSF). The dissenters adhered to a 'traditional, historical determinist approach to republican-ism',[19] rejecting political engagement short of in a united Ireland but a military wing to RSF did not emerge until 1996. The Continuity IRA membership was estimated at 30–50 in mid-1998[20] and recruitment ap-peared problematic: reports continued to allege that the CIRA was re-cruiting petty criminals.[21] The CIRA made public statements that it would defend Catholic homes in flashpoint areas in conjunction with the Irish National Liberation Army (on ceasefire but opposed to the Belfast Agree-ment) from possible attacks by the UVF.[22] This was part of the noticeable attempt by dissident republicans in the period following PIRA decom-missioning to position themselves as the defenders of Catholic urban zones not only from internal threats (anti-social behaviour) but external.

However, the developing peace negotiations led to a major split in 1998. The Real IRA, as it was later dubbed, was formed in opposition to the renewal of the Provisional IRA ceasefire and the impending partici-pation of Sinn Féin in peace negotiations with the British and Unionists. Michael McKevitt, the leader of the dissidents, took a number of senior figures with him. A political wing developed, the 32 County Sovereignty Movement. However the RIRA were strong in only a few areas such as Dundalk and parts of Belfast. The RIRA had at one stage between 120–200 members but how many were activists is unclear,[23] because although a number of experienced men followed McKevitt, recruitment was also strengthened by petty criminals, some of whom 'had no knowledge of the IRA'.[24] It should be noted here that this has been a constant criticism of republican recruitment by 'old hands' already in the organisation.

Politically and militarily the RIRA has been incoherent. Its most seri-ous attack took place in the first year of its operation. In August 1998 the RIRA exploded a car bomb in the town of Omagh, killing 29 people. This was an unmitigated disaster after which the organisation called a ceasefire. The RIRA further factionalised around the two major figures in prison, McKevitt himself and Liam Campbell, after McKevitt had made overtures to the Irish state. McKevitt and his supporters issued a state-ment from Portlaoise prison condemning Real IRA criminality: 'this Army leadership's financial motivations far outweigh their political commitment to our struggle at this time'.[25] But this was labelled a ploy to gain leniency (McKevitt was awaiting sentence for directing terrorism and terrorist membership) and prisoner releases, since RIRA smuggling had been a well-known long-term practice.[26]

Apart from internal instability, the structural context has not been promising for the RIRA. The RIRA has faced the formal opposition of the PIRA. Initially there was concern from within the republican movement about whether there would be defections to the RIRA following the Belfast Agreement, particularly in the South Armagh area. These tensions were reflected in delicate internal politics which saw hardliners who were supportive of the peace process in a majority on the Provisional IRA Army Council. Although internal manoeuvring continued, the Army Council remained unified. The continuation of the PIRA was a failsafe against a serious split. The PIRA also took direct action, allegedly murdering leading Belfast city RIRA member Joseph O'Connor.[27] The shootings of other RIRA members have been linked to the PIRA. However, at times the RIRA appear to have had informal links with some in the PIRA at the micro level, and the INLA. Like the CIRA, the RIRA have attempted to take up the space left by the decline in Provisional IRA punishment attacks, and have apparently been called upon to tackle local anti-social elements in north Armagh (Craigavon and Lurgan).[28] Nonetheless, these organisations' political space is limited practically, since with regard to tackling anti-social behaviour there are already Community Restorative Justice schemes operating in republican areas. Generally the dissidents have been marginalised with regard to the overall success and impetus of republicanism since 1998. Splits were evident within Sinn Féin and the PIRA in 2006–2007 over the leadership's call to support policing and opposition voices were evident. Gerry Adams, Martin McGuinness and Sinn Féin members did receive threats, and the PSNI warned McGuinness of a substantially increased threat to his life by dissident republicans.[29] However the opposition to Gerry Adams's strategy did not convert into a major political surge for the Real or Continuity IRA or for any widespread support for a return to violence.

Attacks

Tonge argues, 'the "military" performance of the ultras has often been abject'.[30] The main impact has been the Omagh bomb in 1998, responsible for 29 deaths and 300 injured. This attack had assistance from the CIRA. The RIRA were also responsible for the death of former Ulster Defence Regiment man David Caldwell at Caw Territorial Army base in Derry in 2002. He died after picking up a lunchbox containing explosives. Supporters of the ultras were responsible for the desecration of Caldwell's grave in 2006. A string of attacks and bomb threats on police installations took place after 1998 but were largely unsuccessful. Later attacks by the RIRA and CIRA were evident after acts of Provisional

IRA decommissioning and on anniversaries such as that of the introduction of internment.[31] The new policing arrangements became an important theme of attack, including an RIRA plan to kill a Catholic recruit to the PSNI,[32] an attack on Denis Bradley, then vice chair of the Policing Board, and the intimidation of members of the new District Policing Partnerships, seen in Derry, Larne, Newry and Mourne, Strabane, Fermanagh and Cookstown.[33] As mentioned the dissidents attempted intimidation in the run up to Sinn Féin's decision to support policing. But these attacks are not part of any long- term coherent strategy. Barring a truly monumental turn-around in the peace process, they appear to represent the last fluttering of the standard of physical force republicanism.

Funding

The Real IRA (like Republican Sinn Féin after the 1986 split) sought funds from the USA.[34] Apparently foreign sources could not provide the funds required to rapidly expand and mount attacks on security targets. Other tactics involved armed robbery, via a specific unit tasked with this (including a spectacular failure that had been the subject of Irish police surveillance),[35] fuel laundering[36] and extortion. Dissidents of both groups became involved in cigarette smuggling and counterfeiting.[37] The Jonesborough market before its closure was used by mainstream and dissident republicans to sell counterfeit goods. Dissident republicans also apparently traded weapons for drugs with mainland criminal organisations. Although such claims must be treated with caution,[38] there are reliable claims that the CIRA has sold undercar bombs to drug gangs in return for cash.[39]

Policing the dissidents

Although public officials and organisations such as the British government, PSNI and the IMC stated that dissidents were a capable threat to the peace process, it was not enough to prevent the demilitarisation and security normalisation outlined earlier. The political context has all but extinguished the dissidents, and in practical terms counter-terrorist policing has played a major role in undermining their capabilities. British and Northern Ireland security actors have played a central role here, but a contextual view of the overall structure of enforcement might identify the 'cutting edge' as arising from action by the PIRA in preventing a split in its ranks and its 'police' actions against dissidents in addition to the policy of the Republic's government in policing down the dissidents (combined with openings to the RIRA).

The disruption of a high proportion of planned dissident attacks was accompanied by a high number of convictions.[40] A number of these operations signalled the extent of informing within the dissidents. In Split, Croatia, weapons, ammunition and explosives were seized in 2000, and the CIRA leader arrested.[41] Elsewhere, a joint CIRA–RIRA weapons purchase was allegedly a set-up by an MI5 agent inside the CIRA.[42] Three RIRA men were jailed in an MI5 sting in Slovakia in which the RIRA men thought they were brokering Iraqi support for funds and arms.[43] Five RIRA men were convicted of conspiring to cause explosions at the BBC, elsewhere in London and in a failed attack in Birmingham.[44] Two dissidents were jailed for 17 years for explosives offences after a device was found outside a Belfast tax office.[45] Perhaps as a response to security force penetration the RIRA had taken to recruiting younger members, aged around 16, but 'clean' individuals were still betrayed by informants. The student trio of Hyland, Grogan and Mulholland were arrested in 1999 and convicted for planning a firebombing campaign in London.[46] The main difficulty in prosecution appears to have been under the Terrorism Act 2000, when convictions for Real IRA membership were overturned on appeal because the group's name did not appear on the government's list of proscribed organisations. However, a later judgement reversed this, arguing that the legislation was drafted with precisely an eye to those organisations that were opposed to peace.[47]

Enforcement in the Republic was evident. As well as Irish police raids there has been a regular stream of convictions at the Special Criminal Court in Dublin of individuals for RIRA membership and other offences, including six jailed for firearms training offences in 2001. Liam Campbell was convicted of RIRA membership, and five were convicted at another session including one described as the RIRA leader in Munster.[48] There were larger numbers of republican prisoners in the South than the North (67 to 28) including the dissidents, reflecting the Republic's counter-terror policy.[49] Irish and French police have also cooperated in investigations into RIRA links in France.[50]

Although counter-terror operations against the dissidents have been effective, the biggest investigation, Omagh, has been shot through with problems. Criticism from the Police Ombudsman for Northern Ireland centred on a warning apparently ignored or not passed on by RUC Special Branch before the bombing took place. The BBC pushed the issue with a programme identifying the individuals allegedly involved. A civil action by the families of the victims was supported by the British government. Colm Murphy was convicted in Dublin in 2002 for 14 years in relation to the attack but was granted a retrial. Sean Hoey was tried in Northern Ireland with offences in relation to the bombing in late 2006–2007, but the trial was marked by defence criticism – and police admission of – problems in the management of forensic evidence.

General enforcement

A central variable in the enforcement of terrorist legislation is whether groups are specified by the executive as being off ceasefire. Once they are classed as off ceasefire the government and police take a harder line on enforcement, and since they remain proscribed this opens up a wider range of charges such as membership, collecting money or providing organisational support. Following respecification of the UVF, John Irwin, a Liverpool based member of the UVF was charged with membership of a proscribed organisation in addition to possessing items for the purposes of terrorism.[51] Following the derecognition of the UDA's ceasefire in 2001, members were charged with membership. Membership of a proscribed organisation made up the second greatest number of charges (60) laid under the Terrorism Act 2000 since it began operation. In the first convictions of their kind under the Act, in March 2004 four men received 4–5 month sentences as a result of their displaying LVF flags in Hollywood in 2003.[52] The other main charges laid under the Act have been making contributions to a proscribed organisation, which made up 30 charges, and also effectively covered some extortion offences.

General charges under the Terrorism Act were also evident. The greatest number of charges (89) were made for s57, the possession of items of use for terrorist purposes, and possessing information of use for terrorists under s58 and s103 (53 charges). Most standard criminal charges as a result of initial terrorist investigations are serious public order and criminal offences such as firearms and explosives offences, and murder/attempted murder.[53]

National security and the conflict with devolution

Regardless of devolution, the British government retains control of national security policy. MI5 assumed control of counter-terror policy and operations from Special Branch in 2007, and although the PSNI still officially led them, MI5 was already conducting operations alongside the PSNI in 2006 in preparation for its lead role. One result was a joint report to the Independent Monitoring Commission concerning the retention of arms by the Provisional IRA.[54]

The proximate cause of this transfer was the lack of security exposed by the break-in at Castlereagh police station in which intelligence documents were stolen, including lists of informants. The Castlereagh affair raised questions, with some concern over the actual responsibility for the break-in.[55] However, former Northern Ireland Office permanent secretary Sir John Chilcot's post-mortem on the break-in apparently recommended the transfer of intelligence-gathering/national security to MI5.[56] However, more long-term movements were at work. MI5 had been trying to garner a greater role in the province since the 1990s.[57] This was reinforced by ideas in the post-9/11 period about standardising counter-terrorist intelligence across the UK and by the case of an al Qaeda sympathiser convicted in Northern Ireland of terrorist offences.[58] However, there was also a specific Northern Irish political component at work. Should policing and justice functions be devolved, despite the fact that the police would still report to the Secretary of State in London on national security issues, the replacement of Special Branch by MI5 means that there is a direct link to London 'from the ground up'. Thus political representatives linked to republican or loyalist paramilitaries no matter how 'reformed', are firmly shut out of the loop.

The role of MI5 raises a number of questions, the major one being accountability, since MI5 is not subject to questioning by the Policing Board in the manner that operations by PSNI counter-terrorist units would be. Under the existing system as just mentioned, there are already limits on the local accountability of the Chief Constable where national security is concerned, because s/he reports directly to a British government minister. However, the physical presence and questioning which the Policing Board has with regard to the PSNI on all other matters (many of which may still be relevant to national security) is missing with regard to MI5. Indeed, the Security Minister's response to a question concerning MI5 accountability presented a blank wall: 'complaints of criminal wrongdoing by security service personnel whether in Northern Ireland or Great Britain are a matter for the police'.[59] In 2006 the SDLP raised accountability concerns based on the idea that MI5's role in the North is likely to expand via the long entrenched principle of 'mission creep' i.e. it will move beyond gaining intelligence on terrorism because paramilitary groups are also involved in crime and MI5 will seek intelligence on this.[60] Conversely, there is an issue of whether in practice MI5 will be deeply interested in republican and loyalist commanders apart from the dissidents. This may be an area where the PSNI retains effective responsibility.[61] Whatever the case, according to critics the role of MI5 will damage the stability of policing and accountability structures if a human rights breach occurs. Initially Peter Hain issued no directives with regard to MI5–PSNI relations[62] but in the gap the PSNI issued a series of principles – apparently agreed to at the St. Andrews negotiations on the restoration of devolution in late 2006 – on the human rights proofing of MI5 handling of informants, the proper distribution of intelligence via PSNI procedures (a point raised by politicians from more than one party), and the provision of information to the PSNI on all counter-terror operations.[63] This was capped by a Commons statement by Prime Minister

Tony Blair in which he stated the PSNI and the security services would be 'completely distinct and entirely separate'. [64] However, it has been suggested that a buttress to accountability might be ensured by appointing a Northern Irish MP to the House of Commons Intelligence and Security Committee.[65]

Further, on a technical level queries have been raised about the lack of experience of the new MI5 intelligence cadre. This is not an issue restricted to Northern Ireland since the same issues have been raised with regard to investigating jihadist elements on the UK mainland following the large recruitment after 9/11 of young graduates to MI5. Apparently the average age of MI5 recruits despatched to Northern Ireland is 28 years, the average age of Special Branch is 45. The government is apparently planning to encourage the movement of Special Branch members across to MI5.[66]

Finally, although Northern Ireland's political parties may generally agree on the importance of the PSNI as lead agency particularly because its intelligence is relatively more quality controlled than that of MI5 (an important development in itself) the debate illustrates the continuing controversy over security/intelligence and its relation to 'Britishness'. The role of MI5 on a symbolic level represents a strengthening of the Britishness of the province. Indeed, the SDLP in its wish to maintain distance from Sinn Féin were actually more hardline on MI5 than Sinn Féin who accepted British government assurances on the agency's role in the province, a remarkable development given the history of the last 30 years. Whatever the case, Northern Ireland is being brought into line with the rest of the United Kingdom, particularly after the weakening of Special Branch as an interest group following the Mull of Kintyre crash in 1994 which extinguished a number of important Special Branch figures, and following reforms to the police after 1999.

Conclusion

The British state's continuation of security normalisation demonstrated that it did not need the traditional physical security infrastructure to neutralise the dissidents. The PSNI and MI5 penetrated the groups in Northern Ireland and on the UK mainland. Garda–PSNI cooperation was also evident, which raises the question of the role of the Republic in counter terror policing. The Republic of Ireland's activity against the mainstream and dissident republican movement has often been criticised for its varying intensity. Some of the criticisms have centred on the sympathetic attitude of individuals in the Irish state towards Irish unity and their antipathy to 'the Brits', which hampered security cooperation in decades past. Some critiques on the micro level concerned active collaboration between Garda officers and the PIRA on the border in the 1980s (the subject of an oncoming inquiry).[67]

However, the same fluctuation is true of the British state, for different reasons,[68] and the latest examples have been detailed in Chapters 2, 3 and 7. The commitment to the peace process by the Irish state led to a hardline approach on security matters reminiscent of the Border War period of the 1950s, when vigorous activity from both sides of the border had constricted the IRA. Following 1998 this was particularly the case towards dissidents, and was clearly represented in the Republic's attitude to the Real IRA. The Republic's general approach was not solely a result of the fact that 'the Irish system is smaller and has certain in-built efficiencies because of its size'[69] including more direct control of law enforcement. The Irish government's perception was that if the dissidents reached a certain size they had the potential to suck the sand from under the feet of Sinn Féin. New legislation gave the Garda wide powers; Garda Special Branch was active and effective and the dissidents were quickly riddled with informants. As Tonge has pointed out, there were wider political reasons why the dissidents failed, including the overall impetus of Sinn Féin, 'policing' by the PIRA and the lack of a credible political programme offered by the ultras. Thus a structure of enforcement included a range of actors from the Irish and British states to the mainstream republican movement and solidified the unfavourable political context for the dissidents.

Notes

1 P. Hillyard, 'The normalisation of special powers: From Northern Ireland to Britain', in P. Scraton (ed.), *Law, Order and the Authoritarian State* (Milton Keynes: Open University, 1987), pp. 279–312.

2 G. Hogan and C. Walker, *Political Violence and the Law in Ireland* (Manchester: Manchester University Press); C. Walker, 'Terrorism and Criminal Justice: Past, Present and Future', *Criminal Law Review* (May) 2004, 311–327.

3 C. Walker, 'Intelligence and anti-terrorism legislation in the United Kingdom', *Crime, Law and Social Change*, 44:4/5 (2005), 400.

4 D. Godson, *Himself Alone. David Trimble and the ordeal of Unionism* (London: Harper Perennial, 2005), p. 389.

5 Godson, *Himself Alone,* p. 389.

6 As a result of the judgment in *A v Secretary of State for the Home Department* 2004 UKHL 56, since the Lords held that applying preventative detention to non-nationals only was discriminatory.

6 J. Moran, 'State power and the war on terror: A comparative analysis of the UK and USA', *Crime, Law and Social Change*, 44:4/5 (2005), 344.

8   IMC, *Second Report of the Independent Monitoring Commission* (London: The
    Stationery Office, 2004), p. 46, IMC, *Eleventh Report of the Independent Moni-
    toring Commission* (London: The Stationery Office, 2006), p. 17.
9   IMC, *2nd* Report, p. 22; IMC, *11th Report,* p. 20.
10 IMC, *2nd Report,* p. 23.
11 IMC, *11th Report,* p. 21.
12 House of Commons Written Answers, 5 June 2006, Hansard, Col. 471W.
13 For these episodes and targeting generally see: R. Cowan, 'Police discover
    updated IRA "target" list with 200 names', *Guardian* (27 June 2002); T.
    Harding, 'Trimble warned of IRA terror list as talks go on', *Daily Telegraph* (7
    March 2003); 'Man convicted on spy charge', *BBC News Northern Ireland* (9
    July 2004) http://news.bbc.co.uk/1/hi/northern_ireland/3880469.stm; S.
    Knight, "Shock as Stormont 'spy ring' investigation dropped", *The Times* (8
    December 2005).
14 Interview: Hugh Orde, *The Blanket* (25 October 2004). The point was not
    made by Orde.
15 IMC, *Eighth Report of the Independent Monitoring Commission* (London: The
    Stationery Office, 2006), p. 18.
16 IMC, *Tenth Report of the Independent Monitoring Commission* (London: The Sta-
    tionery Office, 2006), pp. 14–15.
17 IMC, *Twelfth Report of the Independent Monitoring Commission* (London: The
    Stationery Office, 2006).
18 J. Tonge, '"They haven't gone away, you know." Irish republican "dissidents"
    and "armed struggle"', *Terrorism and Political Violence,* 16:3 (2004), 671–693.
19 Tonge, '"They haven't gone away, you know"', 681.
20 R. English, *Armed Struggle. The History of the IRA* (London: Pan, 2004), p. 316.
21 S. Breen, 'Fear as CIRA rebels link up', *Sunday Life* (23 April 2006).
22 S. Breen, 'CIRA warns of "vicious and violent response to attacks"', *Sunday
    Life* (18 September 2005).
23 J. Wilson, 'How the Real IRA recruits boys into a life of terror', *Guardian* (18
    November 2000).
24 J. Mooney and M. O'Toole, *Black Operations. The Secret War Against the Real
    IRA* (Ashbourne: Maverick House, 2003), p. 39.
25 T. Harding, 'Real IRA men tell "corrupt" leaders to wind up group', *Daily
    Telegraph* (21 October 2002).
26 Mooney and O'Toole, *Black Operations,* pp. 302–303.
27 English, *Armed Struggle,* p. 320; Mooney and O'Toole, *Black Operations,* pp.
    267–268.
28 S. Breen, 'Real IRA target hoods', *Sunday Life* (19 June 2005).
29 *BBC Digital News Northern Ireland* (26 January 2007).
30 Tonge, '"They haven't gone away, you know"', 677.
31 Tonge, '"They haven't gone away, you know"', 680, 682; J. Cusack, '"Old
    guard planning a new terror wave"', *Sunday Life* (23 April 2006); 'Real IRA
    admits city bomb attacks', *BBC News Northern Ireland* (11 August 2006), http:/
    /news.bbc.co.uk/1/hi/northern_ireland/4783953.stm.
32 R. Cowan, 'Police trainee flees after death threat', *Guardian* (29 July 2002).
33 R. Cowan, 'Renegades declare war on Catholic members of police body',

      Guardian (20 September 2003); *BBC Digital News Northern Ireland* (29 Octo-
      ber 2005); *BBC Digital News Northern Ireland* (10 October 2005).
34   Mooney and O'Toole, *Black Operations*, pp. 49–50.
35   Mooney and O'Toole, *Black Operations*, pp. 84–91.
36   BBC, 'Terror witness escapes jail', *BBC News* (21 October 2003), http://
      news.bbc.co.uk/1/hi/england/west_yorkshire/3211492.stm.
37   Author interviews, Detective Chief Inspector, PSNI and attached to the
      Organised Task Force, Stormont House annexe, 24 July 2003; Detective Chief
      Inspector [a] and Detective Inspector [b], PSNI, Belfast, 24 July 2003 and 24
      February 2004.
38   J. Moran, 'Paramilitaries, "ordinary decent criminals" and the development
      of organised crime following the Belfast Agreement', *International Journal of
      the Sociology of Law*, 32 (2004), 266.
39   J. Cusack, '"Old guard planning a new terror wave"'.
40   For the split between intelligence based and conviction based approaches to
      counter terrorism see C. Walker, 'Intelligence and anti-terrorism legislation
      in the United Kingdom', *Crime, Law and Social Change*, 44:4/5 (2005).
41   J. Mullin, 'Police seize republican arms shipment', *Guardian* (July 29 2000).
42   C. McGuigan, 'CIRA boss "set up weapons sting"', *Sunday Life* (2 July 2006).
43   J. Steele, 'Real IRA men snared by MI5 given 30 years', *Daily Telegraph* (8
      May 2002).
44   J. Bennetto, 'Real IRA team convicted of plotting BBC bomb blast', *Indepen-
      dent* (9 April 2003).
45   *BBC Digital News Northern Ireland* (1 July 2005).
46   J. Wilson, 'How the Real IRA recruits boys into a life of terror', *Guardian* (18
      November 2000).
47   R v Z (On appeal from the Court of Appeal in Northern Ireland (Northern
      Ireland) [2005] UKHL 35.
48   *BBC Digital News Northern Ireland* (13 June 2005).
49   H. McDonald, 'Most IRA prisoners held in Irish jails', *Observer* (29 August
      2004).
50   J. Henley, 'Bretons "linked with real IRA"', *Guardian* (5 November 2003);
      'France to seek extradition of man in IRA smuggling operation', *Sunday Life*
      (24 December 2006).
51   *BBC Digital News Northern Ireland* (22 October 2005).
52   *BBC Digital News Northern Ireland* (31 March 2004).
53   D. Lyness, 'Northern Ireland Statistics on the Operation of the Terrorism Act
      2000: Annual Statistics 2005', *Research and Statistical Bulletin*, 4 (2006), tables
      4 and 5.
54   C. Thornton, 'MI5 in move to step up Ulster activity', *Belfast Telegraph* (14
      February 2006).
55   Some argued discontented Special Branch officers had facilitated the break-
      in. T. Harding, 'Police helped IRA raid special Branch', *Daily Telegraph* (28
      September 2002).
56   'The spying game: who's pulling the strings in Ulster?', *Belfast Telegraph* 14
      February 2006.
57   J. Holland and S. Phoenix, *Phoenix. Policing the Shadows* (London: Hodder

and Stoughton, 1996), Chapter 9.

58   'Al Qaeda terror suspect is jailed', *BBC News Northern Ireland* (20 December 2005), http://news.bbc.co.uk/1/hi/northern_ireland/4545692.stm.

59   Written Answers, House of Commons, 14 March 2006, *Hansard*, Col. 2154W.

60   Author interview, Alex Attwood, SDLP MLA, and Policing Board member, Belfast, 7 October 2006.

61   Author interview, Danny Kennedy, UUP, MLA, and Policing Board member, Belfast, 4 October 2006.

62   Author interview, Alex Attwood, SDLP, MLA, and Policing Board member, Belfast, 7 October 2006.

63   B. Rowan, 'Government backs PSNI's principles on MI5 relations', *Belfast Telegraph* (13 October 2006).

64   *BBC News* (10 January 2007).

65   Author interview, Ian Paisley Jr., DUP, MLA and Policing Board member, Belfast, 5 October 2006.

66   Ben Wallace, Conservative MP quoted in C. Thornton, 'MP warns MI5 will not have tools to cope with terrorism', *Belfast Telegraph* (17 July 2006); C. Thornton, 'MI5 is seeking to recruit ex-RUC officers: SDLP', *Belfast Telegraph* (21 December 2006).

67   D. Godson, *Himself Alone. David Trimble and the Ordeal of Unionism* (London: Harper Perennial, 2005) p. 389; T. Harnden, *Bandit Country. The IRA and South Armagh* (London: Hodder and Stoughton, 2000), pp. 213–237; M. Ingram and G. Harkin, *Stakeknife* (Dublin: O'Brien, 2004).

68   P. Taylor, *Brits. The War Against the IRA* (London: Bloomsbury, 2002); T. Geraghty, *The Irish War. The Military History of a Domestic Conflict* (London: Harper Collins, 1998), Parts 1 and 2; Holland and Phoenix, *Phoenix*.

69   Godson, *Himself Alone*, p. 389.

9

Conclusion

For years we stayed outside policing structures because that was the best way to bring about change. Now we want to move into those structures because that is now the best way to maximise that change.[a]

The UDA is giving a lead saying they want bread and butter issues tackled, and they want to create an environment in which there is no longer a need for paramilitarism. The IRA hasn't gone away and the UDA is exactly the same.[b]

'UDA "still involved in extortion"'[c]

A curtain sided heavy goods lorry adapted to carry a tank for transporting fuel, a fuel tanker, three metal storage tanks, and six other storage tanks containing toxic waste along with a generator, pumps and filtration equipment were also seized. Customs said a roadway had been built to a nearby lake which bore evidence of contamination.[d]

[a]   Gerry Adams, quoted in C. Thornton, 'Adams backs PSNI as he honours IRA men', *Belfast Telegraph* (2 January 2007).

[b]   David Nicholl, UPRG spokesman, quoted in W. Allen, 'UDA accepts Catholic suffered', *Belfast Telegraph* (22 February 2007).

[c]   *BBC News Northern Ireland* (23 March 2007), http://news.bbc.co.uk/1/hi/northern_ireland/6483555.stm.

[d]   '"Sophisticated" fuel plant seized', *BBC News Northern Ireland* (2 February 2007), http://news.bbc.co.uk/1/hi/northern_ireland/6324397.stm.

In the rapidly changing environment of Northern Ireland after the Belfast Agreement of 1998, crime and policing were central and volatile issues. From the outset, policing was core to consolidating the peace. The police underwent a major reform process which had seen their acceptance by the SDLP in 2001, but their continuing rejection by Sinn Féin. Meanwhile, paramilitary groups engaged in a number of criminal activities. Murders continued at a lower level. Extortion worsened. Punishment beatings and shootings rose. At points crime threatened to destabilise the peace. By 2007 the wheel was turning full circle. The PIRA had declared its war was over in 2005 and the leadership was apparently closing down criminal activity. Loyalist paramilitaries refused to decommission but were making moves to control crime. The two biggest parties after the March 2007 Northern Ireland Assembly elections, the Democratic Unionists and Sinn Féin were poised to form the backbone of a devolved government. Sinn Féin accepted policing and justice structures in such a devolved government. While other variables were involved, issues of crime and its control were deeply embedded in the political evolution of Northern Ireland, from the processes of British–Irish diplomacy, political negotiation and security policy to formal politics in the province and informal politics and the space for community development.

Crime as a general issue created some rumblings in Northern Irish society. Volume crimes such as burglary and car theft and low-level robbery appeared to signal the negative effects of peace and social change. However, the main issue with regard to crime involved the role of paramilitaries. Northern Ireland was, and is, disproportionate in the types and scale of organised crime it experiences. The dynamism behind this distortion has been the activities of paramilitary groups. The political ramifications of paramilitary crime glowed with a greater intensity than expected. Indeed the issue of crime came close to destabilising the embedding of the peace despite recurrent efforts to manage it down on the part of paramilitaries, their political wings and the British and Irish governments.

Crime also reflected the nature of paramilitary groups, particularly the depth and breadth of their legitimacy. Both republican and loyalist paramilitaries continued to defend and manage 'their' territories. Violence was 'managed' at interface areas. Punishment attacks rose as paramilitaries responded to concerns about anti-social behaviour and drug dealing. However, in Shirlow's terms the territories also turned to 'prisons' as punishment attacks and intimidation continued as tools of social control. The issue of crime continued to cause problems in terms of legitimacy for republicans but particularly loyalists. Both sides' inability to deal delicately with the issue led to distorted responses to the problem when it challenged their authenticity as community 'managers'. Thus the

PIRA offered to shoot the killers of Robert McCartney; the LVF offered to shoot a drugs dealer to 'prove' he had no association with them; and in 2006 UDA members allegedly hacked to death a man identified as a drug dealer. In their attempts to wrest back legitimacy some groups even, like the INLA, mirrored the language of the police, in stating they had 'dismantled' a 'criminal gang' dealing in drugs and 'confiscated' a specified haul of ecstasy tablets.[1] Paramilitary representatives repeatedly used the same language as police spokesmen when referring to anti-social behaviour.

The fact that paramilitary groups engaged in crime appeared to be treated as a minor issue detracting from the real process of political transformation, not only by their spokesmen but some academics. Indeed, the marginalisation of crime by the PIRA and the use by loyalists of terms such as 'conflict transformation' and 'moving to non-violent responses' was a form of Unspeak[2] which detracted from a focus on the fact that crime was clearly important to both groups for perfectly logical reasons. Crime was employed as a method of maintaining or even building capacity in the uncertain environment after 1998, in terms of recruiting members, providing funds for volunteers and procuring weapons of various sorts. Crime was also important in gaining 'pension funds' for senior figures should the war be finally over for good. It seems that groups like the PIRA continue to tolerate lower level criminality as part of a stabilisation policy to ensure those lower down the organisation do not become too disenchanted. Crime was/is central to estimations of whether paramilitaries were/are undergoing genuine demobilisation. In terms of the paramilitaries' political representatives, crime was one of the few issues which threatened to undermine Sinn Féin's political progress. The murder of Robert McCartney was the prime example of this. However, following the changes outlined above from 2005 in the PIRA, after the 2007 Northern Ireland Assembly elections Sinn Féin was the second biggest party. In terms of loyalists, the UDA's political wing, the UDP ceased to exist as a political party in 2001 and the political counterpart to the UVF, the PUP polled 0.6 per cent of the vote in the 2007 Assembly elections. The attitude towards crime on the part of loyalist paramilitaries and their political representatives remains limited in terms of genuine engagement with the issue. This is to be expected, since they are in a delicate process of change. But it should not prevent a clear analysis of the criminality in which the UDA and UVF are still involved.[3]

The British state was central to the process of transition and the control of crime. But British policy was unplanned and often affected by the unintended consequences of previous decisions. Partly this stemmed from the structural contours of British policymaking, particularly in responding to political violence. But it also stemmed from the mode of policy making adopted under Prime Minister Tony Blair and New Labour governments from 1997. This 'occasionalism' in which responding to single events rather than via a long-term strategy (or even overview) and relying heavily on media reactions to initiatives led to a stagestruck response to paramilitary activity.[4] The British government alternated between accommodation and targeting via law enforcement (amongst other penalties). The government placed some stress on treating crime as an activity that was at an 'acceptable level' or tolerable 'in the round' particularly by the Provisional IRA. The murders of Eamon Collins, the attempted murder of Martin McGartland, the murder of Joseph O'Connor of the Real IRA and those alleged to be drug dealers were 'understood' in this framework. However, after the police raids on the alleged Sinn Féin spy ring at Stormont led to the collapse of devolution, the Northern Bank robbery and the murder of Robert McCartney burst asunder the developing framework which aimed to restore devolution. The British government had been warned by the SDLP and others that the PIRA was 'testing' the government in terms of its 'tolerance' of crime before the Northern Bank raid. Following this, PIRA financial structures and other activities were the subject of police and law enforcement attention in Northern Ireland and in the Republic. After moves towards the end of conflict with the PIRA statement in 2005, and Sinn Féin and the republican movement tacitly cooperating with the police in (re)producing public order in republican areas, the subsequent murder of Denis Donaldson by republicans was once again 'read' in a framework of 'acceptability'. Both Irish and British governments quickly stated Donaldson's death would not derail the peace process.

Much attention has been given to these events. Loyalists argued that the British state was 'politicising the Provos, criminalising the Prods' i.e. giving concessions to republicans and tolerating their crime and other activities in contradiction of the Belfast Agreement while treating loyalist paramilitaries as a criminal problem. However, loyalist paramilitaries were given considerable room for manoeuvre. Considerable thought (albeit not necessarily coherent) had been given to the question of returning UFF commander Johnny Adair to prison during the loyalist feud, and similar ruminations were evident with regard to recognising or derecognising the ceasefires of the UVF and UDA at various points. By 2005 public funds were flowing towards loyalist areas. In early 2007 the UDA's political think tank, the UPRG had been allocated £1.2 million over three years to aid its demobilisation. The government statement made mention that crime associated with loyalist paramilitaries must decline or the funding would be withdrawn. But the statement made no mention of the UDA having to decommission.[5] Thus it seems the 'politicisation of the Prods' was in full swing.

Both republican and loyalist paramilitaries have been accommodated, and this was important in the expansion of their operations after 1998. But both have also faced pressure. As mentioned, the PIRA faced investigations into its financial structures after the Northern Bank robbery. Policing has been used as a 'screw-tightening' method on loyalist paramilitaries. From 2005 particularly, this form of policing was evident against the UVF and the North Belfast leadership of the UDA. Policing was more consistently aggressive towards dissidents, such as the Real IRA and the anti-Belfast Agreement Loyalist Volunteer Force.

As paramilitaries began to turn away from crime the level of state control was evident also with regard to the institutionalisation of the paramilitaries. As mentioned, large-scale public investment has been aimed at republican and loyalist areas, the latter particularly from 2005. After a series of meetings with the NIO, the South East Antrim UDA bizarrely estimated it required £8.5 million to assist in its transformation over five years. However, there was a logic to this. Paramilitaries from both sides see the state as the heuristic around which they gravitate. They are not alone. This is a process evident at the formal political level. Both Sinn Féin and the DUP in late 2006 called for a £50 billion package to aid societal transformation, a package extended to £51 billion in March 2007. The public sector in Northern Ireland remains disproportionately large.[6] Whether anti- or pro-state, political actors in Northern Ireland see it as the mechanism to which they turn to engender change.

This process of the transition of the republican movement and developments within loyalist groups raises questions about 'political policing'. Operational independence is jealously guarded by the police in Northern Ireland as it is on the mainland. However, political policing has operated in two ways. Firstly the police have engaged in this in the sense that they have used 'screw tightening' (targeted policing) to manage paramilitary groups towards desistance and political transformation. The talks between the PSNI and the UVF and UDA in 2005–2006 which took place while police investigations were under way into these groups are clear evidence of this. Thus this is strategy within the normal meaning of operational independence: the police are making judgements about the best use of resources. But it is obviously intensely political at the same time. However, the police are clearly affected by the prevailing political climate. PSNI statements such as Hugh Orde's on the difficulty of going after republican assets at the point where Sinn Féin were debating whether to support policing are remarkable and remarkably political. Where, secondly, the spectre of direct political influence on policing appears evident is with regard not only to the police but also to agencies such as the Assets Recovery Agency, which have not targeted the main figures of republican or loyalist paramilitarism. They receive referrals from the PSNI

and the full picture is not clear. However, the pattern shows a disproportionate focus on dissidents of both sides and particularly loyalists in cases.
Following the ARA's merger with the Serious Organised Crime Agency
in 2008, sustained asset recovery into the major financial structures behind the mainstream paramilitary groups and their political counterparts
is highly unlikely. Critics might respond: what does anyone expect? This
is law enforcement in the cause of peace. However, if Northern Ireland
has stumbled over the line to a consolidated peace in 2007, the state's
policy towards crime cannot provide a coherent model for any other polity in transition.

Finally, and linked to this is the question of the effectiveness of policing and law enforcement strategies. Questions of effectiveness became
bound up with the substantial police reform process. The Royal Ulster
Constabulary morphed into the Police Service of Northern Ireland in a
major transition of some controversy. The process of change inspired by
the Patten Report encompassed cultural, organisational and accountability reforms. This development, under which some in the police believed
they were being, via a process of 'cultural revolution', turned into a minor
'county force' had led to large-scale early retirement and demoralisation.
Much debate had centred on whether the RUC had been disbanded,
regenerated or given cosmetic surgery. Whatever the case, the nature of
the police as a continuing Northern Irish force rather than an all-Ireland
one meant police reform would not achieve legitimacy within the republican community but rather acceptance/tolerance. Nevertheless, the fact
that Sinn Féin has accepted the police is remarkable, even if it has not
arisen because they are convinced by police reform but rather stems from
their increasingly difficult position in Northern Irish politics from 2003/
2004 on. This, of course, is a different matter in the streets of Northern
Ireland but the Party received assent for such a move at its *ard fheis* (party
conference) and via its success in the 2007 Assembly elections, when candidates opposing recognition of the police, some of them recent defectors
from the Party, fared poorly.

Further, as the police change process moved beyond organisational,
cultural and accountability reforms it became concerned with the
modernisation of policing. The result of these reforms was ironically to
'mainlandise' the police as a major British urban police service.

The application of New Public Management reforms which the RUC
had avoided in the 1990s was coupled with similar changes brought about
by external inquiries and reports from the Police Ombudsman. These
resulted in the bureaucratisation and modernisation of the police. In terms
of criminal investigation the central process of reform was the creation of
the Crime Department, with crime investigation and Special Branch intelligence under one Assistant Chief Constable. Generally law enforcement

capacity had expanded in the form of the Organised Crime Task Force (instituted in 2000) and the Assets Recovery Agency (2003), part of the modernisation of the state as well as the police. The British Army might have been substantially reduced and army bases closed but the law enforcement state was a presence of some note, bolstered by the role of MI5 in national security from 2007.

How did this modernisation and increased capacity relate to effectiveness? The classic debates about policing involve not only criminal investigation versus disruption, but also centre on the adoption of new tactics. A stress on innovations such as 'follow the money' may combine both investigation and disruption, although with regard to the seizure of financial resources from suspected criminals, this was seen as central to disruption. The UK's experience with asset seizure demonstrated that it is not the magic bullet for organised crime. The Assets Recovery Agency was developed on the basis of the success of similar initiatives in the Republic of Ireland and the United States. However, evidence about these is not as unequivocal as advocates claim. Although the Northern Ireland part of the ARA was its most successful section, the tactic did not work in undermining the operations of organised criminals, and apart from the technical limitations, it was affected by political priorities.

The modernisation of the RUC and the institution of the Organised Crime Task Force and the ARA demonstrate that the keys to effective policing lie in targeted sustained investigations backed by resources. Boring but effective. However, the interaction between law enforcement (and particularly policing) and crime, although important is only one part of a political economy of crime. There are no magic bullets for organised crime, because its growth and development lie in the overall political economy of any given society, and its reduction will also lie (as mentioned throughout this book) not just in policing but with structural developments, bound up for example in the role of the state and the demobilisation of paramilitaries. Indeed the structural and organisational context shows that at the moment it is too early to argue that any paramilitary organisation has desisted from organised criminality. And if they do, there is the issue of whether organised criminality will persist for some as a fruitful method of gaining and dispensing resources for personal rather than political gain, as the shadow of any political justification fades into nothing. This is not to talk of a mafia society; it is simply to analyse the province in the light of other post-conflict situations and in the light of organised crime as a social phenomenon. Northern Ireland remains a complex and unpredictable society in which comparative and detailed research on issues of crime, politics and security will be required.

Notes

1 'INLA dismantles another criminal gang', *Irish Republican Socialist Party Press Release* (7 April 2006), available at www.indymedia.ie.article/75297.
2 S. Poole, *Unspeak* (London, Abacus, 2007).
3 For example, two loyalists were charged over extortion demands made over the 2006/2007 period. BBC, 'Charges follow extortion inquiry', *BBC News Northern Ireland* (6 January 2007), http://news.bbc.co.uk/1/hi/northern_ireland/6236969.stm.
4 See S. Jenkins, *Thatcher and Sons. A Revolution in Three Acts* (London: Allen Lane and Penguin, 2006), especially Chapter 16; the term stagestruck is borrowed from G. Gillespie, 'Noises off: Loyalists after the Agreement', in M. Cox , A. Guelke and F. Stephen (eds), *A Farewell to Arms? Beyond the Good Friday Agreement* (Manchester: Manchester University Press, 2nd edn, 2006), 150.
5 V. Kearney, 'UDA bites at huge cash carrot' *BBC News Northern Ireland* (22 March 2007), http://news.bbc.co.uk/1/hi/northern_ireland/6478329.stm.
6 BBC, 'Nuisance money claim "ludicrous"', *BBC News* (3 November 2006). Academics at Cardiff Business School criticised the claim by Northern Ireland politicians that the British government's proposed public sector funding was limited. They argued that in fact it was a 'huge transfer' and that public spending and the public sector in Northern Ireland is disproportionate compared with that in the rest of the UK.

Glossary

Adair, Johnny

At one time the most notorious loyalist paramilitary in Northern Ireland. The leader of C Company of the Ulster Freedom Fighters, he is alleged to have organised the murders of a number of Catholics and members of Sinn Féin and the Provisional IRA (PIRA) in the 1990s. He was convicted of directing terrorism in 1995. On release from prison in 1998 as part of the peace process he was involved in activities to assume leadership of the Ulster Defence Association (UDA), a move opposed by most UDA brigadiers. This internal conflict led to a number of deaths. Adair was returned to prison but while there allegedly ordered the murder of John Gregg. This resulted in the expulsion of Adair's remaining supporters from Northern Ireland. Adair moved to Scotland on his release from prison.

Assets Recovery Agency (ARA)

Established by the Proceeds of Crime Act 2002 to seize and if possible permanently recover and dispose of the assets of those labelled as having amassed them through criminal conduct. It does this primarily via the civil law. There were constant debates over its effectiveness and it was the subject of a critical report by he National Audit Office. The ARA was merged into the Serious and Organised Crime Agency in 2008.

Belfast Agreement

The Agreement signed in 1998 which formalised the non-violent terms on which the future of Northern Ireland would be negotiated. The

Agreement stipulated that parties adopt democratic and peaceful means to resolve political disagreement and that the future status of Northern Ireland would be decided by majority vote. It established provision for devolved parliament and government via a Northern Ireland Assembly. It made provision for power-sharing with the principle that cross-community agreement would be required for major changes. The Agreement also introduced Republic of Ireland and British government cooperation with regard to the province. A process of police reform and security normalisation was also central to the Agreement and it also called for decommissioning of all paramilitary weapons and the release of prisoners from paramilitary groups that were on ceasefire, both by 2000.

Castlereagh break-in

In 2002 a break-in at the Special Branch offices at Castlereagh saw a number of documents stolen, including details of Special Branch informants. The standard account is that the break-in was enabled by republican sympathisers inside the complex. A number of documents were recovered from the homes of republicans afterwards. Much controversy surrounded the break-in with accusations that it had been facilitated by disillusioned Special Branch or MI5 officers. The inquiry conducted into the break-in recommended the transfer of national security to MI5.

Collins, Eamon

A former member of the Provisional IRA. He wrote a book, *Killing Rage* about his experiences, and also testified in 1998 in a libel trial involving the *Sunday Times* that Thomas 'Slab' Murphy was a member of the PIRA. He also publicly criticised the PIRA. He was murdered in 1999, in all likelihood by members of the South Armagh PIRA.

Combined Loyalist Military Command (CLMC)

The organisation covering the main loyalist paramilitary groups (Ulster Defence Association, Ulster Volunteer Force, Red Hand Commandos), which was established in 1991 and agreed the first major ceasefire in 1994 in response to the PIRA ceasefire earlier that year. The CLMC urged calm following the PIRA breaking of its ceasefire in 1996 and made public statements on loyalist views of the peace negotiations, but in the period before the Belfast Agreement it became less unified and dissolved.

Democratic Unionist Party

Led by Ian Paisley and formed in 1971. The DUP is committed to maintaining the Union and was for a long period implacably opposed to power-sharing with nationalists and republicans. The Party has a strong Protestant religious flavour. Its opposition to the Belfast Agreement eventually saw it surpass the largest Unionist party the Ulster Unionist Party in Assembly elections and in elections to the British parliament in 2005 when the Ulster Unionists were all but extinguished. However, from this position they began negotiations with Sinn Féin for the restoration of devolution. Central to these negotiations were DUP accusations of PIRA involvement in criminality and negotiations over Sinn Féin giving their support to policing in Northern Ireland. After the 2007 Assembly elections, the DUP was the largest party and agreed devolution with Sinn Féin.

Devolution

The practice of returning government to Northern Ireland rather than via Direct Rule from London.

Direct Action Against Drugs (DAAD)

DAAD is the title allegedly employed by the Provisional IRA when they shot or murdered those labelled as drug dealers. DAAD first appeared in the mid-1990s. Estimates vary but the DAAD label has been applied to 15 or so murders from the mid-1990s. One murder in 1998 was attributed to the PIRA and (in addition to the murder of a UDA activist) led to Sinn Féin's brief suspension from peace negotiations. DAAD murders after 1998 did not threaten the recognition of the PIRA's ceasefire.

Direct Rule

The practice of governing the province of Northern Ireland from the United Kingdom central government in London, via a Secretary of State for Northern Ireland and his/her ministerial team. Direct Rule was established in 1972, replacing the local parliament and government that had been in operation in the province since the formation of Northern Ireland by the Government of Ireland Act in 1920.

District Command Unit (DCU)

A police area with its own management structure, planning and staffing functions. There are 29 DCUs in Northern Ireland.

District Policing Partnership (DPP)

Each DCU has its own DPP, an organisation comprised of members of the public, which is meant to secure police accountability. The DCU reports to the DPP every month and answers questions from DPP members or the public. Meetings are open to the public.

Donaldson, Denis

A long-term member of Sinn Féin who worked in the Party's office in the Assembly at Stormont. He was arrested as part of the Stormont spy ring investigations in 2002. The charges against Donaldson and another two individuals were dropped in 2005 amidst much controversy. Shortly afterwards Donaldson admitted to being an informant for British military intelligence. He moved to County Donegal in the Republic of Ireland, lived in a remote cottage without electricity and refused police protection. In 2006, shortly after being discovered by a journalist, he was murdered. The murder remained officially unattributed as of 2007 but members of the Provisional IRA, possibly acting without sanction are believed to have been involved.

Finucane, Patrick

An energetic Belfast solicitor who, amongst many other cases, defended a number of republicans accused of terrorist offences. He was shot dead by members of the Ulster Freedom Fighters (UFF) in 1989. Ken Barrett of the Ulster Freedom Fighters was convicted of his murder in 2004. His murder was central to the investigation by Sir John Stevens of collusion between Special Branch and loyalist paramilitaries.

Gray, Jim

A senior East Belfast UDA figure accused of corruption. He was expelled by the UDA in 2005. He was arrested by police on charges of money laundering as part of an investigation into his financial assets. He was murdered in 2005, in all likelihood by the UDA.

Gregg, John

South East Antrim UDA brigadier who achieved high status through his attempt on Gerry Adams's life in 1984. He opposed Johnny Adair's move for control of the UDA. He was murdered in 2003.

Haddock, Mark

The leader of the UVF on Mount Vernon, an area of Belfast. Haddock was exposed as a long-term police informer in 2006. Shortly afterwards he was the subject of a murder attempt attributed to the UVF leadership. He is at the centre of controversies over the murders he is accused of committing or ordering while working as a police informer.

Historical Enquiries Team (HET)

A unit established to investigate the more than 3600 deaths related to the security situation which occurred during the period of conflict from 1968–

1998. Funded by the Northern Ireland Office (NIO). The HET has a limited life span. The HET is composed of officers from the Police Service of Northern Ireland (PSNI), Garda and the Metropolitan Police Service. The Team is basically formally classifying most of the deaths (for example recording deaths as murder and making a judgement as to which paramilitary group or state security agency, if any, was responsible) rather than reinvestigating all with a prospect of prosecution. However, some cases may see a comprehensive murder investigation leading to charges.

Independent Monitoring Commission (IMC)

A organisation with two main functions: firstly, to monitor paramilitary ceasefires and recommend sanctions; secondly, to monitor the security normalisation measures by the British government in Northern Ireland. The IMC produced its first report in 2004. It produced a number of damning reports on the activities of the republican and loyalist paramilitary organisations. As part of its role it made judgements on the activities and responsibility of the political wings of paramilitary groups. The IMC recommended sanctions on Sinn Féin and the Progressive Unionist Party as a result of the activities of the PIRA and UVF respectively. Its reports in 2006 were central to the negotiations over the re-establishment of devolution as it stated the PIRA were ending criminal activity. The political representatives of both sides subjected it to criticism. It was accused of following the British government line. Its members comprised: Lord Alderdice, former leader of the Alliance Party and first Presiding Officer of the Northern Ireland Assembly; Joseph Brosnan, former Secretary General of the Department of Justice in the Republic of Ireland; John Grieve, former anti-terrorist officer in the Metropolitan Police; and Richard Kerr, former deputy director at the CIA.

Irish National Liberation Army (INLA)

The Irish Republican Socialist Party split from Official Sinn Féin in the mid-1970s, aiming to take republicanism in a more revolutionary socialist direction. Its military wing, the INLA was effective in murdering police officers and the influential Conservative MP Airey Neave in 1979. It was unstable and engaged in a number of violent internal disputes which saw major figures killed. It went on ceasefire in 1998 but remains politically opposed to the Belfast Agreement. Its political counterpart remains the Irish Republican Socialist Party.

Loyalist Volunteer Force (LVF)

A paramilitary organisation formed in 1996 from elements of the Mid-Ulster UVF who were dissatisfied with the political developments in

Northern Ireland which they saw as selling out the Union. Its leader, Billy Wright, was murdered by the INLA in the Maze prison in 1997. In revenge the LVF murdered a number of Catholic individuals. It declared a ceasefire in 1998. It engaged in a violent dispute with the UVF in the 2000–2005 period. The LVF also sided with Johnny Adair in his dispute with parts of the UDA and so the LVF engaged in violent conflict with the UDA. The LVF apparently stood down its members in 2005. It never developed a formal political wing. It was accused of drug dealing by other loyalists and the PSNI.

McCartney, Robert, murder of

The murder of Robert McCartney created global headlines and highlighted the issue of the involvement of the republican movement in crime. In January 2005, Brendan Devine and Robert McCartney were involved in a fight in Magennis's Bar in the centre of Belfast after apparently insulting PIRA members. McCartney was stabbed and Brendan Devine chased down and attacked (he survived). The bar was cleaned by supporters and witnesses did not come forward. Controversy centred on the initial reluctance of Sinn Féin and the PIRA to encourage individuals to provide information to the authorities, especially the police. A number of people were arrested. One man was charged with the murder in 2005. Another was charged with the attempted murder of Brendan Devine. The PSNI were still calling for information in 2007.

McCord, Raymond Jr.

A member of the RAF who was involved with UVF paramilitaries, Raymond McCord Jr. was murdered in 1997 and his body dumped in a local quarry. His father Raymond McCord Sr. argued that the UVF murdered his son. Allegedly his killers were Special Branch informants who were protected by the police.McCord Sr. had been subject to intimidation by paramilitaries before his son was killed and this has continued. This killing was one of a number investigated by the Police Ombudsman for Northern Ireland. The Ombudsman's report found that Special Branch officers had effectively sheltered informants inside the UVF from prosecution for McCord's murder and a number of others. The Report was subject to criticism in a counter report by the Northern Ireland Retired Police Officers' Association.

MI5

The Security Service developed from the Secret Service Bureau, established in 1909 to combat domestic subversion. Its agents have no powers of arrest. Their main jobs include organising operations, surveillance and

running agents. They work closely with the police and Army and may be
present during interrogations. The transfer of national security intelligence
from PSNI Special Branch to MI5 took place in 2006–2007 and was a
subject of some controversy over the devolution of policing and justice.
Symbolically and practically this appeared to be an important signal of
the British presence in Northern Ireland.

Murphy, Thomas 'Slab'

A powerful South Armagh figure who runs an agricultural and oil business. The Murphy farm complex straddles the North–South border.
Murphy sued the *Sunday Times* for suggesting he was a member of the
PIRA and lost. Eamon Collins testified at the 1998 trial that Murphy was
a PIRA member. Murphy has been regularly accused of being the PIRA's
chief fundraiser and Chief of Staff of the powerful PIRA Army Council.
He is accused of organising smuggling and other cross-border criminal
activities. He is also estimated to have a personal worth of £30 million.
Regularly raided by police and customs officers on both sides of the border, in 2006–2007 he was the subject of a major investigation and asset
seizure. Initially a supporter of Gerry Adams, he is a critic of the peace
process, seeing it as betraying republican principles which call for the
unconditional withdrawal of Britain from Ireland.

National Intelligence Model (NIM)

A system for standardising the collection, assessment and dissemination
of intelligence within and between police forces. It seeks to involve all
police officers, including the uniformed level, in the collection of intelligence and seeks to ensure the consistent communication of relevant intelligence throughout the police. The NIM has been a part of the
modernisation of police investigation. It is a model affected by New Public Management.

New Labour

A general term for the Labour Party following its remodelling and
'rebranding' under Tony Blair's leadership from 1994–2007. The Party
won British general elections in 1997, 2001 and 2005 pursuing public
sector modernisation and business-friendly polices coupled with socially
liberal policies on minority rights and an interventionist foreign policy.

New Public Management (NPM)

A general term for the application of reforms to the public sector involving its modernisation and move towards becoming more business-like to
improve performance. This involves treating users of public services as

customers, the use of business planning and reorganisation, and a stress on IT. NPM stresses the use of systems of accountability involving targets, the production of annual reports and monitoring by external bodies. Some term this latter surveillance the 'new regulatory state'.

Northern Bank robbery

In December 2004 in a well organised raid involving 30 individuals and the kidnapping of bank workers over £26 million was stolen from the Northern Bank on Donegal Square in the centre of Belfast. Following a police investigation by the PSNI and Garda Siochána a substantial amount of money was recovered but much remains unaccounted for. A large proportion was burnt. A large proportion was in new notes and could not be used by the robbers. In 2005 the Northern Bank replaced its notes with new designs. £50,000 was discovered after being planted at a police sports club. A number of arrests were made. Three people were charged including a worker at the Bank. Charges against two were later dropped. The raid was attributed to the PIRA by the PSNI and the IMC. The raid ended the possibility of restoring devolution, which had been the subject of talks between Sinn Féin and the DUP in late 2004.

Northern Ireland Assembly

The devolved parliament established as part of the peace process. It has 108 members elected by proportional representation. Its first elections took place in 1999. The members of the devolved government – the First Minister, Deputy First Minister and ministers for major functions – are drawn from the Assembly via the d'Hondt system. It operates under the principle of cross community agreement. Devolution was suspended in 2002 after the Stormont spy ring arrests. The next elections for the Assembly took place in 2003. However since devolution had been suspended the Assembly continued but did not then form the basis for a devolved government. Talks were continually under way to restore devolution but were hampered by the hard line taken by the DUP and the continuing issue of republican paramilitary crime including the Northern Bank robbery, the murder of Robert McCartney and disagreement over policing and justice. Devolution was planned to resume in 2007 following agreement by the two largest parties (the DUP and Sinn Féin), which would under the d'Hondt system form the bulk of the government.

Northern Ireland Office (NIO)

The British government department which governs Northern Ireland directly from London. Even after devolution certain functions such as national security remain the responsibility of the NIO (non-devolved matters) or the Home Office.

Official IRA (OIRA)

That part of the IRA which did not join the Provisionals. The OIRA was committed to a political strategy to secure an independent Ireland centred on a commitment to working-class politics. It announced a cessation of violence against British state figures in 1972, but engaged in feuding with the PIRA and INLA/IRSP (Irish Republican Socialist Party) which had split from the OIRA in the mid-1970s.

Omagh bombing

The largest loss of life in a single attack during the period of conflict in Northern Ireland. In August 1998 the Real IRA exploded a car bomb in Omagh town which killed 29 people including a woman pregnant with twins. Only one person has been brought to trial in Northern Ireland for the attack, Sean Hoey, tried in 2006–2007. The trial was characterised by criticism of the forensic evidence. The police were subsequently criticised by the Police Ombudsman over the warning they apparently received before the bomb went off.

Organised Crime Task Force (OCTF)

A body established in 2000 by Peter Mandelson when he was Secretary of State for Northern Ireland. The Task Force promotes strategy and co-ordination between all relevant law enforcement bodies including the PSNI, Revenue and Customs, and the Director of Public Prosecutions and the private sector (banks, security companies) into areas of organised crime. It has subgroups dedicated to specific crime areas. It is chaired by the Security Minister. It produces annual reports.

Ordinary Decent Criminal (ODC)

A general term which refers to criminals unconnected to paramilitaries.

Patten Report

The shorthand and common term for the Independent Commission on Policing in Northern Ireland, established in 1998 to make recommenda-tions for the future of policing in Northern Ireland. It was chaired by Chris Patten, former Governor of Hong Kong. The other eight members were drawn from policing, academe and public life. It reported in 1999 and its report was the blueprint for the police reform which saw the Po-lice Service of Northern Ireland come into being.

Police Ombudsman for Northern Ireland (PONI)

Set up following the Patten Report, the PONI is an independent body established to ensure PSNI accountability. It has a budget, investigators and is empowered to launch investigations into matters involving the PSNI such as deaths in custody, the discharge of rubber bullets and the discharge of police firearms. It can also initiate investigations proactively. It has investigated the use of intelligence with regard to the Omagh bombing, and a number of unsolved murders as a result of complaints from individuals, including Sean Brown and Raymond McCord Jr.

Police Service of Northern Ireland (PSNI)

The new police service formed as part of the Belfast Agreement. It came into being in 2001 accompanied by a major reform programme which included its new name, a new oath and insignia, a reduction in the size of the force, early retirement provisions for police officers and recruitment policies to increase the number of Catholics in the police.

Provisional IRA (PIRA)

The largest republican paramilitary group. It formed as a result of the split in the IRA which occurred in the 1969–1970 period with regard to the correct strategy to end British rule in Northern Ireland. The Provisional name came from the all-Ireland elections for the Parliament (Dáil) in 1918 that were dominated by Sinn Féin who formed an alternative parliament and government which declared independence. This move was unsuccessful and the subsequent political compromise resulted in the partition of Ireland in 1920 by the Government of Ireland Act. The North remained as part of the United Kingdom. The South of Ireland eventually gained independence from Britain as the Republic of Ireland in 1948. However, the IRA took their authority from this 1918 Dáil, regarding it as the only legitimate all-Ireland government. When the IRA split via the formation of the Provisionals they took this mantle as the continuing defenders of the only legitimate parliament. Exact estimates vary but the Provisional IRA murdered over 1700 people from 1968–1998. The organisation displayed notable organisational and logistical capacity, and developed bomb- and mortar-making skills, formed an impressive financial structure and reportedly still had 1,500 volunteers in 2005. The PIRA was particularly strong in Belfast, Tyrone and South Armagh. The other result of the split was the Official IRA. In 2005 the PIRA announced its military acttivity was at an end and urged members to engage in 'political and democratic programmes'.

Real IRA (RIRA)

A splinter group from the PIRA which rejected the idea of negotiating with the British government over the future of Northern Ireland and argued that the new political arrangements brought no prospect of a quick withdrawal of the British from Northern Ireland, particularly since they maintained the Unionists' effective influence over the future of Northern Ireland. The RIRA remained committed to the use of political violence to force a British withdrawal. The RIRA exploded the Omagh bomb which murdered 29 people. This severely reduced support for it in republican areas. It has been undermined by the security forces in the Republic and in Britain, and apparently has a number of informants inside it. Its political wing is the 32 County Sovereignty Committee.

Red Hand Commando (RHC)

Loyalist paramilitary group linked to the Ulster Volunteer Force. First appeared in the early 1970s. Assessed to have murdered 13 people. Strong in Belfast and North Down.

Republican Sinn Féin (RSF)

A splinter group that split from the PIRA in 1986 over the issue of Sinn Féin politicians taking seats in the parliament of the Republic of Ireland (the Dáil). Its politically violent wing is the Continuity IRA. It has worked with the RIRA to mount attacks on security forces and allegedly assisted in the Omagh bomb. The Continuity IRA (CIRA) regard the Sinn Féin-dominated parliament which resulted from elections in 1918 and which declared Irish independence in 1919 as the only legitimate parliament of Ireland, rejecting the Northern and Southern regimes.

Royal Ulster Constabulary (RUC)

The police force of Northern Ireland following the partition of Ireland in 1920. The RUC were formed in 1922 largely from elements of the former Royal Irish Constabulary. The RUC were effective in countering terrorist operations, in penetrating paramilitary organisations and in developing surveillance and criminal investigation. They were also criticised on human rights grounds. The force's Special Branch was subject to a number of criticisms over the way it placed informants inside paramilitary organisations, particularly in the 1980s and 1990s. Other specialist units of the RUC such as the Headquarters Mobile Support Unit were involved in the 'shoot to kill' controversy of the 1980s when a number of suspected terrorists were shot by members of the unit and two innocent individuals were shot in a hayshed which was under security forces' surveillance. During the period of conflict (1968–1998), 302 officers were killed and

7,000 injured. The police were superseded by the Police Service of Northern Ireland in 2001.

Shoukri, Andre

Identified as the leader of the North Belfast UDA who assumed the position following the ouster of Johnny Adair. Shoukri had been an Adair supporter. He solved his differences with the UDA leadership but remained a critic of the Belfast Agreement. By late 2005 he was facing a number of charges including money laundering and blackmail, and his brother Ihab was facing charges of membership of a proscribed organisation (the UDA).

Sinn Féin

The political wing of the Provisional IRA (although the use of the term 'wing' is controversial). It famously declared that it might take power in Ireland with an Armalite in one hand and a ballot box in another. The Party shared personnel with the PIRA and allegedly continued to do so after 1998. The Party has alternated between nationalism and socialism. It implacably opposed British rule in Northern Ireland and regarded the Republic of Ireland as illegitimate. It occupied a junior position to the 'military wing' the PIRA. But under the skilful leadership of figures such as Gerry Adams and Martin McGuiness it became the leading edge of republicanism. Over time it softened its attitude to participation in the parliament of the Republic of Ireland, to participation in politics in Northern Ireland and then, following the Belfast Agreement and its success in the Assembly elections, took up a role in running the government of Northern Ireland until devolution was suspended in 2002. The negotiations for restart centred on Sinn Féin's complaints about the extent of police reform and alternatively on calls for its support for policing and justice structures which it agreed to in 2007. Later in the year, after elections, it joined the DUP in running the devolved government.

Social Democratic and Labour Party (SDLP)

The constitutional nationalist political party, i.e. it seeks to end British rule in Northern Ireland via peaceful means. It entered talks with Sinn Féin in the 1980s to encourage the party down the exclusively political line. SDLP leader John Hulme was central to the negotiations for what became the Belfast Agreement. After initial criticism the SDLP joined policing arrangements in Northern Ireland in 2001. Its relationship with Sinn Féin became particularly fractious after Sinn Féin eclipsed the SDLP in Assembly and – nearly – in 2005 elections to the British Parliament.

Special Branch

The section of the British police which deals with threats to national security. Established in the early twentieth century as Irish Special Branch to counter Irish terrorism but also anti-colonial and national liberation movements and other political violence such as anarchism. In Northern Ireland the RUC Special Branch was deeply involved in combating republican and loyalist organisations. This was highly controversial. Special Branch was accused of running agents inside organisations and protecting them when they committed serious crimes including murder, and Special Branch was even more seriously accused of soliciting murder by these agents. Alternatively, Special Branch is credited with preventing a number of attacks, many of them on senior republicans who later became major figures in the peace process, and of effectively constraining the operations of terrorist groups. Following reform the Special Branch was renamed Intelligence Branch and brought under the Crime Department and the authority of the Assistant Chief Constable Crime.

Stormont spy ring

In 2002 the police raided the Northern Ireland Assembly at Stormont, arresting three members of Sinn Féin and removing a number of documents. The police were investigating suspected offences against national security. Charges were brought against three individuals. The charges were dropped in 2005 amidst much controversy. At this time one of those charged, Denis Donaldson admitted to working for British military intelligence.

Ulster Defence Association (UDA)

The largest loyalist paramilitary group, formed from a series of self defence associations in Belfast in the early 1970s which had been established to protect Protestant areas from attack, and to launch attacks on Catholic/republican areas. It developed a 'military wing', the Ulster Freedom Fighters (UFF), who carried out political murders. The UDA/UFF murdered over 250 people during the period of conflict. The organisation was prone to internal disputes because of its decentralised organisation under the six brigadiers responsible for different areas. Its strength was concentrated in Belfast. It displayed political innovation in the 1970s and 1980s in tandem with violence, producing proposals for peace with republicans and nationalists, devolution and even Ulster independence. Its political wing the Ulster Democratic Party ceased to exist in 2001. The UDA supported peace in 1994 and 1998 but its factions have displayed differing attitudes to the peace process. Its personnel have been regularly accused of corruption. It underwent a serious and violent internal dispute centred on Johnny Adair in the 2000–2005 period.

Ulster Democratic Party (UDP)

Formed in 1989 but had previous history as the Ulster Loyalist Democratic Party (ULDP) and New Ulster Political Research Group, which had developed innovative political thinking early on. The political party closely associated with the Ulster Defence Association. It never achieved the political support of the Progressive Unionist Party (PUP) and performed poorly in the first Assembly elections in 1999. It ceased to exist as a Party in 2001 but the Ulster Political Research Group, a think tank, emerged in its place.

Ulster Freedom Fighters (UFF)

The 'military wing' of the UDA. The UFF was divided into Companies. Its members undertook a series of attacks against Catholics, members of Sinn Féin and the Provisional IRA. It was particularly effective in attacking the latter targets in the late 1980s. This raised issues of collusion with the security forces, as apparently republican operators were targeted on the basis of leaked police and military intelligence. Others argue internal developments made the UFF more professional in its targeting. In November 2007 the UDA announced it was standing down the UFF and putting its weapons 'beyond use'.

Ulster Unionist Party (UUP)

For a long period the main Unionist Party. Moderate. It led the negotiations in the peace process which led to the Belfast Agreement. Initially popular, its support slumped as the Unionist community saw it as making too many concessions to Sinn Féin and being unable to pressure the British government into taking action against the violence and criminality associated with the Provisional IRA. It was eclipsed by the Democratic Unionist Party in elections for the Assembly in 2003 and the British parliament in 2005, losing all but one of its seats. David Trimble, its leader since 1995, resigned in 2005.

Ulster Volunteer Force (UVF)

A paramilitary organisation originally established to oppose Home Rule (the proposal to devolve power to Ireland). It smuggled weapons into Northern Ireland in 1914. It was estimated to have 30,000 members. A number of these formed the 36th Ulster Division and fought in the First World War. It was re-established in 1966 as a more traditional, small-scale paramilitary group. However, it is generally regarded as the most disciplined paramilitary group on the loyalist side and perhaps outside the PIRA. It murdered over 420 people during the period of conflict. It is strong in Belfast and semi-rural and rural Northern Ireland, particularly in mid-Ulster. It developed a political wing, the Progressive Unionist Party in the late 1970s. It declared a ceasefire in 1994 and in 1998. It is the paramilitary organisation most committed to the peace process, indeed its early commitment to the peace process led to a breakaway faction forming the Loyalist Volunteer Force. In 2007 the UVF announced it would cease to exist as a military organisation and encouraged members to engage in civilian roles.

Interviews

All interviews were undertaken by the author and notes were taken contemporaneously, following which an electronic copy was provided to the interviewee who could then suggest corrections and add comments. Anonymity was provided where requested. When no reply was given anonymity was provided as a safeguard. Three of the police officers spoken to were under threat from paramilitaries at the time of the interview, or had been shortly before.

NIO official [d] involved with the OCTF, Belfast, 25 February 2003.
Detective Chief Inspector, PSNI, Belfast 22 July 2003.
Detective Constable, PSNI, Belfast, 23 July 2003.
Detective Chief Superintendent, PSNI, Belfast, 24 July 2003.
Detective Chief Inspector [a] and Detective Inspector [b], PSNI, 24 July 2003.
Detective Chief Superintendent, PSNI attached to the OCTF, Stormont House annexe, 25 July 2003.
NIO official involved in financial matters, Stormont House annexe, 25 July 2003.
NIO official [d] involved with the OCTF, Belfast, 26 July 2003.
Chief Officer, PSNI [c], Belfast, 24 February 2004.
Detective Chief Inspector [a] and Detective Inspector [b], PSNI, Belfast, 24 February 2004.
Chief Officer, Police Federation, Belfast, 25 February 2004.
Chief Officer, Superintendents Association, Garnerville, Belfast, 26 February 2004.
Chief Officer, PSNI [c], Belfast, 13 April 2005.

Detective Chief Inspector [a], Belfast, 10 November 2005.

Two NIO officials, Stormont House annexe, 10 November 2005.

Chief Officer, PSNI [c], Belfast, 26 January 2006.

Danny Kennedy, UUP, MLA and Policing Board member, Belfast, 4 October 2006.

Ian Paisley Jr., DUP, MLA and Policing Board member, Belfast, 5 October 2006.

Alex Attwood, SDLP, MLA and Policing Board member, Belfast, 7 October 2006.

Bibliography

Books, journals, reports

Adair, E., 'To pay or not to pay: The extent of paramilitary extortion within the construction industry', M.Sc. dissertation, University of Leicester, 2005.

Alldridge, P., *Money Laundering Law* (Oxford/Portland: Hart, 2003).

Anderson, C., *The Billy Boy* (Edinburgh: Mainstream, 2002).

Anderson, D., *Histories of the Hanged: Britain's Dirty War in Kenya and the End of Empire* (London: Weidenfeld and Nicholson, 2005).

Anderson, D. and D. Killingray (eds), *Policing and Decolonisation. Nationalism, Politics and the Police 1917–65* (Manchester: Manchester University Press, 1992).

ARA, *Annual Report 2005–06* (London: ARA, 2006).

Audit Commission, *Helping with Enquiries. Tackling Crime Effectively* (London: HMSO, 1993).

Audit Commission, *Cheques and Balances. A Management Handbook on Police Planning and Financial Delegation* (London: HMSO, 1994).

Audit Commission, *Detecting Change. Progress in Tackling Crime* (London: HMSO, 1996).

Aughey, A., 'The 1998 Agreement: three unionist anxieties', in M. Cox, A. Guelke and F. Stephen (eds), *A Farewell to Arms? Beyond the Good Friday Agreement* (Manchester: Manchester University Press, 2nd edn, 2006), pp. 89–108.

Barton, A., *Illicit Drugs: Use and Control* (London: Routledge, 2003).

Beck, U., *The Risk Society* (London: Sage, 1992).

Berman, M., *All That is Solid Melts into Air* (London: Verso, 1983).

Bichard Inquiry Report (London: The Stationery Office, 2004).

Bowling, B., 'The rise and fall of New York murder: Zero tolerance or crack's decline?', *British Journal of Criminology*, 39:4 (1999), 531–554.

Braithwaite, J., 'Following the money trail to what destination?', *Alabama Law Review*, 44:3 (1993), 657–668.

Brewer, J. (ed.), *Restructuring South Africa* (London: Macmillan, 1994).

Brewer, J. (*et al.*) (ed.), *Police, Public Order and the State* (London, Macmillan, 1996).

Brewer, J. and K. Magee, *Inside the RUC* (Oxford: Oxford University Press, 1991).

Brewer, J., B. Lockhart and P. Rodgers, 'Crime in Ireland since the Second World War', *Journal of the Statistical and Social Inquiry Society of Ireland*, 27:3 (1996).

British Irish Rights Watch, *Conflict Related Deaths 2000*, http://www.birw.org/Deaths%20since%20ceasefire/deaths%2000.html.

British Irish Rights Watch, *Conflict Related Deaths 2001*, http://www.birw.org/Deaths%20since%20ceasefire/deaths%2001.html.

British Irish Rights Watch, *Conflict Related Deaths 2002*, http://www.birw.org/Deaths%20since%20ceasefire/deaths%2002.html.

British Security Industry Authority, 'BSIA and Greater Manchester Police join together in Operation Hawk-Eye' (2002), www.bsia.co.uk/cgi-bin/WebObjects/BSIA.woa/wo/39.0.12.3.28.3.

British Security Industry Authority, 'BSIA teams up with north west police forces' (2003), www.bsia.co.uk/cgi-bin/WebObjects/BSIA.woa/wo/30.0.12.3.9.3.

Brogden, M. and C. Shearing, *Policing for a New South Africa* (London: Routledge, 1997).

Brookman, F., *Understanding Homicide* (London: Sage, 2005).

Brown, J., *Into the Dark. 30 Years in the RUC* (Dublin: Gill and Macmillan, 2005).

Bruce, S., *The Red Hand: Protestant Paramilitaries in Northern Ireland* (Oxford: Oxford University Press, 1992).

Bruce, S., 'Loyalists in Northern Ireland: Further thoughts on pro state terror', *Terrorism and Political Violence*, 5:4 (1993), 252–265.

Bruce, S., *The Edge of the Union. The Ulster Loyalist Political Vision* (Oxford: Oxford University Press, 1994).

Bruce, S., 'Loyalist assassinations and police collusion in Northern Ireland: An extended critique of Sean McPhilemy's "*The Committee*"', *Studies in Conflict and Terrorism*, 31:1 (2000), 61–80.

Bruce, S., 'Turf War and Peace: Loyalist Paramilitaries since 1994' *Terrorism and Political Violence* 16:3 (2004), 501–521.

Catanzaro, R., *Men of Respect: A Social History of the Sicilian Mafia* (New York: Free Press, 1992).

Chatterton, P., 'Governing nightlife: Profit, fun and (dis)order in the contemporary city', *Entertainment Law*, 1:2 (2002), 23–49.

Chivite-Matthews, N., A. Richardson, J. O' Shea (*et al.*), 'Drug misuse declared: Findings from the 2003/04 British Crime Survey', *Home Office Statistical Bulletin* (May) 2005.

Clarke, L. and K. Johnston, *Martin McGuinness: From Guns to Government* (Edinburgh, Mainstream, 2001).

Cohen L. and M. Felson, 'Social change and crime rate trends: a routine activity approach', *American Sociological Review*, 44:4 (1979), 588–608.

Cohen, S., *Visions of Social Control* (Cambridge: Polity, 1985).

Coleraine District Policing Partnership, *Report of the Coleraine District Policing Partnership Public Meeting* (23 June 2003).

Coles, N., 'It's not what you know – it's who you know that counts', *British Journal of Criminology*, 41 (2001), 580–594.

Collins, E., *Killing Rage* (London: Granta, 1998).

Connolly, J., *Drugs and Crime in Ireland. Overview 3* (Dublin: Health Research Board, 2006).

Connolly, M., J. Law and I. Topping, 'Policing structures and public accountability in Northern Ireland', *Local Government Studies*, 22:4 (1996), 229–244.

Coupe, T. and M. Griffiths, 'Catching offenders in the act', *International Journal of the Sociology of Law*, 28:2 (2000), 163–176.

Crawford, C., *Inside the UDA. Volunteers and Violence* (London: Pluto Ireland, 2003).

Cribb, R., *Gangsters and Revolutionaries. The Jakarta People's Militia and the Indonesian Revolution 1945–49* (Australia: Allen and Unwin, 1991).

Cuellar, M., 'The mismatch between state power and state capacity in transnational law enforcement', *Stanford Public Law and Legal Theory Research Paper*, 70 (2003).

Cusack, J., and H. McDonald, *UVF* (Dublin: Poolbeg, 2000).

Darby, J., 'A truce rather than a treaty? The effect of violence on the Irish peace process', in M. Cox, A Guelke and F. Stephen (eds), *A Farewell to Arms? Beyond the Good Friday Agreement* (Manchester: Manchester University Press, 2006), pp. 212–223.

Davis, M., *City of Quartz.. Excavating the Future in Los Angeles* (London: Vintage, 1990).

Davis, M., *Ecology of Fear. Los Angeles and the Imagination of Disaster* (London: Picador, 2000).

Dennis, N., G. Erdos and D. Robinson, *The Failure of Britain's Police. London and New York Compared* (London: Civitas, 2003).

Dickson, B., 'Miscarriages of justice in Northern Ireland', in C. Walker and K. Starmer (eds), *Miscarriages of Justice* (London: Blackstone, 1999).

Dickson, B., 'Policing and human rights after the conflict', in M. Cox, A. Guelke and F. Stephen (eds), *A Farewell to Arms? Beyond the Good Friday Agreement* (Manchester, Manchester University Press, 2006), pp. 170–186.

Dodd, T., S. Nicholas, D. Povey and A. Walker, 'Crime in England and Wales 2003/04', *Home Office Statistical Bulletin* 10/04 (2004).

Doig, A., 'Mixed signals? Public sector change and the proper conduct of public business', *Public Administration*, 73 (1995), 191–212.

Doig, A., 'Joining up a response to terrorism? And agency shall speak unto agency', *Crime, Law and Social Change*, 44: 4/5 (2005), 423–440.

Doig, A. and R. Theobald (eds), *Corruption and Democratisation* (London, Frank Cass, 1999).

Donohoe, J., 'Did *Miranda* diminish police effectiveness? *Stanford Law Review*, 50, April (1998), 1147–1180.

Druglink, 'Street Drug Prices', *Druglink*, Jan/Feb (2004).

Druglink, 'Street Drug Prices', *Druglink*, Sep/Oct (2005).

Dunnighan, C. and C. Norris, 'The detective, the snout, and the Audit Commission: The real costs in using informants' *Howard Journal of Criminal Justice*, 38:1 (1999), 67–86.

Eaton, G., 'Drug Use in the Population', in G. Eaton, M. Morleo, A. Lodwick (*et al.*) (eds), *UK Drug Situation 2005 edition* (European Monitoring Centre for Drugs and Drug Addiction/Department of Health, 2005).

Edwards, A. and P. Gill, 'The politics of "transnational organised crime": Discourse, reflexivity and the narration of "threat"', *British Journal of Politics and*

International Relations, 4:2 (2002), 245–270.

Ekblom, P. and N. Tilley, 'Going equipped: criminology, situational crime prevention and the resourceful offender', *British Journal of Criminology*, 40 (2000), 376–398.

Elliott, M., *The Catholics of Ulster* (London: Penguin, 2001).

Ellison, G. and J. Smyth, *The Crowned Harp. Policing Northern Ireland* (London: Pluto, 2000).

English, R., *Armed Struggle. The History of the IRA* (London: Pan, 2004).

Erlich, I., 'The deterrent effects of capital punishment', *American Economic Review*, 65 (1975), 397–417.

Erlich, I., 'Capital punishment and deterrence', *Journal of Political Economy*, 85 (1977), 741–788.

Evason, E., and R. Woods, 'Poverty, deregulation of the labour market and benefit fraud', *Social Policy and Administration*, 29:1 (1995), 40–54.

Ewing, E., and C. Gearty, *The Struggle for Civil Liberties. Political Freedom and the Rule of Law in Britain, 1914–1945* (Oxford: Oxford University Press, 2001).

Farrell, M., *Northern Ireland. The Orange State* (London: Pluto, 1976).

French, B., D. Donnelly and M. Willis, 'Experience of crime in Northern Ireland', *Research and Statistical Bulletin*, 5 (2001).

French, B., and P. Campbell, 'Crime victimisation in Northern Ireland: Findings from the 2003/04 Northern Ireland Crime Survey', *Research and Statistics Bulletin*, 4 (2005).

Furedi, F., *The Culture of Fear: Risk Taking and the Morality of Low Expectations* (London: Continuum, 2002).

Garland, D., *The Culture of Control. Crime and Order in Contemporary Society* (Oxford: Oxford University Press, 2001).

Gaylor, D., *Getting Away with Murder. The Reinvestigation of Historic Undetected Homicide* (Centrex/Home Office, 2002).

Geraghty, T., *The Irish War. The Military History of a Domestic Conflict* (London: Harper Collins, 1998).

Gill, M., 'The craft of robbers of cash-in-transit vans: Crime facilitators and the entrepreneurial approach', *International Journal of the Sociology of Law*, 29 (2001), 277–291.

Gill, P., *Policing Politics. Security, Intelligence and the Liberal Democratic State* (London: Frank Cass, 1994).

Gillespie, G., 'Noises off: Loyalists after the Agreement', in M. Cox, A. Guelke and F. Stephen (eds), *A Farewell to Arms? Beyond the Good Friday Agreeement* (Manchester: Manchester University Press, 2nd edn, 2006).

Gilmour, R., *Dead Ground. Infiltrating the IRA* (London: Little Brown, 1998).

Goddard, C., *POCA 2002: Implementation and Financial Awareness Training Within the PSNI* (PSNI, 2005).

Godson, D., *Himself Alone. David Trimble and the Ordeal of Unionism* (London: Harper Perennial, 2005).

Goldstock, R., *Organised Crime in Northern Ireland. A Report for the Secretary of State and Government Response*, www.nio.gov.uk/government_response_to_goldstock_report.pdf.

Griffiths, H., 'Smoking guns: European cigarette smuggling in the 1990s', *Global*

Crime, 6:2 (2004), 185–200.

Gunst, L., *Born Fi Dead* (Edinburgh: Payback Press, 1999).

Hadfield, P., *Bar Wars* (Oxford: Oxford University Press, 2006).

Harnden, T., *Bandit Country. The IRA and South Armagh* (London: Hodder and Stoughton, 2000).

Hillyard, P., 'Popular justice in Northern Ireland', in S. Spitzer and A. Scull (eds), *Research on Law, Deviance and Social Control* (Greenwich: Jai, 1985).

Hillyard, P., 'The normalisation of special powers: From Northern Ireland to Britain', in P. Scraton (ed.), *Law, Order and the Authoritarian State* (Milton Keynes: Open University, 1987), pp. 279–312.

Hillyard, P. and M. Tomlinson, 'Patterns of policing and policing Patten', *Journal of Law and Society,* 27:3 (2000), 394–415.

Hillyard, P., J. Sim, S. Tombs and D. Whyte, '"Leaving a stain upon the silence": Contemporary criminology and the politics of dissent', *British Journal of Criminology,* 44 (2004), 369–390.

Historical Enquries Team, *Policing the Past. Introducing the Work of the Historical Enquiries Team* (PSNI, n.d.).

HM Customs and Excise, *The Misuse and Smuggling of Hydrocarbon Oil* (London: The Stationery Office, 2002).

HMIC, *2000/2001 Inspection: Royal Ulster Constabulary* (London: HMIC, 2001).

HMIC, *2002 Inspection: Police Service of Northern Ireland* (London: Home Office, 2002).

HMIC, *Baseline Assessment of the Police Service of Northern Ireland* (London: HMIC, 2004).

Hobbs, D., *Doing the Business: Entrepreneurship, Detectives and the Working Class in the East End of London* (Oxford: Clarendon, 1988).

Hobbs, D., 'Criminal collaboration: Youth gangs, subcultures, professional criminals and organised crime', in M. Maguire, R. Morgan and R. Reiner (eds), *The Oxford Handbook of Criminology* (Oxford: Oxford University Press, 1997), pp. 801–840.

Hobbs, D., P. Hadfield, S. Lister and S. Winlow, *Bouncers: Violence and Governance in the Night Time Economy* (Oxford, Oxford University Press, 2003).

Hogan, G. and C. Walker, *Political Violence and the Law in Ireland* (Manchester: Manchester University Press).

Holland, J. and S. Phoenix, *Phoenix. Policing the Shadows* (London: Hodder and Stoughton, 1997).

Holloway, K. and T. Bennett, 'The results of the first two years of the NEW-ADAM programme', *Home Office OnLine Report,* 19/04 (2004), http://www.homeoffice.gov.uk/rds/pdfs04/rdsolr1904.pdf.

Home Office, 'Crime and Police Effectiveness', *Home Office Research Study,* 79 (London: HMSO, 1984).

Hood, C., 'A public management for all seasons?', *Public Administration,* 69:1 (1991), 3-18.

Horgan, J. and M. Taylor, 'Playing the "green card" – financing the Provisional IRA', *Terrorism and Political Violence,* 11:2 (1999), 1–38.

Horgan J. and M. Taylor, 'Playing the "green card" – financing the Provisional IRA Part 2', *Terrorism and Political Violence,* 15:2 (2003), 1–60.

Hughes, D., 'The Spivs', in M. Sissons and P. French (eds), *Age of Austerity 1945–51* (Oxford: Oxford University Press, 1986), pp. 69–89.

IMC, *Second Report of the Independent Monitoring Commission* (London: The Stationery Office, 2004).

IMC, *Fourth Report of the Independent Monitoring Commission* (London, The Stationery Office, 2005).

IMC, *Fifth Report of the Independent Monitoring Commission* (London: The Stationery Office, 2005).

IMC, *Sixth Report of the Independent Monitoring Commission* (London: HMSO, 2005).

IMC, *Eighth Report of the Independent Monitoring Commission* (London: The Stationery Office, 2006).

IMC, *Tenth Report of the Independent Monitoring Commission* (London: The Stationery Office, 2006).

IMC, *Eleventh Report of the Independent Monitoring Commission* (London: The Stationery Office, 2006).

IMC, *Twelfth Report of the Independent Monitoring Commission* (London: The Stationery Office, 2006).

IMC, *Thirteenth Report of the Independent Monitoring Commission* (London: The Stationery Office, 2007).

Ingram, M., and G. Harkin, *Stakeknife* (Dublin: O'Brien, 2004).

Innes, M., *Investigating Murder. Detective Work and the Police Response to Criminal Homicide* (Oxford: Clarendon, 2003).

Jackson, A. and A. Lyon, 'Policing after ethnic conflict', *Policing*, 24:4 (2001), 563–585.

Jenkins, S., *Accountable to None. The Tory Nationalisation of Britain* (London: Penguin, 1996).

Jenkins, S. *Thatcher and Sons. A Revolution in Three Acts* (London: Allen Lane and Penguin, 2006).

John, T. and M. Maguire, 'The National Intelligence Model: Early implementation experience in three Police Force areas', *Cardiff School of Social Sciences Working Paper*, 50 (2004).

Johnston, L. and C. Shearing, *Governing Security. Explorations in Policing and Justice* (London: Routledge, 2003).

Kauzlarich, D., R. Matthews, W. Miller, 'Towards a victimology of state crime', *Critical Criminology*, 10 (2001), 173–194.

Kelly, L. and L. Regan, 'Stopping Traffic', *Home Office Police Research Series Paper*, 125 (2000).

Kennedy, A., 'Civil recovery proceedings under the Proceeds of Crime Act 2002', *Journal of Money Laundering Control*, 9:3 (2006), 245–264.

Kennedy, L., 'They shoot children don't they? An analysis of the age and gender of victims of paramilitary punishments in Northern Ireland', *Report Prepared for the Northern Ireland Committee Against Terror and the Northern Ireland Affairs Committee*, http://cain.ulst.ac.uk/issues/violence/docs/kennedy01.htm.

Knox, C. and B. Dickson, *An Evaluation of the Alternative Criminal Justice System in Northern Ireland*, ESRC research project L133251003 (2001).

Knox, C., 'See no evil, hear no evil: Insidious paramilitary violence in Northern Ireland', *British Journal of Criminology*, 42:1 (2002), 164–185.

Law, J., 'Accountability and Annual Reports: The Case of Policing', *Public Policy and Administration*, 16:1 (2001), 75–90.

Leishman, F., B. Loveday and S. Savage (eds), *Core Issues in Policing* (Essex: Longman, 1996).

Leman-Langlois, S. and C. Shearing, 'Repairing the Future: The South African Truth and Reconciliation Commission at Work', in G. Gilligan and J. Pratt (eds), *Crime, Truth and Justice. Official Inquiry, Discourse and Knowledge* (Devon: Willan, 2004), pp. 222–242.

Levi, M., 'Evaluating the "new policing": Attacking the money trail of organised crime', *Australian and New Zealand Journal of Criminology*, 30:1 (1997), 1–25.

Levi, M., Perspectives on "organised crime": An overview', *Howard Journal of Criminal Justice* 37:4 (1998), 335–345.

Levi, M. and M. Maguire, 'Reducing and preventing organised crime: An evidence based critique', *Crime, Law and Social Change*, 41 (2004), 379–469.

Lister, D. and H. Jordan, *Mad Dog. The Rise and Fall of Johnny Adair and 'C Company'* (Edinburgh: Mainstream, 2003).

Loader, I., 'Democracy, justice and the limits of policing: Rethinking police accountability', *Social and Legal Studies*, 3:4 (1994), 521–544.

Loader, I., 'Consumer culture and the commodification of policing and security', *Sociology*, 33 (1999), 373–392.

Loveday, B., 'The impact of performance culture on criminal justice agencies in England and Wales' *International Journal of the Sociology of Law*, 27 (1999), 351–377.

Loveday, B., 'Managing crime: Police use of data as an indicator of effectiveness', *International Journal of the Sociology of Law*, 28 (2000), 215–237.

Lustgarten, L., 'Human rights: Where do we go from here?', *Modern Law Review*, 69:5 (2006), 843–854.

Lyness, D., 'Northern Ireland Statistics on the operation of the Terrorism Act 2000: Annual statistics 2005', *Research and Statistical Bulletin*, 4 (2006).

Lyness, D., P. Campbell and C. Jamison (eds), *A Commentary on Northern Ireland Crime Statistics* (National Statistics, 2005).

MacDonald, R. and J. Marsh, 'Crossing the Rubicon: Youth transitions, poverty, drugs and social exclusion', *International Journal of Drug Policy*, 13 (2002), 27–38.

McAuley, J., '"Just fighting to survive": Loyalist paramilitary politics and the Progressive Unionist Party', *Terrorism and Political Violence*, 16:3 (2004), 522–543.

McCamant, J., 'Governance without blood: Social science's antiseptic view of rule', in M. Stohl and G. Lopez, *The State as Terrorist. The Dynamics of Governmental Violence and Repression* (London: Aldwych, 1984).

McCoy, A., *The Politics of Heroin* (USA: Lawrence Hill, 1991).

McDonald, H. and J. Cusack, *UDA* (Dublin: Penguin Ireland, 2004).

McElrath, K., *Prevalence of Problem Heroin Use in Northern Ireland* (Belfast: Drug and Alcohol Information and Research Unit, 2002).

McEvoy, K. and H. Mika, 'Restorative justice and the critique of informalism in Northern Ireland', *British Journal of Criminology*, 42 (2002), 534–562.

McEvoy, K., P. Shirlow and K. McElrath, 'Resistance, transition and exclusion: Politically motivated ex-prisoners and conflict transformation in Northern

Ireland', *Terrorism and Political Violence*, 16:3 (2004), 646–670.

McIntosh, M., 'Changes in the organisation of thieving', in S. Cohen (ed.), *Images of Deviance* (London: Pelican, 1971), pp. 98–134.

McIntyre, A., 'Out of the ashes of armed struggle arose the Stormonistas. And they fought … Ardoyne youth', *The Blanket* (5 September 2002).

McIntyre, A., 'CRJ – new name for the IRA?', *The Blanket* (December 2005).

McIntyre, A., 'Catching the monkey', *The Blanket* (4 April 2006).

McMullan, S. and D. Ruddy, 'Experience of drug misuse: Findings from the 2003/ 04 Northern Ireland Crime Survey', *Northern Ireland Office Research and Statistical Bulletin*, 10 (2005).

Maguire, K., 'Policing the black economy: the role of C13 of the RUC in Northern Ireland', *Police Journal*, LXVI: 2 (1993), 127–135.

Maguire, M., 'Crime statistics: The "data" explosion and its implications', in M. Maguire, M. Morgan and R. Reiner (eds), *The Oxford Handbook of Criminology*, Oxford: Oxford University Press, 2002), pp. 322–376.

Marks, T., *Maoist Insurgency since Vietnam* (London: Frank Cass, 1996).

Matthews, R., *Armed Robbery* (Devon: Willan, 2002).

Matthews, R., 'Armed robbery: Two police responses', *Police Research Group Crime Detection and Prevention Series Paper*, 78 (1996).

Matthews R. and J. Young (eds), *The New Politics of Crime and Punishment* (Devon: Willan, 2003).

Mawby, R., *Policing the City* (England: Saxon House,1979).

Miller, A. and N. Damask, 'How myths drive policy: The dual myths of narco-Terrorism', *Terrorism and Political Violence* 8:1 (1996), 114–131.

Moloney, E., *A Secret History of the IRA* (London: Penguin).

Mooney, J. and M. O'Toole, *Black Operations. The Secret War Against the Real IRA* (Ashbourne: Maverick House, 2003).

Moran, J., 'Paramilitaries, "ordinary decent criminals" and the development of organised crime following the Belfast Agreement', *International Journal of the Sociology of Law*, 32 (2004), 263–278.

Moran, J., 'State power and the war on terror: A comparative analysis of the UK and USA', *Crime, Law and Social Change*, 44:4/5 (2005), 335–359.

Moran, M., *The British Regulatory State. High Modernism and Hyperinnovation* (Oxford: Oxford University Press, 2003).

Moran, M., 'The rise of the regulatory state in Britain', *Parliamentary Affairs*, 54 (2001), 19–34.

Morrison, D., 'What measures can be taken to increase confiscation of criminal assets in Scotland?' MA Dissertation, Business School, University of Teesside, 2006.

Mulcahy, A., *Policing Northern Ireland. Conflict, Legitimacy and Reform* (Devon: Willan, 2006).

Muncie, J., 'Decriminalising criminology', *British Criminology Conference: Selected Proceedings*, Vol.3 (2000), http://lboro.ac.uk/departments/ss/bsc/bccsp/vol03/muncie.html&gt.

Munck, R., 'Repression, insurgency and popular justice', *Crime and Social Justice*, 21/22 (1984), 81–94.

Murray, G. and J. Tonge, *Sinn Féin and the SDLP. From Alienation to Participation*

(Dublin: O'Brien, 2005).

National Statistics, *Recorded crime and clearances 1st April 2005–31st March 2006*, www.psni.police.uk/1._recorded_crime.pdf.

National Statistics, 'Statistics relating to the security situation 1st April 2005–31st March 2006', *Statistical Report*, 6 (2006), www.psni.police.uk/6._statistics_relating_to_the_security_situation-2.pdf.

Ní Aoláin, F., *The Politics of Force. Conflict Management and State Violence in Northern Ireland* (Belfast: Blackstaff, 2000).

NIO, *A Commentary on Northern Ireland Crime Statistics 1997* (Belfast: TSO, 1997).

NIO, *A Commentary on Northern Ireland Crime Statistics 2004* (Belfast: NIO, 2005).

NIO, 'Changing patterns of drug use in Northern Ireland – some recent survey findings', *Research Findings*, 1 (1997).

Noble, R. and C. Golumbic, 'A new anti-crime framework for the world: Merging the objective and subjective models for fighting money laundering', *New York University International Journal of Law and Politics*, 1/2:30 (1997/98), 79–144.

Norman, P., 'The Terrorist Finance Unit and the Joint Action Group on Organised Crime: New organisational models and investigative strategies to counter "organised crime" in the UK', *Howard Journal of Criminal Justice*, 37:4 (1998), 375–392.

Northern Ireland Affairs Committee, *The Financing of Terrorism in Northern Ireland*, Vol. 1, HC 978-1 (London: The Stationery Office, 2001–02).

Northern Ireland Affairs Committee, *The Illegal Drugs Trade and Drug Culture in Northern Ireland*, Vol. 1, HC 1217-I (London: The Stationery Office, 2003).

Northern Ireland Affairs Committee, *The Functions of the Northern Ireland Policing Board: Responses by the Government and the Northern Ireland Policing Board to the Committee's Seventh Report of Session 2004–05*, HC 531 (London:The Stationery Office, 2005).

Northern Ireland Affairs Committee, *Organised Crime in Northern Ireland, Third Report of Session 2005–06*, Vol. I HC 886-II (London: The Stationery Office, 2006).

Northern Ireland Assembly, 'Report on [1] grants paid to Irish Sport Horse Genetic Testing Unit Ltd. and [2] National Agriculture Support: Fraud', *Fourth Report of the Public Accounts Committee* (PAC, 2001).

Northern Ireland Assembly, 'Report on internal fraud in the Local Enterprise Development Unit', *Eleventh Report of the Public Accounts Committee* (PAC, 2002).

Northern Ireland Policing Board, *Policing Board backs recommendations on Special Branch* (2002). http://www.nipolicingboard.org.uk/text_only/to_pr_nov02.htm.

Northern Ireland Policing Board, *The Life and Times of the Northern Ireland Policing Board 4 November 2001–31 March 2006* (Belfast: NIPB, 2006).

Northern Ireland Retired Police Officers Association, *A Rebuttal of the Statement by the Police Ombudsman for Northern Ireland on her investigation into the circumstances surrounding the death of Raymond McCord Junior and related matters* (Belfast: NIRPOA, 2007).

Northern Ireland Statistics and Research Agency *Northern Ireland Abstract of Statistics OnLine*, www.nisra.gov.uk/archive/uploads/publications/abstract_online/Table%206.2.xls.

O'Brien, J., *Killing Finucane* (Dublin: Gill and Macmillan, 2005).

O'Doherty, M., *The Trouble with Guns. Republican Strategy and the Provisional IRA* (Belfast: Blackstaff, 1998).

O'Donnell, I., 'Violence and social change in the Republic of Ireland', *International Journal of the Sociology of Law*, 33 (2005), 101–117.

O'Donnell, I. and S. Morrison, 'Armed and dangerous? The use of firearms in robbery', *Howard Journal of Criminal Justice*, 36:3 (1997), 305–320.

Orde, Hugh, 'PSNI Chief Constable interviewed', *The Blanket* (25 October 2004).

Orde, Hugh, PSNI Chief Constable, oral evidence to the Northern Ireland Affairs Committee, *BBC Parliament* (9 November 2005).

Organised Crime Task Force, *Confronting the Threat. Strategy 2001–2* (Belfast: OCTF, 2001).

Organised Crime Task Force, *Threat Assessment* (Belfast: OCTF, 2002).

Organised Crime Task Force, *Strategic Response. Serious and Organised Crime in Northern Ireland* (OCTF, 2003).

Organised Crime Task Force, *Threat Assessment. Serious and Organised Crime in Northern Ireland* (Belfast: OCTF, 2003).

Organised Crime Task Force, *Confronting the Threat. Serious and Organised Crime in Northern Ireland* (Belfast: OCTF, 2004).

Organised Crime Task Force, *Serious and Organised Crime in Northern Ireland. Threat Assessment and Strategy* (Belfast: OCTF, 2004).

Organised Crime Task Force, *Confronting the Threat. Serious and Organised Crime in Northern Ireland* (Belfast: OCTF, 2005).

Organised Crime Task Force, *Annual Report and Threat Assessment 2006* (Belfast: OCTF, 2006).

Parker, H., L. Williams and J. Aldridge, 'The normalisation of "sensible" recreational drugs use: Further evidence from the North West of England', *Sociology*, 36:4 (2002), 941–964.

Patten Report, *A New Beginning: Policing in Northern Ireland. The Independent Commission on Policing in Northern Ireland* (Belfast: The Stationery Office, 1999).

Patterson, H., *The Politics of Illusion. A Political History of the IRA* (London: Serif, 1997).

Pearson, G., *Hooligan. A History of Respectable Fears* (London: Macmillan, 1983).

Pearson, J., *The Cult of Violence* (London: Orion, 2002).

Penna, S., 'The Children Act 2004: Child protection and social surveillance', *Journal of Social Welfare and Family Law*, 27:2 (2005), 143–157.

Performance and Innovation Unit, *Recovering the proceeds of crime* (London: Cabinet Office, 2000), www.strategy.gov.uk/downloads/su/criminal/recovering/03.htm.

Pollitt, C., J. Birchall and K. Putman, *Decentralising Public Service Management* (London: Macmillan, 1998).

PONI, *Statement by the Police Ombudsman for Northern Ireland on her Investigation of Matters Relating to the Omagh Bombing on August 15th 1998* (PONI, 2001).

PONI, *First Annual Report November 2000–March 2002* (PONI, 2002).

PONI, *Police Ombudsman statement following the withdrawal of a judicial review by the Police Association for Northern Ireland to Quash her Report into Events Surrounding the Omagh Bombing* (Thursday 23 January 2003).

PONI, *The Investigation by Police of the Murder of Sean Brown on 12 May 1997* (PONI, 2004).

PONI, *Annual Report and Statement of Accounts April 2004 to March 2005* (Ireland: The Stationery Office, 2005).

PONI, *Statement by the Police Ombudsman for Northern Ireland on her Investigation into the Circumstances Surrounding the Death of Raymond McCord Junior and Related Matters* (Belfast: PONI, 2007).

Power to the People. An Independent Inquiry into Britain's Democracy (York: The Power Inquiry, 2006).

Prenzler, T., 'Civilian oversight of police. A test of capture theory', *British Journal of Criminology*, 40 (2000), 659–674.

Presdee, M., 'Volume crime and everyday life', in C. Hale, K. Hayward, A. Wahidin and E. Wincup (eds), *Criminology* (Oxford: Oxford University Press, 2005), pp. 185–201.

Progressive Unionist Party, *Rebuttal of the First Report of the International Monitoring Commission* (April 2004).

PSNI, *Report on Murder Investigation Procedures Presented to Policing Board*, www.psni.police.uk/index/media_centre/press_releases/pg_press_releases_2003.

PSNI, *Annual Report of the Chief Constable 2001–2002* (PSNI: Belfast, 2003).

PSNI, *Annual Report of the Chief Constable 2002–2003* (PSNI: Belfast, 2003).

PSNI, *Annual Report of the Chief Constable 2003–2004* (PSNI: Belfast, 2003).

PSNI, *Annual Report of the Chief Constable 2004–2005* (PSNI: Belfast, 2005).

PSNI, *Chief Constable's Annual Report 2005–2006* (PSNI: Belfast, 2006).

PSNI, *Number of Persons Charged with Terrorist and Serious Public Order Offences 1990/91–2005/06* (2005), www.psni.police.uk/persons_charged_fy-19.doc.

Reiner, R., 'Media made criminality: The representation of crime in the mass media', in M. Maguire, R. Morgan and R. Reiner (eds), *The Oxford Handbook of Criminology* (Oxford: Oxford University Press, 1997), pp. 189–231.

Reiner, R., *The Politics of the Police* (Oxford: Oxford University Press, 3rd edn, 2000).

Reiner, R., 'Police Research', in R. King and E. Wincup (eds), *Doing Research on Crime and Justice* (Oxford, Oxford University Press, 2000), pp. 205–235.

Reno, W., *Corruption and State Politics in Sierra Leone* (Cambridge, Cambridge University Press, 1995).

Reno, W., 'Clandestine economies, violence and states in Africa', *Journal of International Affairs*, 53:2 (2000), 433–459.

Reynolds, J., 'The new US anti-money laundering offensive: Will it prove successful?', *Cross Cultural Management*, 9:3 (2002), 3–31.

Rogerson, P., 'Performance measurement and policing: Police service or law enforcement agency?', *Public Money and Management*, Oct–Dec (1995), 25–29.

RUC, *Annual Report of the Chief Constable 1997–1998* (Belfast: RUC, 1998).

RUC, *Annual Report of the Chief Constable 1998–1999* (Belfast: RUC, 1999).

RUC, *Annual Report of the Chief Constable 1999–2000* (Belfast: RUC, 2000).

RUC, *Annual Report of the Chief Constable 2000–2001* (Belfast: RUC, 2000).

Ruggerio, V., *Crime and Markets. Essays in Anti-criminology* (Oxford/Clarendon: Oxford University Press, 2001).

Ruggerio, V., 'War markets: Corporate and organised criminals in Europe', *Social and Legal Studies*, 5 (1996), 5–20.

Ryder, C., *The RUC. A Force Under Fire 1922–2000* (London: Arrow, 2000).

Ryder, C., *The Fateful Split. Catholics and the Royal Ulster Constabulary* (London: Methuen, 2004).

Ryder, C. and V. Kearney, *Drumcree* (London: Methuen, 2001).

Serious and Organised Crime Agency Annual Plan 2006/07 www.soca.gov.uk/downloads/annualPlan.pdf

Sáiz, P. A., 'Use of cocaine by secondary school students in Northern Spain', *European Addiction Research* 9:3 (2003), 138–143.

Shearing, C., 'A "new beginning" for policing', *Journal of Law and Society*, 27:3 (2000), 386–393.

Shirlow, P., 'Mapping the spaces of fear: Socio-spatial causes and effects of violence in Northern Ireland', ESRC research project L133251007 (Economic and Social Research Council, 2001).

Shover, N. and D. Honaker, 'The socially bounded decision-making of persistent property offenders', *Howard Journal of Criminal Justice*, 31 (1982), 276–293.

Silke, A., 'In defense of the realm: Financing loyalist terrorism in Northern Ireland: Part one,' *Studies in Conflict and Terrorism*, 21:4 (1998), 331–361.

Silke, A., 'Rebel's dilemma: The changing relationship between the IRA, Sinn Féin and paramilitary vigilantism in Northern Ireland', *Terrorism and Political Violence*, 11:1 (1999), 55–93.

Silke, A., 'Drink, drugs and rock 'n' roll: Financing loyalist terrorism in Northern Ireland: Part two', *Studies in Conflict and Terrorism*, 23:2 (2000), 107–127.

Simon, J., 'Governing through crime', in L. Friedman and G. Fisher (eds), *The Crime Conundrum* (Boulder, CO: Westview, 1997), pp. 171–189.

Simpson, M., 'The relationship between drug use and crime: a puzzle inside an enigma', *International Journal of Drug Policy*, 14 (2003), 307–319.

Sinn Féin, 'The king is dead. Long live the king. Chief Constables come and go but the central problem remains', *Sinn Féin Press Release* (13 April 2002).

Sinn Féin, 'Durkan clutching at straws', *Sinn Féin Press Release* (29 August 2002).

Sinn Féin, 'Special Branch: Still untouchable', *Sinn Féin* (8 August 2002).

Sinnerton, H., *David Ervine* (Dublin: Brandon, 2002).

Smith, K., 'Explaining variation in State level homicide rates. Does crime policy pay?', *Journal of Politics*, 59:2 (1997), 350–367.

Smyth, M., 'The process of demilitarization and the reversibility of the peace process in Northern Ireland', *Terrorism and Political Violence,* 16:3 (2004), 544–566.

Smyth, M., 'Lost lives: Victims and the construction of "victimhood" in Northern Ireland', in M. Cox, A. Guelke and F. Stephen (eds), *A Farewell to Arms? Beyond the Good Friday Agreement* (Manchester: Manchester University Press, 2006), pp. 170–186.

Sproat, P., 'The new policing of terrorist finance in Northern Ireland', paper delivered to the British Society of Criminology Annual Conference, University of Leeds, July 2005.

Sproat, P., 'The social impact of counter terrorist finance policies in the UK', *Crime, Law and Social Change*, 44:4/5 (2005), 441–464.

Sterling, C., *The Terror Network* (New York: Berkeley, 1983).

Stevens, J., *Stevens Enquiry 3. Overview and Recommendations* (2003).

Stohl, M. and G. Lopez (eds), The State as Terrorist. The Dynamics of Governmental Violence and Repression (London: Aldwych, 1984).

Stone, M., *None Shall Divide Us* (London: John Blake, 2004).

Taylor, I., *Crime in Context. A Critical Criminology of Market Societies* (London: Polity, 1999).

Taylor, P., *Provos. The IRA and Sinn Féin* (London: Bloomsbury, 1998).

Taylor, P., *Brits. The War Against the IRA* (London: Bloomsbury, 2002).

Thoumi, F., 'Illegal drugs in Colombia: from illegal economic boom to social crisis, *Annals of the American Academy of Political and Social Science*, 582:1 (2002), 102–116.

Tilly C. (ed.), *The Formation of National States in Western Europe* (Princeton, Princeton University Press, 1975).

Tilly, C., 'Urbanisation, criminality and collective violence in nineteenth century France', *American Journal of Sociology*, 79 (1973), 296–318.

Tilly, C., 'War making and state making as organised crime', in P. Evans, D. Rueschemeyer and T. Skocpol (eds), *Bringing the State Back In* (Cambridge: Cambridge University Press, 1985), pp. 169–191.

Tilley, N. and J. Burrows, 'An Overview of Attrition Patterns', *Home Office Online Report* 45/05 (2005), www.homeoffice.gov.uk/rds/pdfs05/rdsolr4505.pdf.

Tombs, S. and D. Whyte, *Unmasking the Powerful: Scrutinising States and Corporations* (New York: Peter Lang, 2003).

Tonge, J., '"They haven't gone away you know". Irish republican "dissidents" and armed struggle', *Terrorism and Political Violence* 16:3 (2004), 671–93.

Topping, I., 'The police complaints system in Northern Ireland: a repeated transplant?', in M. Connolly and S. Loughlin (eds), *Public Policy in Northern Ireland; Adoption or Adaptation?* (PRI: Belfast, 1990).

University of Glasgow Centre for Drug Misuse Research, *Estimating the Prevalence of Problem Opiate and Problem Cocaine Use in Northern Ireland* (Belfast: Drug and Alcohol Information and Research Unit, 2006).

UNODC, *World Drugs Report* 2006 (Slovakia: UN, 2006).

Urban, M., *Big Boy's Rules* (London, Faber, 1992).

van Duyne, P., 'The phantom threat of organised crime', *Crime, Law and Social Change*, 24 (1996), 341–377.

van Duyne, P., 'Organised crime, corruption and power', *Crime, Law and Social Change*, 26 (1997), 201–238.

van Duyne, P., 'Money laundering: Pavlov's dog and beyond', *Howard Journal of Criminal Justice*, 37:4 (1998), 359–374.

van Duyne, P., 'Organising cigarette smuggling and policy making: Ending up in smoke', *Crime, Law and Social Change*, 39:3 (2003), 285–317.

Waddington, P. A. J., *The Strong Arm of the Law* (Oxford, Oxford University Press, 1991).

Walker, C., 'The Patten Report and post-sovereignty policing in Northern Ireland', in R. Wilford (ed.), *Aspects of the Belfast Agreement* (Oxford University Press, Oxford, 2001) pp. 142–165.

Walker, C, 'Terrorism and criminal justice: Past, present and guture', *Criminal Law Review* (May) 2004, 311–327.

Walker, C., 'Intelligence and anti-terrorism legislation in the United Kingdom', *Crime, Law and Social Change*, 44:4/5 (2005), 387–422.
Wilford, R. (ed.), *Aspects of the Belfast Agreement* (Oxford, Oxford University Press, 2001).
Wood, I. S., *Crimes of Loyalty. A History of the UDA* (Edinburgh: Edinburgh University Press, 2006).

Newpapers and news television programmes

Belfast Telegraph
The Blanket
Daily Telegraph
Guardian
Independent
Independent on Sunday
Observer
Sunday Life
Starry Plough
Sunday Times
The Times
BBC Digital News Northern Ireland
BBC News Northern Ireland

Cases

A v Secretary of State for the Home Department [2004] UKHL 56.
R v Z (On appeal from the Court of Appeal in Northern Ireland (Northern Ireland) [2005] UKHL 35.

Index